ENDPAPERS:

Stratford in 1872
when three-dimensional
civic maps were popular.
Drawn by H. Brosius.

THE STORY OF STRATFORD

By the same author

The Great Canoe

Canada, Young Giant of the North

Lukey Paul from Labrador

Mainstream

Flightline North

The Visible Past: The Pictorial History of Simcoe County

The Blue Roan

Into the High County: Dufferin, the Last 12,000 Years

Floodtides
of
Fortune

The Story of Stratford
and the progress of the city
through two centuries

by
Adelaide Leitch

Published by
The Corporation of The City of Stratford
Stratford, Ontario, Canada

Acknowledgments

The words of young Thomas A. Edison quoted in Chapter 4 are from "Edison: His Life and Inventions", by Frank Lewis Dyer and Thomas Commerford Martin. The "Vista of Stratford" map in Chapter 15 is used with the kind permission of its creator, Duncan Macpherson. Acknowledgment is made to the Perth County Archives for inclusion of the C. A. Mayberry material in Chapter 17; and to Dr. James Reaney for permission to use the excerpt and sketch from "Twelve Letters to a Small Town" in Chapter 20.

ISBN   0-9690047-0-2

Production, printing and binding:
The Beacon Herald Fine Printing Division, Stratford, Ontario.
T. H. Best Printing Company Ltd., Toronto, Ontario.
Printed and bound in Canada.

CONTENTS

Part II: THE SUPPORTS

PREFACE

When Stratford City Council authorized the city's first major history, it launched no ordinary tale of southern Ontario life.

For here is a city small, unique, and altogether remarkable, in its origins and in its development. Stratford was always a city that knew where it was going. Charting that progress through the decades has taken thousands of hours of research, many interviews and endless checking that involved many people, and turned up a wealth of information, along with a few scandals, some romance and even violence with troops brought in to quell it.

There are many Stratfords in the world, in addition to Canada's Festival City and England's Stratford-upon-Avon. In United States are several, including a town in Connecticut and a borough in New Jersey. Robert E. Lee was born in "Stratford", an estate in Virginia, and Stratford in Texas is named for a Virginian. Others are in California, Iowa, New Hampshire, Oklahoma, South Dakota and Wisconsin. In New Zealand, Stratford is a borough in North Island. There is a Stratford also in southern Australia. And one more Avon River, a tidal stream, flows through Hants County, Nova Scotia.

Canada's Stratford, nearly ten degrees farther south than its English namesake, is at Latitude 43° 22' 12'' N, and 80° 58' 57'' W. It has more people, with a population a bit over 27,000 in 1980. And it is higher, at 1,194 feet above sea level, to make it the highest city in Southern Ontario. Its area is a trifle smaller than that of the English borough.

It picked up a whole covey of names in the progress along the road to cityhood. It appeared just once as "Appin" on a rare and curious old map. To surveyors, squatters and early settlers, it was "Little Thames" after the river of the same name. In exasperation, they called it "Muddy Stratford" in the 1850's. They named it, proudly, "The Classic City" in 1885, cityhood year. Now, because of the Shakespearean plays, they call it "The Festival City". The townspeople prefer not to remember — or, if they do, prefer not to tell you — that once it was "Slowford-on-the-Sluggard" in a 19th century novel.

Early in the 19th century, where the river curved gently through the flats, shanties of Canada Company surveyors stood on the north side of the river. The excellent riverside soils produced lush wild vegetation for the pioneers, then orderly flower beds as shanties gave way to homes.

The Avon, which began as a squiggle on a map, grew in importance. Because of the river, the mightiest railway in the country would be sent packing — and this without any foreknowledge that Stratford would parlay the river and its setting into the location for an internationally famous theatre. The city, the Avon, the Shakespearean names and the swans were all there before the players for the Shakespearean Festival even were born.

In order not to jar the reader too greatly by plunging him back and forth over the decades, the orientation of past sites and present buildings has, usually, been omitted in the text but, for the curious, some of these progressions are collected at the back of the book in an "Inventory of History". Writing this book has been a challenge; sorting fact from fiction in old accounts has not always been easy. Along the way, assistance has come from many sources.

Very special appreciation goes, first of all, to city historian, Tom Dolan, who spent endless hours laying the groundwork and assembling a wealth of material; and who later was unfailingly helpful in answering many more questions for me. He recruited others to help with specific areas of research: E. G. Neigh, Harold M. "Winger" Thomas, Zeta Rivers, Barbara Miller, Mary Jane Lennon, John McCarroll and Molly Graham. The vast amount of data collected by them is held by the city, for the use of future historians and students.

I am also much indebted to Jim Anderson, curator of the Perth County Archives, for taking valuable time to help with my research and also for arranging for the reproduction of priceless illustrative material from the Archives collection. The Stratford Public Library and its microfilm collection also were invaluable.

Many nuggets of Stratford history came, too, from the Metropolitan Toronto Library, particularly with the assistance of the staffs of the Baldwin Room, the map department, the fine art section and the theatre department. My thanks to the staffs of the Ontario Archives, the National Archives and the Archives of the Department of Agriculture, Ottawa. The Surveys Branch of the Ministry of Natural Resources made available for study rare old maps along with surveyors' diaries and field notes; these added depth to the early part of the book. For further help with the research and illustrations, my thanks to: the Canadian National Railway, at Toronto, Montreal and Stratford; Bell Canada; the Edison National Historic Site in the United States, and the Regional Collection, University of Western Ontario, London, Ontario.

So many individuals have, at one time or another, helped provide information it is foolhardy to try to single out a few. However, I greatly appreciated the help of Jim Burns, Secretary of the Stratford and District Labour Council, in unravelling the story of the unions; also I thank the staff of the Stratford Shakespearean Festival, particularly Anne Selby, Director of Publications, and Archivist Daniel Ladell. Details of the history were filled in by the Board of Park

Management and its superintendent, Ed Martin; and by both the police and the fire departments. My thanks to Beverly Neeb at the *Beacon Herald,* who located some special pictures for me; and to Rev. E. J. Laverty, P. H., Chancellor of the Diocese of London, who sent me valuable material. My thanks also to Mary Cjaskowski, for a tape recording and a rare picture from the days when slaves sought peace in Stratford. And a very special bow to cartoonist Duncan Macpherson, who so graciously gave permission to reprint his outrageously funny map of Stratford after the arrival of the Festival.

At city hall, I appreciate the privilege extended to me by city clerk Ron Schulthies and his staff in permitting my poking and prying through old documents that survived the fire in the earlier market building. And a very special thank you to the clerk's secretary, Judy Purcell, who never lost patience with me for what sometimes must have seemed endless and odd questions! Also involved were the councilors and mayors who (sometimes with trepidation) smoothed the course of a lengthy project. Particularly, I would thank, for his unstinting work, Alderman Jack Hamilton, my liaison with the City and to a large extent the sparkplug for the printing of the book.

The special printing committee also included former mayor Betty McMillan, Alderman Delmar Smythe and Rev. Ross Cumming of Cumming Press. For advice, for checking copy, for putting up with all a book entails, my husband, Jim Lennox, deserves credit; as does my typist, Lee Knight, who caught discrepancies I might have missed. They all helped get the history between covers.

If, inadvertently, I have omitted some names and neglected some people, I am truly sorry — and assure them their help was appreciated both by the City and by myself.

Here then, with the help of many of its citizens, is the sometimes stormy saga of "Little Thames" and the subsequent Corporation of the City of Stratford.

1980   Adelaide Leitch

History is reflected in the Avon, and the brick smokestack of the Dufton Woollen Mills now is part of the Shakespearean Garden.

PART
1

THE HAMLET AND THE CITY

There is a tide in the affairs of men,
Which, taken at the flood, leads on to fortune . . . .

Julius Caesar, Act IV, Scene 3.

Cleeve Horne's head of Shakespeare, commissioned for the Parks Board in 1949.

PROLOGUE

England

IN THE OFFICES of the Canada Company at 13 St. Helen's Place, London, England, the Court of Directors met regularly to discuss the enormous lands in the colony.

Under control of the company, in addition to the Guelph Block and a scatter of crown lands in Upper Canada, was a tract of more than a million acres lying in the lee of Lake Huron. It was, judging by the reports and survey maps coming across the ocean, as fine a piece of land as could be wished for, rich of soil, well endowed with water and, save for a squatter or two, immediately available for settlement and ripe for development at a handsome profit.

The directors impatiently awaited the coming of each sailing ship bearing its packets of information from overseas. They digested the reports, often were guided by them, but they were the ones who issued the final orders, decisively and — considering the distance—usually with intelligence.

The first necessity of settlement they had taken care of: ordering a road to be punched through virgin forest to link their new community of Guelph with the known harbor of Goderich on Lake Huron. On the advice of "Tiger" Dunlop, their man in the field in Upper Canada, it would have connections with Dundas, rather than with York, and, over it, settlers' wagons would soon be bumping along on the way to surveyed lots. Before long, (thought the London-based directors) they could expect to recoup handsomely, for the shareholders, their investment in the Huron Tract!

The new company received copies of all survey maps, along with written reports and journals. As these began to show that the first small, wayside inns were inadequate, the directors made plans for the third Company settlement, midway on the road between Guelph and Goderich. When it came time to lay out a townsite, they called the shots and decided where and when — and the size of it. And they named it.

The location chosen on the east branch of the Thames was excellent — set in the midst of good wheat-growing lands, located on a swift-running stream, and on the Huron Road. The geographical similarity of this site at the river crossing to another nearer at hand could scarcely escape the notice of anyone in England, and, when the town plot was laid out, "Stratford" was the name that went on the map.

It was a name as apt for it as for their own Stratford-upon-Avon, the old municipal borough built where an ancient Roman road once had forded the river. The name was of Saxon-Latin origin, derived from *straeta* (or *strata*), meaning a road or street, and from *ford,* a crossing. It could not have been more graphic for the new hamlet in the bush.

Whoever actually settled upon the name, it was hardly Superintendent John Galt, already in disfavor with the directors in 1828-29 and being replaced. Dr. William "Tiger" Dunlop, the company's adventurous developer, could have had a hand in it. Or the idea may even have started with a bright young man, Thomas Mercer Jones, who was in the employ of one of the directors and who, in 1829, was slated for promotion to replace John Galt. Conceivably, it could just have been an anonymous and influential shareholder, throwing out an obvious suggestion over a glass of hot toddy. But, whoever hit on the name, there was no question who had the final say — the omnipotent directors of the Canada Company in London, most of whom — Edward Ellice excepted — had never set eyes upon Upper Canada, let alone the settlement whose future they manipulated like a pawn on a chess board.

These astute, capitalistic, and decisive men had, from the start, proven themselves jealous of their prerogative of name-giving. There had been an earlier difference of opinion with their superintendent, John Galt, over the naming of Guelph and Goderich.

Periodically, they sent off long, detailed memoranda to him regarding names to be attached to rivers and places in the Huron Tract. Galt had been considerably hurt when his own name had not been placed on a township, since there were three or four townships left over after all the directors had been taken care of.

Three of the directors had been immortalized in the names of the townships that encircled the proposed new townsite: Montreal-born Rt. Hon. Edward Ellice, who had extensive business interests in North America; Sir John Easthope, owner of London's important *Morning Chronicle;* and Robert Downie, M.P. It was at the junction of Ellice, Downie, and North and South Easthope Townships, that they located "Stratford".

While the prime purpose of the Company was simply to make a profit, yet the Canada Company had had a curious and philanthropic origin. It came into being to provide the Government with funds for the settlement of war claims resulting from the War of 1812-14. Veterans, some near-destitute, had enlisted the sympathies of the Scottish novelist John Galt, who, with Edward Ellice, became their London agents in 1820. Looking around for ways to raise money for them, Galt hit upon the idea of selling to a colonizing company crown lands and clergy reserves which were lying fallow in the Canadas. The government could then use the proceeds of the sale to make reparation to the war veterans. In the English financial community, there was considerable enthusiasm for Galt's scheme, but, naturally, it did not sit well with the Upper Canada clergy, led by powerful Bishop John Strachan at York. To him, it seemed the price offered the Church was too little.

In place of the Church's lands, the company finally acquired, instead, a huge block of 1,100,000 acres in the lee of Lake Huron — the Huron Tract, recently bought from the Chippewa Indians, and covering, roughly, the areas of the future Perth and Huron Counties. The land was good; it was a very good deal.

Land purchased by the Canada Company at an average of 3s 6d an acre was to sell to settlers at a 100% mark-up, for an average of 7s to 10s, although prices could fluctuate with the desirability of the location. The Canada Company still had, besides, scattered crown lands, making 2,484,013 acres in all.

The Canada Company was incorporated August 19, 1826, by Royal Charter. John Galt was its first Secretary, and, the following year, its Superintendent. Somehow, the needs of the war veterans were permanently shelved. The government used the proceeds of its land sale, paid to it annually, for other purposes, and Galt turned his sympathies and efforts to the problems of incoming settlers.

In 1827, when development of the Huron Tract began, the London interests controlled it lock, stock and barrel, and their prime concern was simply to fatten the London coffers. John Galt was the Company's man in Canada, and it was, in a way, a perfect job, at least in the beginning, for the sensitive novelist and humanitarian. To help the underdog and, at the same time, to hold a responsible job suited John Galt well.

He envisioned building in the wilderness "an asylum for the exiles of society." But he also recognized the financial soundness of the undertaking, and had no qualms about its future. As he would write in his *Autobiography*, with happy conviction, "The Canada Company . . . . is an institution which only calamity can prevent from obtaining great prosperity."

When Galt arrived at the Huron Tract, "Stratford" was not even a paper town. The road had yet to be built, the lots yet to be surveyed. And when the first settlers came, they would neither know nor care what the men in London had named the place. They would call it "Little Thames" as the road builders and itinerants earlier had done.

Traffic would gradually increase along the first communication road through the bush, and others would follow in the wake of the first white man to set foot on the actual site of Little Thames, the Canada Company's colorful Warden of the Woods, Dr. William "Tiger" Dunlop.

Out of the wilderness of the Huron Tract, rose a remarkable city. Part of the reason for the rise of its fortunes was the 19th century arrival of the Grand Trunk Railway's locomotive repair shops, shown in operation, bottom right.

1

Running The Proof Line

THE LITTLE SETTLEMENT that grew up at the river crossing was a company town — a *Canada Company* town — and the men in the field who shaped its early destiny were some of the most colorful men at work in the early Canadas.

There was a triumvirate of enormous Scots, all over six feet tall: John Galt, Scottish novelist, visionary, founder and superintendent of the Canada Company; Dr. William "Tiger" Dunlop, wilderness developer on the grand scale; "Stout Mac" — John McDonald, the surveyor. A little later, there was also Colonel Anthony Van Egmond, the road builder, a rich and respected Dutchman from Pennsylvania who later would be jailed on a charge of treason.

Most colorful by far was the youthful Dunlop, tramping through the bush in the summer of 1827, criss-crossing his own exploration trails, keeping his journal, directing his wide-ranging survey party.

Exploration of the million-acre Huron Tract was his first major assignment for the Canada Company in his new capacity as "Warden of the Company's Woods and Forests in Upper Canada," and "Tiger" Dunlop liked his job. He was perfectly suited for it.

This man was an instinctive pioneer, and the Huron Tract was his third and last assignment in clearing the way for settlement of the wilderness. He had volunteered in 1814 to cut a military road from Lake Simcoe to Penetanguishene in mid-winter but, before his work was finished, had received what he called "the appalling intelligence" that peace had been declared between Britain and United States. A few years later, while in Calcutta, India, he had been approached by the Saugor Island Society on a matter of clearing the island of tigers. The venture was a failure; the tigers still plagued Saugor Island, but Dunlop dined out for years on a fund of colorful stories, many of them quite outrageous.

When he returned to England, he wrote articles for *Blackwoods,* the popular magazine published in Edinburgh in the 1820's. The top editors and contributors, somewhat affectedly, used pseudonyms, each choosing the name of an animal. Inevitably, Dunlop became "The Tiger", and so he was known for the rest of his life. Although he held a degree in medicine, he was always more raconteur than doctor, and more adventurer than either.

He was still in his mid-30's when he came to work for the Canada Company, a big, red-haired, bewhiskered man whose lifestyle increasingly attracted — and who personally nurtured — some wild legends based loosely on his exploits. He himself had a deft way with words. In the spring of 1827, the 33-year-old Dunlop sat down and wrote home to his sister:

> I am now preparing to make a dive into the woods, and shall not emerge, most probably, until midsummer, unless something extraordinary occurs in the way.

His "dive into the woods" was exploration for a colonization road through the dark and forested Huron Tract, and first step was to be the running of the proof line — an exploratory survey line that might, or might not, be part of the completed road. Dunlop was in charge.

Dunlop assembled his party in mid-May. With him went two of the most respected surveyors at work in the Canadas: the near-legendary Mahlon Burwell, whose surveys already had opened up much of Upper Canada, and John McDonald, who soon would become the architect of the whole Huron Tract. Chain bearers, explorers, and some Mohawk guides, completed the group that set out from Galt.

The horses were left at a settler's farm along the way, and the party proceeded on foot, bedding down, first night out, at Smith's Creek, which had just been renamed the River Nith by John Galt. The second night out, they bunked in a hastily built shanty on the eastern rim of the Huron Tract and, next morning, the Dunlop party started work inside the Tract itself.

The proof line was begun at the boundary of Wilmot Township a little north of the point designated later as the start of the "proposed road" through the Huron Tract. Through land impossible for pack animals and forests completely uncharted, working with instruments primitive by later standards, they set out toward a site many miles distant but already known: a harbor on Lake Huron, surveyed in 1819-23 by Henry Wolsley Bayfield, R.N.

Two days into the survey, the diary of Mahlon Burwell recorded problems:

> Thursday, 17th May, 1827. Surveyed on the Proof Line four miles and a half — the last half in a cedar Swamp, the waters of which appear (although not positively) to trend Westerly. . . .

Friday, Saturday, Sunday, the entries were monotonously the same. There was nothing but swamp. Monday was worse. They camped in swamp, without shelter, "and it rained in the night." Soggy and fly-bitten, this little party of men was seeing the source of the Upper Thames. And it was no place for a road.

That was abundantly clear, long before they emerged from swamps and forests

Key men
at Stratford

*DUNLOP: "The Tiger"
was first to set foot on the site of
Little Thames.*

*GALT: The Canada
Company superintendent,
John Galt, wanted to call it "Appin".*

*VAN EGMOND: The road contractor
amassed acreage in town. No picture of
Anthony Van Egmond exists, but his son,
Augustus, (right) resembled him.*

to reach Lake Huron exactly where Burwell had aimed his line.

Legend persisted for over a century that the Mohawk Chief, John Brant, son of the famous *Thayendanegea,* Chief Joseph Brant, was a member of Dunlop's party. But Brant, cultured friend of John Galt, sophisticated visitor in English drawing rooms and better educated than half the people in Upper Canada, went more comfortably. While the survey party was slogging through swamp, Chief Brant also was on his way toward Goderich, up Dunlop's old military route, the Penetanguishene Road, in the company of Superintendent John Galt. At Penetanguishene, Galt's party went aboard the naval vessel *Bee,* bound for Goderich harbor, and there that meticulous scribe, Mahlon Burwell, recorded that they "came ashore, Friday, June 29, 1827, at about 2 p.m."

The originator of this long-lived rumor about Brant (grown more colorful over more than a century of retelling) was almost certainly John Mactaggart, an engineer and geologist working on the Rideau Canal project, and a self-appointed historian. He had, at times, traveled with Dunlop, and had perhaps seen portions of Dunlop's reports.

Mactaggart's book describing the colonial experience, *Three Years in Canada (1826-28),* contained the frequently quoted account of the Chief of the Mohawks accompanying the Dunlop party as all of them went "wandering about" and "penetrating the huge untraveled wilderness in all directions". Later, the Lizars sisters of Stratford embellished the account in a book of their own — gratuitously adding some Indian braves "with tomahawks and scalps at belt".

It was monumental nonsense — not at all the gospel according to the day-by-day field notes and diaries of survey of the veteran surveyor, Mahlon Burwell! Nor was either Galt or Brant in the party that began the return trip through the Tract in early July.

Burwell by then had begun opening a bridle road — a first primitive track that would link Goderich with Guelph. The chosen route lay south of the big swamp and, as it laboriously advanced, it circumnavigated the physical obstacles that lay in its way. Later, route changes would have to be made but, for the moment, the word from London, passed on by John Galt, was "All speed ahead!"

The Dunlop party set out. Behind came the pack animals, with baggage and also with provisions acquired at the Lake Huron port. John McDonald before long headed north of the swamp. The explorers, also, were sent ranging into the bush. One such exploration took the Mohawk, John Fish, north from a point near Stratford. Monday, July 9, "Tiger" Dunlop himself left the road party, tramping south and taking a huge triangular swing he calculated would bring him back, approximately two days later, to intercept Burwell's advancing bridle road.

Wednesday, July 11, it was pouring rain as Dunlop hurried toward the rendezvous. He slogged along a stream where the raindrops danced and sputtered on the coffee-colored water, and his heavy boots left marks in the soft river mud. It was the first time such boots had walked the north shore of the still-unnamed Avon at the site of the future Stratford. It was a bit after noon.

The footprints lasted only so long as it took the rain to blur them and the river to obliterate them, filling them with silt it had brought down from its swampy

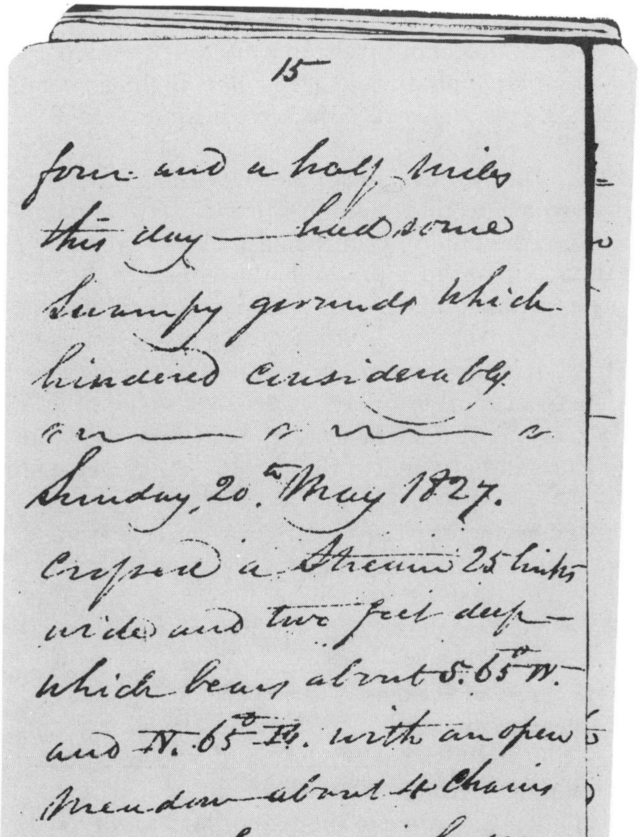

four and a half miles
this day — had some
swampy grounds which
hindered considerably

Sunday, 20ᵗʰ May 1827.
Crossed a Stream 25 links
wide and two feet deep —
which bears about S. 65 W.
and N. 65 E. with an open
Meadow about 4 Chains
wide which can be seen
for a mile above; and
appears to come from a
large Swamp not far
distant; and this, I sup-
pose to be the North Branch
of the River Thames — Proceeded the line towards
Lake Huron, then

ONTARIO ARCHIVES

*Sunday, 20th May, 1827:
Mahlon Burwell, running
his proof line through the
swamp north of Stratford,
updated his diary of survey.*

source to the north. In the wake of this man's passing were only trodden grasses and crushed vegetation, a few blazes on ancient trees, and flights of mallards returning to the river to feed. The passenger pigeons were again free to descend, in thousands, on the trees.

But, that summer day in 1827, the primeval era of the river ended.

Dunlop emerged from the woods to find Mahlon Burwell and his party had already gone by. He turned into the muddy trail recently left by men and pack animals, and set out after them. Up ahead, Burwell had finally given up for the day. *"July 11 . . ."* he wrote. "It rained and continued to rain until one o'clock p.m. Struck up a camp. . . .''

Here, around 3 p.m., "Tiger" Dunlop came tramping out of the southwest and joined him — "wet and fatigued", as Burwell noted.

Two days later, the party was out of the Tract. McDonald returned from the north and, for days, he and Burwell "wrought at the map", as they documented the summer's work.

The working map of that summer of 1827, with its separate surveys and explorations, was a spiderweb of activities. There was not yet so much as a dot to mark a city site on the Avon, only the dotted line showing Dunlop's route alongside a nameless river and the "proposed" road between Guelph and Lake Huron crossing his trail where, a few years hence, would be built the bridge of Little Thames. Mahlon Burwell's bridle road skirted around a future city's northern perimeter, and the lean-to shelters of the rendezvous may even have been the first buildings at or near the site of a yet-to-be country club.

A copy of the exploratory map reached John Galt and, at the speed of the ships crossing the ocean, the information also came to the real proprietor of the whole Huron Tract — the Canada Company.

Before long, Mahlon Burwell received his orders from the Surveyor General for the running of the purchase line on the Company's north boundary. John McDonald, at times assisted by other surveyors, from then on did most of the work in the Huron Tract. One of his assistants was surveyor Samuel Smith; another, his own youthful kinsman, Donald McDonald, whom he trained, as the surveys went forward through the forested land.

In the years that followed the Dunlop "dive in the woods", there was much activity in the Huron Tract, with many goings and comings in and around the area of Stratford.

On the maps, the site began to materialize:

> *1827* . . . a dotted line where "Tiger" Dunlop had tramped along the
> river.
> *1828* . . . "tavern to be", a tentative memo, on the summer map.
> *1829* . . . a small town plot marked out, and a curious label,
> "Appin" . . .

Surveyor John McDonald's "Appin" map of the winter of 1828-29 was a huge document, lined with cloth, and encompassing the whole length of the Huron Road. By order of John Galt, he was working on the townships and the range of lots along the road to Goderich, and he was spending Christmas eve of 1828 near the river crossing at the previously labelled "East Branch of the River Thames".

"Today," he wrote on December 24th, "I erected Monuments for the S.E. Angle of Ellice & N.E. Angle of Downie & got 2½ Miles forward with the Lots. Frosty day & some snow in the latter part of the evening. Sent 2 men off today for provisions & they were met on the way by a man from Zorra with a good supply." Such was Christmas Eve near a future Stratford.

Christmas Day . . . and again it was a day "bitterly frosty", as he "took the bearings of a departure which the present Road makes to the North of the line." He got forward a mile and a half with the survey of the lots, and moved forward to the 20th mile log shanty.

Methodically, like the fine surveyor he was, he worked on toward Goderich. When it was time for the return trip, he sent off most of his men and, with one assistant, explored more carefully the rivers he had observed along the way. On one stream he found a "good mill seat" and a salt lick much frequented by deer, and noted these observations on the map. The winter sky was dark and cloudy, the weather closing in. He hurried past the East Branch of the Thames, where the road angled northwest. And so he hastened on to Guelph.

He was out of the Tract by the middle of January, completing his field notes, putting the cloth backing on the map, and making additional copies for the Surveyor General and for England. By January 27th, his diary noted he was "putting the names of the different Townships on the Draft in characters imitating print". He next "put the names of places on the Draft according to the instructions of Mr. Galt", and completed copies of the map for the Surveyor General and for England.

In addition to "Appin", there were other names of places spaced along the Huron Road: to the west, "Alipore" . . . farther west, "Balangeigh". . . . They may have surprised, then angered the Court of Directors, who had ordered nothing of the sort.

Appin? . . . Alipore? . . . Balangeigh? Where did these ephemeral names *come* from? "Appin" was familiar enough as a place in Scotland; "Balangeigh" also had a Scottish ring. (And there *were* those three huge Scots busy in the tract at the time: Galt, Dunlop and McDonald!) There was also "Alipore". This, interestingly enough, was the name of a suburb of Calcutta, almost certainly known to Dunlop, who once had been busy ridding an island of tigers not far from the Indian city.

The finished map was dated February 28, 1829, and certified at Guelph a few days later, on March 4. Shaded "sold" were: Lot 48, North Easthope; Lot 1, Ellice; and Lot 1, Downie — all of them converging to the point of "Appin", all of them now almost certainly owned by Anthony Van Egmond, beginning his work of road building in the Huron Tract.

McDonald's finalizing of the maps coincided with a change of policy by the Canada Company superintendent who, himself, had just returned from one last trip over the Huron Road. Perhaps because of the cold and discomfort, and the fact that, in the blinding snow, he and his driver had floundered off the sleigh road between stop-over houses, John Galt had come to a new way of thinking.

He now felt that communities, and clusters of settlers, would be better than homes and farms strung out along a lonely bush road. Such settlements would make easier the establishment of churches and schools, to which the Canada Company was committed.

About this time, John Galt ordered "the names of places" to be put on the map, and, for one brief period, Stratford was "Appin".

Up to this time, little attention had been given to the need for a town between Guelph and Goderich, and only a "tavern to be" had been provisionally indicated at this site the previous summer. It may have been Galt, overstepping the powers the Canada Company allowed him, who first directed the attention of the Court of Directors to this particular spot. If so, he may have been the real founder of Stratford, in the "Appin" of McDonald's map.

Without this curious name on a long ago map, perhaps the Canada Company's third planned community might have been placed at the "mill seat" and "saltish spring" on a branch of the river farther west — at Sebringville. "Appin" never again appeared on a map of the Huron Tract. Nor did the other names. But there was one footnote to the story.

John Galt went back to England that April to find his position abolished. In London, among the Canada Company directors he went to see on his rounds, was a man he much respected, and his name was — "Mr. Downie *of Appin*".

While the surveyors and road gangs had been working through the Huron Tract, there had been considerable activity afoot elsewhere.

In the spring of 1828, as the ice ground and buckled in the St. Lawrence and finally freed Quebec harbor, the ships and the immigrants began to arrive, and the Canada Company put on the pressure to have the Huron Road passable.

Galt had been hounding Dunlop to open up at least a rough trail of access by July 4, and Dunlop was coping with an exceptionally rainy summer with its attendant insects, as well as a shortage of good woodsmen and available oxen. A four-day work week was good — a three-day one more common, and Dunlop, the doctor, was as busy with the accidents and illnesses of his men as Dunlop the Canada Company man was busy with his road.

By August, there were immigrants at Guelph, living as best they could, cooking outdoors, washing (as need grew dire) in the river. The Company was generally fair in providing credit and supplies for those going on to choose land, and this speeded outbound traffic.

There entered the affairs of the Huron Tract about this time the Dutchman who would be of enormous help: Colonel Anthony Van Egmond.

Van Egmond was already located in the area, having come up from Pennsylvania and rented — not bought — land in what would later become Waterloo County. He was of noble Dutch descent. His ancestors were still revered in the Netherlands, and had been immortalized in Goethe's drama and in Beethoven's music.

He knew many of the surveyors, including John McDonald who had stayed at his place, and he was familiar with the making of roads — a pioneer process always much the same in Upper Canada.

Van Egmond observed the efforts of Galt's work parties, and, in 1828, approached Galt, offering his help to make this sorry, meandering "sleigh road" passable. Galt appointed him "honorary agent" of the Company. And so Van Egmond began his long-term and mutually satisfactory association with the Tract. Before long, he had a contract to build 45½ miles of the road, while lesser contracts went to other men. As he and his sons labored, Anthony Van Egmond was able to amass thousands of acres of land through the Tract — as much as 800 acres of it around Stratford.

As the Huron Road snaked and stumbled and worried its way through the country toward Goderich — 60 miles of it opening up the Tract itself — it had not a single inn or tavern.

Galt proposed to erect, every 20 miles, inns that he called, interestingly, "Houses of Entertainment". Innkeepers in that wild country would, he knew, have to be subsidized, and the bonus he dangled as inducement was 40 pounds the first year to the men willing to dispense primitive hospitality along the Huron Road. Before Christmas, 1828, Col. Anthony Van Egmond had found two such sturdies: Sebastian Fryfogel and Andrew Seebach. A third inn, nearest Goderich, he would build and operate himself, apparently without extra payments.

Settlement did not get far along the Huron Road that year but, as winter closed in, it heralded the arrival, in December, of the tavern keepers. John McDonald, laying out lots along the Huron Road, found Fryfogel's tavern already "abuilding" on December 18, a night that was "severe frosty".

The innkeepers had a lonely time of it the first few years, with only a straggle of settlers — most of them headed for Goderich — and the occasional visits of Canada Company officials such as "Tiger" Dunlop, Anthony Van Egmond, Charles Pryor and Samuel Strickland.

Fare at the hostels was primitive, albeit the hospitality was warm. An exasperated Dr. Dunlop, although possessed of a strong stomach, sometimes found his palate offended by the offerings — steaks awash in grease, peas served in a wash basin, or cucumbers pickled in whisky. As for the fastidious Canada Company clerk, Samuel Strickland, traveling the Huron Road in 1828-1831, he complained of being "doomed to stop" at Seebach's. One of his stop-overs at this "center house" was particularly disastrous:

> Not that I expected anything better than tea, fried pork and bread and butter, to which, hungry as I was, I should no doubt have done ample justice. Judge, then, of my astonishment and disappointment, when mine hostess placed before me a piece of dirty-looking Indian meal-bread, and a large cake of beef-tallow, and, to wash down this elegant repast, a dish of crust coffee without either milk or sugar, assuring me at the same time in her broken English, "That she had nothing better in the house till the return of her husband, who had gone fifty miles to the mill and store for a supply of flour, groceries, and other fixings." Not being a Russian, I rejected the tallow with disgust, and made but a sorry meal of the other delicacies.

One of the first women over the terrible Huron Road was Strickland's own wife who, tired of being left alone in Guelph, set out in an oxcart, with her child and a nursemaid, bound for Goderich to join her husband. The inns were spaced too widely apart for the slow progress of the poor lady, and she slept two nights along the way in the bush.

After John Galt took his lonely leave, two commissioners were appointed to replace him: Hon. William Allan, a pillar of the Family Compact in Upper Canada and, sent out from England, 30-year-old Thomas Mercer Jones, vouched for by Director Ellice and eager to take on the supervisory chores. The *Colonial Advocate* took a dim view of the new man — "an individual totally ignorant, we presume, of the colony, its inhabitants, or its capabilities".

It was Jones, in February, 1830, who gave Van Egmond and his son the contract to build three quarters of the new road, including the bridge across the Little Thames. Before long, mail was moving from Guelph to Goderich twice a week, and the Stricklands, in February, took their last trip across the Avon, on their way home to Peterborough. Strickland had left the Canada Company partly because his salary had been cut after Galt's departure.

Now came the time of the pioneers, the era of oxcarts laboring through the forest, and of families hacking out clearings for their homesteads.

The land to which the early Stratford settlers came was river land, the flats and banks incredibly rich with silts and nutrients brought down from the great swamp to the north.

"E. Branch of the Thames ½ chain wide, one ft. deep runs swift." That was the description of the river marked on surveyor John McDonald's map in the summer of 1828, again on his winter map of 1828-9. It was little more than a stream in size, a branch of the larger river flowing west into the Great Lakes system at Lake St. Clair. Rain falling on it or snow melting into it would eventually find its way into the Thames and, through it, into the Great Lakes and so, finally, reach the Atlantic Ocean.

The Huron Road emerged here from the deep, green gloom of forests and, across the bridge, disappeared into the forests again. Trees had been slashed for the road, huge trees, their stumps still there. Some of the standing trees were over a hundred years old. There had been an elm "6 links in girth" (nearly four feet in diameter) blazed and notched, in the easterly angle of Downie, and "a birch tree, 8 links in girth" — more than five feet thick — in the southerly angle of Ellice. These trees would be felled to make way for settlement.

There was a mixture of growth in the swale and there were century-old butternuts and immense black cherry trees in the forest. In Lot #1 of Downie, surveyors found maple, birch, elm, and basswood, and called it "Very Fine Land". Dunlop, too, described the country in an assessment he sent to John Galt, and he catalogued not just one but *four* kinds of swamp along the proof line: cedar swamp, spruce swamp, black ash swale and mixed swamp. He further noted the existence of the "dry swamp", no swamp at all but simply a cluster of cedar trees. So deeply associated with swamps were cedars in the minds of settlers in Upper Canada that they "would apply the term to Mount Lebanon!"

Little Thames was 1,194 feet above sea level. Geologically it was on what would later be called the Stratford Plain, a broad, sloping plain of well over a thousand square miles lying between London and Listowel, and extending, also, around the Grand River. Goderich people always would speak of going ''up'' to Stratford.

On the Stratford Plain, the slope lay from northeast to southwest, dropping from about 1500 feet to 900 feet above sea level. The till, a brown silty clay, was a product of the raking action (literally the *tilling*) by the Huron ice lobe during the last great ice age. An old spillway trough, cut across the plain, in time provided the route for the Little Thames, which became the Avon River.

The site of Stratford once had been frozen beneath the Wisconsin glacier, which, at its peak, covered all of Ontario and stretched into Ohio. As the wasting glacier uncovered the land, the site emerged from the great wash of seas a little later than the first land, in the area of Orangeville, 60 miles to the northeast.

Because of the slope of the plain, which is part of the slope east of Lake Huron, about five inches more rain and snow fall here than in Southern Ontario as a whole — an annual average of 38 inches, according to the Stratford weather station.

The rainfall would make for good farmlands, eventually, but was of no interest to the earliest hunter Indians, who spurned the inland country and made their encampments near navigable waters. In the 17th century, there were some highly advanced Huron villages around the Georgian Bay. There also was a French mission, the first white settlement of Ontario: Sainte Marie Among the Hurons, the Jesuit Fathers' ''Abode of Peace''. It was distant by a few days' moccasin travel, but was light years away in communication. Hurons from around Sainte Marie, Petuns to the west, Neutrals from Lake Erie, possibly also a few Iroquois, may have occasionally hunted inland, but did not remain.

In 1649, the Iroquois wiped out Sainte Marie, slaughtering the Hurons and their allies, and leaving a smoking ruin of villages and fields. Becalmed in the central plain, in the eye of the holocaust, in the area of Stratford, nothing much changed.

The trees still stood tall and untouched, and the small birds sang and nested and migrated as before. Only, for a long, black age, no hunting parties strayed through the area. After 1649, there was a blackout of nearly a hundred years.

Eventually coming in trickles down from the north, the next men into southern Ontario were the Ojibwa (Chippewa) and their offshoot, the Mississauga, perhaps, also, a few Algonquins drifting over from the east. Iroquois from time to time expanded their hunting territory, and a few hunting parties once again began to penetrate north of the Great Lakes. Surveyors wisely used Indian guides, and the copper-skinned people were helpful also to the incoming settlers.

There were salt beds on the flats below the early Avon mills, on the south side of the Little Thames. Here the deer came and they, in turn, drew the Indian hunters from Lake Huron. In the fall, there often was a Mississauga camp nearby, and the ground would be coated with hair left where they dressed the skins. It was strange to the early villagers, and they would walk down to the

*Surveyor John McDonald, the six-foot
Scot they called "Stout Mac", mapped
the area and laid out Stratford itself,
with one of the most attractive plans in
Upper Canada.*

ASSOCIATION OF ONTARIO LAND SURVEYORS

camp in the evening to watch, and then to exchange goods for a haunch or two of
venison or bear, for maple sugar or baskets.

Another little camp sometimes was set up farther downstream, and "Tiger"
Dunlop once reported finding a red man's grave in the area — probably that of a
hunter accidentally killed on the trail. Flint arrowheads sometimes were turned
up by incoming settlers.

However, the interior land, without navigable waterways, had little attraction
for the Indians, and the people of a growing Stratford seldom saw them, except
on the occasional trading trips they made from the permanent villages near
Goderich. Barter was mutually profitable, for the settlers needed basic articles of
Indian manufacture, and many a Mississauga broom swept clean the hearth of a
Stratford pioneer. It was replaced by another, when a new house was built, and
would stand by the door for many moons, for the Indian brooms were
beautifully and sturdily made. Finely crafted too were their baskets woven of
pliant strips of black ash.

Everyday moccasins of deerskin could be bought from the Indians for 2s 6d,
Halifax currency, but it would cost up to 5s — around a dollar — for the finest,
decorated with porcupine quills. They would last almost forever.

But, by the time the settlers arrived, the Ojibwa and the Chippewa, who once
had owned the land in the Huron Tract, had given it up by Treaty 27½, on April
25, 1825. It was this treaty that opened the door for the Canada Company, and
for the community that grew out of the surveyors' shanties on the banks of the
Little Thames.

Stratford
On
The
Canada
Company
Maps

1828 — "Tavern to be".

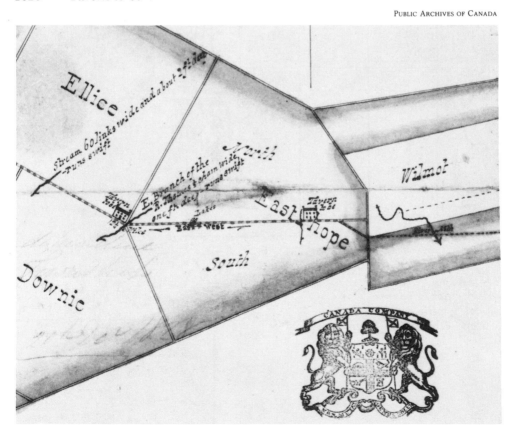

*1829 — "Appin", the name
that never stuck. The
additional detail was added on
the 3rd and 4th concessions in
1830.*

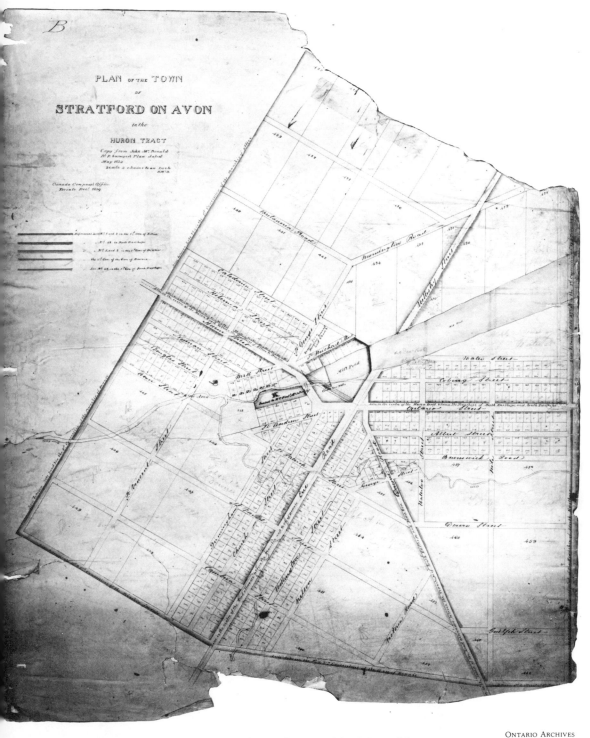

*1839 — Plan for a city of 35,000, drawn by Donald McDonald
from the 1834 survey of John McDonald. The Canada Company agent in Stratford
got a redrawn copy from York.*

Stratford, 1972, from 13,600 feet, looking south.

2

"Little Thames"

THE RIVER SHANTIES closed their doors to no one.

They were dark little huts, covered with elm bark, and little better than lean-tos, but travelers going to Goderich knew that, at Little Thames, they would at least have some protection from the snow or rain, and a roof over their heads. For this they could thank the Canada Company, and the surveyors who originally had built them on the river flats. Soon, they were also sheltering the road builders, Company men, and any stray travelers through the Huron Tract who could not — or would not — go the extra six miles to Seebach's.

By the river was a good place for a settler to break the trip at noon. It was not a bad spot either to have to spend the night, for, around the evening fires, there was warmth and conviviality in abundance, especially if "Tiger" Dunlop was on an inspection tour of the Huron Road.

The Dunlop recipe for the whisky punch was meant to alleviate the bitter cold:

> Put a spoon into a glass and fill the glass with boiling water. When
> the glass is well heated, pour out the water, fill the glass with
> whisky and drink it before the glass cools.

Here, by the river, stopped the first two white women to enter the Huron Tract, Betsy Hill and Jane Good, on their way to Goderich. Before going on, they cooked lunch for their party, using the fires and cooking pots loaned — with surly grace — by Anthony Van Egmond's son, Constant, in charge of a work gang.

The shanties often were shared for days on end by those planning to settle in or around Little Thames. In the first cautious trickle of settlement, they sheltered adventurous men like Charles Cawston and his son Richard, who came looking for river land, and young John A. McCarthy, whose wagon had broken down and left him stranded. McCarthy, with his wagon mended, moved on to farmlands in North Easthope, but others stayed right at Little Thames.

One particularly strange entourage arrived early. William Berwick and his family came from England, complete with a retinue of servants, hunting dogs

23

and much inappropriate equipment. Backwoods life brought rapid disenchantment, and he was one who packed up and left — his exit not unnoticed by the Warden of the Forests.

Dr. Dunlop shortly was to publish his *Statistical Sketches* for immigrants to Canada. It may have been the presence of Berwick's bizarre retinue at Little Thames that resulted in one sage bit of advice. "Make a present of your setter to your cousin, who is going to the north next season for the grouse season," he counselled. Smooth-haired pointers "and maybe a spaniel" he felt would be better suited to the bush life around Little Thames.

The shanties sheltered all alike: those going to Goderich, heads of families who had come to select their land, settlers proceeding to homesites already chosen in the Easthopes, Ellice and Downie. But no one settled in Little Thames until, one day late in the winter of 1831-32, there arrived William Sargint and his family, possessed of land by the river, on the understanding that there they would build a hotel. Sargint had been given some inducement to come, as the Canada Company finally considered establishing its third townsite. And here he was, this

The Shakespeare Hotel was first permanent building, first church,
first schoolroom and first hamlet hall. . . .
It survived religious riots in 1845, but succumbed to fire in 1849.

Irishman, out from County Tipperary, setting about erecting the first permanent building, and with him his wife, his brother, his brother's wife and possibly some others.

During the first winter, the Sargints lived in the river shanties, while William and his brother cut timber for the two-storey frame building and the women kept house and coped as best they could.

The spring of 1832 was an early one for Upper Canada, with snow off the ground before the first day of April and, as the days lengthened and the forest shadows shortened, travelers on the Huron Road noted that the inn at Little Thames was "abuilding" nicely. Mrs. Sargint, fresh out from Ireland, trustingly put in the settlement's first garden; then had to put it in twice more because of unexpected, killing frosts.

The Sargints soon had the little hotel about ready for business. Thomas Mercer Jones may or may not have had word from England about the imminent establishment of a town to be called "Stratford," but local folklore says he arrived with a sign for the inn — first commercial sign along the Huron Road — and thus he christened the settlement.

The day of the opening of the "Shakespeare Inn" was undoubtedly lively, and perhaps as recorded nearly 65 years after the event by Kathleen MacFarlane Lizars and Robina Lizars, in their book, *In the Days of the Canada Company.* Although the Stratford sisters were not noted for their adherence to fact, they caught the flavor of the times as few other writers did.

> By the time all was finished it was thought high time to christen the village. Mr. Commissioner Jones bought a sign for the inn, a presentment of Shakespeare, to follow up the leading idea which his whim has resolved should govern the nomenclature of the new village. No doubt it was a very convivial gathering; there is no record of Dunlop having honored the occasion with a full Indian costume, with blanket wrapped round him and eagle's feathers decorating his fiery locks, as he did elsewhere; but internal evidence, analogy, and contemporary history warrant one in supposing the event was not a dry christening. No one knew better than Mrs. Sargint how to cater and minister to a guest's wants. . . .
> She even knew the Mysteries of Plotty, when port wine could be got. (Mulled, or rather burnt port, "and very delectable as a night-cap.")

Outgoing Mrs. William Sargint was an asset to the little pioneer community. As the settlers straggled in, she gathered the children together and taught them in the hotel. She helped make the inn the center of business and social life, and she readied "the big room" for the first Anglican church services, held by Canon William Bettridge from Woodstock.

Everyone who possibly could, made it over the bush trail that Sunday, among them Dr. William Dunlop, who contributed handsomely to the collection, and, afterwards, congratulated the minister—

"Goddam good sermon, sir!"

ADELAIDE LEITCH

*A granite boulder
marks an historic site on Ontario
Street.*

Other members of the Sargint family found their way to Upper Canada, either with the first group or afterwards, for early records show a sprinkling of Sargints and their relations. Like her sister-in-law, Mrs. Thomas Sargint, also, was a fitting pioneer. A Roman Catholic in a family of liberal Anglicans, she helped many of her Catholic friends come to the Huron Tract, and settle in, easing their fears and sharing in their backwoods joys.

June, 1833, was a happy month, with a marriage and a baptism, the first Roman Catholic sacraments in the Huron Tract. Father Dempsey, the priest at St. Thomas, came riding up through the forest and performed the marriage of Julia Coffey and Richard O'Donnell. Baptized that same day, June 4, was young Edward Stinson, who may or may not have been born in the settlement.

In the pioneer group of Catholics were also Mr. and Mrs. John Stinson, John Phelan with his wife and five sons, Patrick Cashen, and two unwed ladies, Margaret Anglin and Alice Daly. Village life was not for the Thomas Sargints themselves, however. Shortly, they moved out to a farm on the Huron Road in the township of North Easthope.

In the enormous, hand-written register of contracts that the Canada Company kept, there began to emerge the pattern of settlement: pioneers going through Little Thames to take up land in Goderich; settlers buying up lots all along the Huron Road; first-comers locating on Concession 1, later ones taking up land in the second and third concessions. All the time, some shrewd pioneer speculators were quietly assembling large blocks of land around a future city — among them Anthony Van Egmond, the road builder, as well as the Sargint brothers who, between them in 1833, acquired some 620 acres in South Easthope adjoining two choice lots bought earlier by Van Egmond.

John Sebring, on orders of the Canada Company, built a sawmill in 1832 on the south side of the river, before moving on to build another at the "mill seat" which eventually would be Sebringville. The Company added a grist mill at Little Thames that winter.

The directors of the Canada Company concerned themselves a great deal with the community named Stratford but known as Little Thames, and the second man they sent to settle there was their agent, John Corry Wilson Daly. This quick-tempered, short-statured Ulsterman, born 37 years before in England, was in a fine position to make himself something of a little dictator, and this he proceeded to do — and continued to do — for about the next decade.

He had reached Canada by way of Cooperstown, New York, and joined the Canada Company in Hamilton. He had been the Company's doctor-clerk for a time in Guelph, before he arrived in Stratford in the summer of 1833. Choosing the most commanding location he could find, he built the hamlet's second frame building on the vacant site alongside the wooden bridge; here he would look straight down the Huron Road, the main street.

Taking over the company's mills, he added a machine for carding wool, to attract the farmers who were establishing themselves in the surrounding townships. Before long, he could provide sawn lumber for buildings, flour and oatmeal for food, and yarn for clothing. He became the first postmaster, the closest post office up to that time being in Wilmot Township. He was the local medical authority, the local banker, and an officer of the militia. As a justice of the peace, he performed marriage ceremonies. He took over just about all the responsibilities and occupations of a newly formed community, except that of hotel keeper.

His wife saw to it that they lived in a suitable manner, and the lifestyle of the Dalys was elegant for the time and place. They ate from good china, poured wine from glass decanters, used elegant white chamber pots, and threw their broken glass and crockery into their ash pile — shards which later would be unearthed when modern watermains were being dug in the lawn of the Perth County building.

Daly's prickly disposition did not appeal to early settlers, nor did his wife's attitudes endear her to all the women. Dinner guests were seated in strict protocol, and it was an insult to be seated "below the salt" at the Daly table or, worse still, banished for dinner into the barn. Autocrat he might be, but John Daly would always work single-mindedly for the advancement of his village, and, for that, has sometimes been called its founder. Stratford was the star to which he hitched his wagon, as he, too, assembled choice acreage in the area. In his opinion, what was good for Daly was good for Stratford, and vice versa. They were indivisible.

At the Shakespeare Inn, the Sargints bought a stock of goods and opened a store. The Van Egmonds completed their section of road well ahead of their deadline and the wooden bridge across the river began to bear the weight of heavy wagons. From a nucleus of industrious people, the population grew, not exactly by leaps and bounds, but steadily.

Early in settlement days, George Worsley opened the first general store in a surveyor's shanty near the bridge. John Monteith opened another store on the south side of the river, and then there was George Gowanlock's at what would later become the Bank of Nova Scotia corner. Cobblers came. Then a cabinet maker, William Way. With this arrival, J. C. W. Daly before long had a fine new couch for his cottage, made from cherry wood when a tree was cut down to make way for a post office.

By 1834, there were 39 souls there, as John McDonald arrived with orders from the Canada Company to lay out a plan for a city intended to accommodate, eventually, 35,000 people.

When the Huron Road had been planned, the line had been run from Goderich to a point near the Little Thames. A second line coming west from Wilmot intersected it, and there a stake had been driven, just south of the river. McDonald had used this stake earlier as a reference point in surveying boundaries of the five surrounding townships. Now, he used it to lay out the streets in the "Plan of the Town of Stratford on Avon", rearranging the spokes somewhat to create an attractive downtown, but still keeping the original character of the junction. It was the third Canada Company city the brilliant Scot had designed, following Guelph and Goderich, and all three were exceptional examples of early town planning.

The Huron Road now was Huron Street, as it passed out of this new city, and three main arteries pointed to three Great Lakes: Huron, Erie and Ontario.

On the plan, a sizeable block of land south of the dam was marked as "deeded to Wm. Fredk. McCulloch, Esq." In the center core were streets called Mill, Norman and Douglas, as well as a clutch of saints — St. Andrew, St. Patrick, St. George, St. Michael. One lot by the river was left unnumbered, probably intended for the market square.

To create this wilderness metropolis, land had to be expropriated from Anthony Van Egmond, who was given other lots elsewhere. However, it was a while before this new town proved lucrative to its owners. A Canada Company tabulation from its town lots to December 31, 1837, showed how the revenues were coming in from land sales: in Goderich £1,987; in Guelph, £2,328.5; and in "Stratford on Avon" — £15.

The map was copied, dated at Toronto, 1839, by Donald McDonald, John McDonald's young cousin and earlier his apprentice. He was no longer a boy, but now 23 years old, married for a year, and a promising young man coming to the attention of the Canada Company. His knowledge of the Stratford area would later be put to most lucrative use!

It had been the intention of Galt and Dunlop — and it now was the aim of Thomas Mercer Jones — to bring in the better grade of settler, including the "working artisans". And the working artisans were coming, along with the tradesmen and professionals.

But the most essential early arrival for the backwoods settlement was the English blacksmith, John Sharman, for not only were there the horses and oxen to be shod, but also hinges, bolts and nails to be made, as well as rough tools and

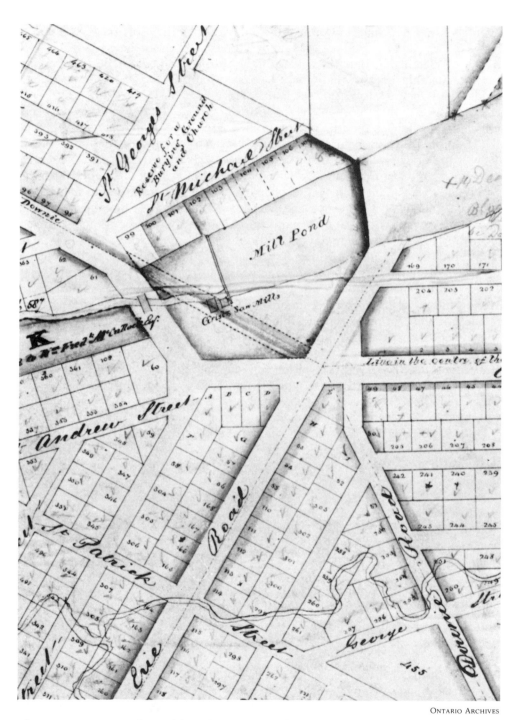

*The center core, as planned by John McDonald in 1834. The map
was copied by Donald McDonald in 1839.*

even cooking pots. Sharman came out from Bedfordshire with about 100 pounds in his pocket, and he used part of it to buy the first lot in the new town plan — a nice little clearing north of the bridge on the Huron Road, where he operated the first blacksmith shop in what would be Perth County. He also served as crown lands agent, for the lots outside the Huron Tract.

His son, Joseph, was born in 1841, one of a new generation who knew only this village. His wife was the first person to die there. But the Sharmans prospered, bought more land and, before long, would own also a foundry and a hotel.

Over the bridge to town, the ox carts and wagons came rumbling in from the prospering farms of Ellice and Downie and the two Easthopes. Produce from the newly-cleared fields could be exchanged for goods and, increasingly, for services. The mills were busy. The pump, across from the Shakespeare Hotel, became, by mutual necessity, the gathering place on a summer afternoon.

Stratford was fortunate in having mills within the community. The straggle of small mills throughout the Huron Tract was soon proving woefully inadequate for the isolated pioneers. In the first ten years of Company reign, Commissioner Jones' indifference to mills seemed criminal, and some settlers beyond Stratford were grinding wheat in coffee grinders nailed to their walls.

The Canada Company was not the only organization lax in its duties. Unrest throughout Upper Canada and antagonism to the governing and despotic Family Compact were growing and, at last, boiled over. News of the Mackenzie Rebellion of 1837 arrived in the Huron Tract the only way it could — over the Huron Road. There were those who sympathized with the fiery William Lyon Mackenzie and his cause, and the rebel attack and defeat on December 7 at Montgomery's Tavern outside York had local implications.

One of the men fighting on the side of the government was "Stout Mac's" young cousin, Donald McDonald. Supporting the rebels — and jailed by the time news of the defeat had reached Stratford — was the man the hamlet could thank for its road and its first bridge over the Avon — Colonel Anthony Van Egmond.

Disillusioned with the bigotry of both Canada Company and Family Compact, and fired by the rightness of William Lyon Mackenzie's cause, he had set out to join the attack on Montgomery's Tavern, and been taken prisoner. When news reached Goderich, Captain Daniel Lizars marched his men down from the lake port and surrounded Van Egmond's Tavern, defended only by poor Mrs. Van Egmond. Some papers were confiscated, a few chairs overturned and smashed, and then the soldiers left, shame-faced. The Van Egmonds, in better times, had been friends and neighbors. Anthony Van Egmond never came back to the Huron Tract he had helped to open. Taking sick in the lonely prison of York, he was transferred to hospital and there he died, a charge of treason hanging over his head.

By the bridge that the Van Egmonds had built across the Little Thames, there began to be signs of civic responsibility: a small, log place of worship for the Presbyterians and any others who wished to attend . . . a log school going up. The community got its first, rudimentary police force, as John Augustus McCarthy returned from the Easthopes.

This young Australian-born pioneer had been only 21 years old, when his wagon had broken down near the river, but he had already had a lifetime of adventure behind him. Son of a military officer with overseas postings, he had had a chance to see the world as few other youngsters had. His childhood had been full of real events that were far beyond any other boy's wildest dreams — seeing Napoleon walking in exile on St. Helena; being given an elephant and a monkey as pets in Ceylon. Life back in England palled. He found keeping the peace around Stratford was more to his taste, and he would still be associated with the law until he died full of years at the age of 87. His firstborn son also would be a policeman. Thomas Brittiff McCarthy, born in 1841, became the High County Constable of Perth. Another son, John A. McCarthy Jr., became police chief of Stratford.

Many early settlers, like the elder McCarthy, came by way of the British Isles. English, Irish, Scots and a few Welshmen brought Old Country customs to flavor the life of a growing community.

Stratford was not a particularly superstitious settlement, although perhaps it was the predominence of Irish in the population that did give it a ghost or two along the way. Most awesome was the one that appeared in the 1870's. A traveler hurrying past the floating log bridge by the McCulloch farm could very well meet this disturbing apparition — a grisly fellow, from all accounts, and minus his head. To some, he appeared in a primitive coffin tied to a plank. Of others he inquired if they had found a missing head. Fleeing this horror, a man could fall over a pale, soft, lumpy object lying on the wooden sidewalk near the dam, and he could fair die of fright before finding out it was only a cow.

Citizens at the time walked abroad with foreboding, and with minds receptive to the notion of a headless haunt. Before the ghost tales had started, a real headless corpse had been found tied to the logs of the old bridge. It turned out that a medical student had taken the body from a graveyard and removed the head for study purposes. Then, becoming alarmed over the whole macabre business, he had tried to sink the body in the river. The corpse was that of a prisoner who had died in the county jail. The headless torso was buried in potters field at Avondale Cemetery. It was the best ghost story that Stratford ever had.

If the Irish brought ghosts, the Germans brought music, and a deep appreciation of all the arts. Pioneer William Brandenberger from Germany came bringing his country's rich cultural traditions. He was a musician who also made sausages, and his wife, Caroline, carried on the business after he died. A son, many years later, provided Stratford with its opera house and first legitimate theatre.

The German immigrants in time would make up about 30% of Perth County's population. The brothers Seegmiller (sometimes *Siegmueller*) would regularly come driving over the rough Huron Road with a four-horse team and wagon loaded with flour, pork and whisky, to exchange in Goderich for salt, fish, hides or money. A descendant would own a tannery in Stratford, and Adam Seegmiller would eventually become the county treasurer.

German settlers were strongly attracted to the area, and both John Galt and

Thomas Mercer Jones encouraged these tidy and industrious people, first recruiting them from the overflowing German settlements of Massachusetts, Pennsylvania and Vermont, later from Germany itself. Early arrivals were founders of new Stratford families — men such as John and George Kalbfleisch, who left Germany in the 1830's; the Wettlaufers, from a later migration.

In the 1840's, the Company approached a man named Rischmiller already in Canada, and had him guide in the German settlers. Although he was not too diligent in his duties, the families he brought that year developed into a thriving German community around the Stratford area. He returned to Germany, but the name remained linked with Stratford. A relative perhaps, William Rischmiller bought a site on which would one day stand the controversial Town Hall and Market Building.

In the 1860's, there was a spilling over of Mennonite families from neighboring and overcrowded Waterloo County; once more, after World War II, there would be an influx of both German and Dutch into Perth. The early arrivals were mainly farmers, keeping to themselves and speaking their own tongue. For a long time, the only man on the South Easthope council who could speak English was the Swiss innkeeper, Sebastian Fryfogel, a man much valued by all who had business within the Huron Tract.

His daughter, Nancy, was promised one of the lots in the new town of Stratford on Avon by Thomas Mercer Jones, who had been at the Fryfogel Inn the night she was born. When she became of age, Nancy came to Stratford to claim her land; the Canada Company honored Jones' promise and she was given Lot 228, a prime piece of residential real estate that proved profitable to her.

Little Thames saw a lot of Commissioner Jones, who had been doing considerable traveling back and forth over the Huron Road — and some said that he had kept a mistress in Goderich until he married — at which point, they said, he handed her over to Charles Pryor, the agent at Goderich.

Jones' marriage took place on November 3, 1832, in St. James' Cathedral at York, where Archdeacon John Strachan, one of the most powerful men in Upper Canada and a force in the Family Compact, saw his daughter, Elizabeth Mary, married to a man twice her age.

Five or six years later, when Commissioner Jones moved to Goderich, he decided to bring with him the trappings of the good life and the lavish home he had enjoyed in York. Shortly, 21 wagons came jolting through Little Thames, a caravan bearing oriental rugs, carved furniture, aged wines, fine linens and elegant clothing for the parties at Goderich — even a huge chandelier brought out from Ireland. All this came trundling down Ontario Street and across the bridge. They ran out from the Shakespeare Hotel and from the shops and mills. They watched, open-mouthed, as the forest swallowed up this remarkable entourage. They marvelled, shrugged, then went back to their businesses.

Incoming settlers shared the usual hardships of Upper Canada pioneers, but they were better off than most. They found Canada Company Agent Daly was, on the whole, a fair man. And Dunlop was to them a godsend, hunting with the settlers, drinking with them, understanding their fears. He was unstintingly generous with his help, both in the wilderness and at dockside in Quebec, where he sometimes met the immigrant boats and steered the best of the new arrivals to his beloved Huron Tract.

January following publication of his *Sketches,* Dunlop had gone to England on Huron Tract business. The Court of Directors of the Canada Company earlier had abolished the office of Warden of the Forests but, in the face of vehement protest from the two commissioners in Canada, had continued to employ him. Convinced of his usefulness, they renewed his salary agreement and sent him back with a new title: "General Superintendent of The Huron Tract in charge of Sales, and General Overseer". He would still be enormously helpful to the genuinely suitable settlers, even after he resigned from his post in 1838.

Prospective settlers had considerable advance information, for the Canada Company was no slouch at advertising:

> Industrious men may look forward with confidence to an improvement in their situation, as they may save enough out of one season's work to buy land themselves. . . .

John Mactaggart, producing a wealth of information for emigrants leaving Britain, told them:

> Gin and rum, of superior quality, may be obtained from wild berries, which grow profusely in the woods, and [from] the sugar maple.

Many a settler was enormously disappointed, on trying it!

The Huron Road, in the 1830's, was still mainly corduroy, awash with mud and dotted with stumps. This did not stop the Canada Company, as soon as the road was passable, from encouraging settlers to take the stage coach from Hamilton to Goderich. Said the alluring advertisement:

> Two good covered Stage Wagons, with Teams of good Horses each, are to be constantly kept traveling between Hamilton, at the Head of Lake Ontario, and through Wilmot to Goderich in the Huron Territory.

This was largely propaganda. Such regular service did not operate through Stratford until around 1841, by which time the daily stage lines were operating east to west across the province, although mainly still just carrying the mails.

By the time the Huron Road was passable, the major routes had already been built along the St. Lawrence and Lower Lakes: Dundas Street . . . the Talbot Road . . . Governor Simcoe's Yonge Street (as well as the Penetanguishene Road built by "Tiger" Dunlop). The Kingston Road extended this highway system to the east.

In the Huron Tract, the Huron Road was one of the three primary access routes aimed at Goderich. The other approaches to the prized Canada Company port on Lake Huron were the road from London and the water route up the lake. Secondary roads were developed with less enthusiasm on the part of the Canada Company, although, in the mid-1830's, the company did slash a sleigh track, the Zorra Road, southeast through Downie and Zorra Townships to Ingersoll.

The log school, the "Auld Kirk" and J. C. W. Daly's
cottage cluster together, in a poetic watercolor by R. Thomas Orr.

The Canada Company built one more road near Stratford, the Mitchell Road, a miserable little thoroughfare designed — as were the others — to provide access to Goderich. There was no connection with Stratford, on its completion in 1844.

And, at that point, the Canada Company bowed out of the road building business. From then on, the people of Stratford and the Huron Tract could jolly well build and finance their own roads. The Company was far more interested in land transactions.

Land alongside the Little Thames River was of prime value, and the Canada Company, in selling lots, took great care to protect its water rights, including the right to raise or lower the mill pond at will. The deeds it issued disclaimed liability for damages to inundated lands at "Avon Mills", on payment of "seven shillings for each acre so overflowed in the Townships of Ellice and eight shillings per acre so overflowed in the townships of North Easthope".

This did not deter the early land baron, William McCulloch, who, upon his arrival from Ireland in 1842, began accumulating riverfront land. One choice piece was a broad estate, the "Grange" property, straddling the river and, on it, he built himself a luxurious home. As other properties became available, he bought them too.

Some who bought from the company on a land-lease — or leasehold — basis, had difficulty keeping up their payments, among them James and Henry

Mitchell. Finally, an 1843 indenture recorded the transfer of their land in North Easthope and Ellice to William McCulloch, on payment of the Mitchells' arrears and on McCulloch's assuming the original provisions allowing the Canada Company to flood the land for stated compensation. It was signed by Thomas Mercer Jones, for the Canada Company, and witnessed by Donald McDonald. The next year, McCulloch also got the mills.

There was much criticism of the Canada Company's leasehold system that had spelt disaster for the Mitchells; yet it allowed many industrious settlers eventually to own their property. More legitimate grievances concerned the lack of mills, bungling by officials in building and repairing the roads, and in the company's known alliance with the Family Compact.

Understandably, and through pure self-interest, the land company would pander to the country's powerful and despotic clique, but the alliance did nothing to aid the struggling settlers, and William Dunlop, once the Company's Warden of the Woods and Forests, increasingly opposed his former bosses. When he narrowly won the 1841 election over the candidate put up by Thomas Mercer Jones, the elated voters of the Huron Tract celebrated the victory of "people over power", sure that the "Tiger" in the Legislature would, as the press put it, "triumph over the daring iniquities of the Canada Company".

There were celebrations throughout the Huron Tract.

In Goderich, Daniel Lizars chaired a celebration dinner at the Goderich Hotel "in honor of the Doctor's glorious return to Parliament". It was a somewhat more sedate affair than the one held on the banks of the Avon!

In Stratford, the victory dinner was in Sharman's Tavern. They worked through the usual toasts — the Queen, the Prince Consort, the Governor General, the Commander of the forces, the Duke of Wellington. Then the celebrants went on to the main toasts: the Health of Dr. Dunlop, Liberal Opinion, Agriculture, The Election and, eventually (as the *British Colonist* correspondent reported in the issue of Sept. 15, 1841), they toasted Themselves:

> As the freeholders of this quarter, notwithstanding much annoyance and it may be said intimidation from the supporters of the defeated candidate, went nobly to the poll, and throughout displayed much spirit . . . their health was proposed and drunk.
> The meeting shortly afterwards separated.

No mention of how they wended their way home, through the autumn evening, over the uneven ground!

Within the Tract itself there had been changes. In the young country, early administrative areas had been huge, and the whole Huron Tract had been within the London District. In 1834, it became the newly-separated District of Huron, with one representative in the Legislature, although it still was ruled from London. In 1842, a district council met in Goderich for the first time — which was some improvement for the people of Stratford, but not much. They now went 45 miles to the district's municipal town of Goderich, instead of 70 miles to London. It was still a long, weary way to go, over the Huron Road, to attend to matters such as taxes, legal problems and education.

There was much work at hand, much planning to do in building a settlement. Old ties weakened; new roots explored new soil, and interests turned increasingly inward to the community. Despatch riders, going back and forth to Goderich, brought snippets of news. The saddlebag preachers stayed the night and filled in the details. The town crier broadcast the more electrifying events.

The Stratford people listened with mild interest to the gossip of Guelph and Galt, and took some interest in the infighting in Goderich between the local elite, the Colborne Clique, and the Canada Company. But they really did not tremendously care. Goderich was, after all, miles distant over rough roads. Nor did they have to live on the doorstep of the sometimes arrogant top officials of the Canada Company.

They had, besides, some local problems of their own developing, and one of them was becoming increasingly unpleasant.

On July 12, 1843, some 80 Roman Catholics assembled at the village square, armed with loaded guns, pitchforks and scythes, and they marched down the Zorra Road to accost the men of Downie on the way up for their annual Orange Parade. The Protestants, ill-prepared and not wanting a fight, scattered, but not without bitter resentment.

A year and a half later, January 6, 1845, the racial antagonisms erupted in earnest at a regular township meeting. It had been called to elect two district councilors from Downie and the Gore of Downie to replace J. C. W. Daly, too busy with other things to continue to represent the townships on the Huron District Council. Two men had agreed to stand in his stead, W. F. McCulloch and James Simpson. However, when the supposedly cut-and-dried meeting got under way at the schoolhouse, Daly — who was not present and no longer wanted the job — also was nominated by his loyal followers.

John Daly, an Irish Catholic who attended church services with the Anglicans, and sometimes with the Presbyterians, was known as a fair man, generally respected, if not cordially liked. On the other hand, McCulloch was a different matter — an *English* Catholic. And Simpson, a Scot, had made no bones about his support of the Orange Lodge. The Irish Catholics of Downie, outnumbered about three to one, were alarmed, and grew even more so when Daly drew a handsome vote but, nevertheless, was defeated.

The smarting Irishmen withdrew, and spent the rest of the afternoon drinking and nursing their grievances. When the meeting broke up, they watched McCulloch and Simpson head toward the village's traditional meeting place, the Shakespeare Hotel, and they followed.

The victorious candidates were celebrating as the Irishmen forced their way in, but they had anticipated an attack, and they were armed with two bayonets and a multitude of axe handles. Chairs were heaved. The tables were sent crashing. They nearly wrecked the Shakespeare Hotel before the fracas finally erupted through the front door onto Ontario Street.

No one was killed in the riots, thanks to the 30 special constables that J. C. W. Daly, as Justice of the Peace, had taken the precaution of appointing for meeting day. Many people were badly injured and there were bloody heads and some

27 arrests in Stratford before it was over. Daly, in a tactless speech, publicly blamed the Orange Lodge for the intolerant situation in Stratford.

Next January, when the township meeting was called and Daly was to be absent, McCulloch asked for, and got, help from Goderich. They sent down John Bignall to keep the peace — and indeed he did. He arrived to find that it was common knowledge that arsenals of arms — guns, knives, scythes and axe handles — were stored within reach. The meeting ended without a repetition of the 1845 confrontation, but it was years before the bitter feelings subsided in Stratford.

There was some constraint, around the town pump, as people exchanged local news, made business deals and operated their village. They still gathered

*The innkeeper's brother and a young son lie
buried beneath a stone on the St. James' Church lawn.*

together in the Shakespeare Hotel for peaceable affairs — such as the organization meeting of the first boat club. Of necessity, in a crisis, they would still band together for mutual assistance, and they still volunteered for the bucket brigade to carry water from the wells and the river to douse village fires.

One fire they could not douse in time was at the Shakespeare Hotel. It burned to the ground in 1849, from causes unknown.

The innkeeper, William Sargint, and his wife had moved away some time before, leaving a brother-in-law, William Jackson, in charge. No one knew where the Sargints had gone. And so exited the founder of Little Thames and of Stratford, a mystery man in a way, a shadowy figure moving in the background in the first inn. Industrious clearly he was, but overshadowed by his wife, of whom some description was written. Although Thomas Sargint remained in the area, and was buried on the lawn of St. James Church, William never returned. The burning of the Shakespeare Hotel marked the end of an era.

Somewhere, in the midst of all the activity that had gone before, Little Thames had quietly become, in everyone's mind, Stratford.

3

The Stormy Road To Independence

ONE MAN WHO DID not exactly fit the mold of the average incoming settler was John James Edmonstoune Linton — a man as brilliant and as single-minded in his way as was J. C. W. Daly. He was, besides, a Scot and, to further compound a touchy situation, he settled across the street from the store of the Irishman, Daly.

John Linton was straight-laced, but he was sincere. His dour, Presbyterian God he followed absolutely, not just when he bowed his head in his church on the Sabbath, but when he went about his business on weekdays. He expected everyone else to follow Him, too, while he himself acted at God's guardian of the public morals.

In the late Victorian era, many straight-laced municipalities enacted bylaws derived from the English "blue laws". Aware of this, John Linton drew up a lengthy list of rules for "The Preservation of the Public Morals", and had no trouble getting county council to endorse them. He then published them with enthusiastic praise in Issue 23 of *The Challenge,* an outspoken temperance periodical "published occasionally and gratis by J. J. E. Linton".

Among a truly formidable list of 24 Shalt-Nots were these:

Clause 5 — No "marbles, cricket, skittles . . . on Sunday."

Clause 17 — "no tippling. . . ." (No "tippling houses" either.)

Clause 21 — "No circus performances. . . ."

Clause 22 — No bowling alley was to be allowed.

Breaking the bylaw would be followed by a fine or by being "committed to Gaol for 20 days with or without hard labor".

Straight-laced he was. Yet this annoyingly upright Scot could be deeply touched by the troubles of others. In the depression days that followed the crop failures of the 1850's, and despite his strong anti-liquor views, John Linton carried a bottle of wine to a dying man, Pat Connors, and later paid two dollars for the funeral expenses. And that was a princely sum in those destitute days.

Linton was the man the settlement needed. He would teach the early pioneer children, and he himself would achieve a permanent place among Stratford's great. But he would travel a stormy, if self-selected, road to get there.

Linton began, quietly enough, as a farmer in Downie Township, one of the few jobs he ever tackled without the necessary qualifications. He was 29 years old and already married when he came to the Huron Tract in 1833, bringing his Scottish wife, Margaret. Born at Rothsay, Isle of Bute, he had been a teacher and a lawyer in Scotland before emigrating to Upper Canada. An agent of the Canada Company directed him to lands near Stratford and there, in Downie Township, he soon learned, to his chagrin, that farming was not his forte.

When he moved into town, he turned to his earlier profession and opened a school in his home. Margaret Linton started one in nearby North Easthope, and both soon were conducting night classes as well. Had he stuck to his books, and not enriched his own personal curriculum, he might not have run afoul of J. C. W. Daly, busy consolidating a little empire.

They were two of a kind, these two driving men of Stratford, and they mistrusted each other completely.

When Linton abandoned farming and entered business in Stratford as a public notary and conveyancer, the ambition of the man did not go unnoticed. John Linton applied for an appointment as a magistrate, and Daly, who had the necessary power and was already irked by a neighbor he considered a radical, blocked the appointment promptly — this in spite of the fact that the Huron Tract sorely needed such educated and qualified men. It was one of the few times Daly's personal interests superseded those of Stratford.

However, John James Edmonstoune Linton, like the Scottish thistle of his homeland, was not to be sat upon, as Daly quickly learned. In the Legislative Assembly, Robert Baldwin and his Reformers were known to favor more independence for local governments, and the early 1840's found Linton complaining by letter to Robert Baldwin about Daly's misuse of public funds. When the racial riots rocked Stratford in 1845, Linton angrily took pen in hand and wrote to the *British Colonist* at York, criticizing the Little King of Stratford for mishandling the whole thing.

When not needling Daly, or teaching, Linton was endlessly busy. Evenings, he worked on three handbooks for the Canada Company, one of them the lovely little volume, "Life of a Backwoodsman", published anonymously. He frequently involved himself in religious disputes. He churned out articles, essays and pamphlets on a number of themes close to his heart: the abolition of slavery, strong anti-Americanism, local morality. He published the short-lived "Voice of the Bondsman" in Stratford in 1856-57, but it attracted few subscribers. It did not last out a year and the only surviving copy of it ended up at the University of Western Ontario.

John Linton also promoted an agricultural society, became its first secretary, and saw the first fall fair in Stratford held October 14, 1842, in Shakespeare Place. He became the first clerk of the 3rd division court and, as he steadily improved his fortunes, he irked J. C. W. Daly increasingly. Then, in 1846, the two arch rivals found themselves suddenly in agreement, and with a cause neither could ignore. It was the promotion and advancement of Stratford as the center of a new district.

J. C. W. Daly first put forward the plan to make Stratford the district capital, an event to follow a hoped-for division of the large and unwieldy Huron District. Like Linton, other villagers buried personal antagonisms towards Daly who, by now, had acquired an awesome number of enemies. One supporter was Stratford's wealthiest landowner, W. F. McCulloch, who had bought the Avon mills. Another was Stewart Campbell from Ellice, who had been beaten by several Roman Catholics in front of Daly's house in the riots of 1845 without Daly lifting a finger, as magistrate. Another recruit was Daly's own 20-year-old son, Tom, enterprising, young, confident to the point of brashness, and ambitious far beyond his years.

Huron District, containing much of the old Huron Tract, had been separated from the London District for some years. Now John Daly, supported by Linton, argued that the eastern section had become big enough for a district government of its own, to be centered on Stratford, since Goderich was so far away. The *real* grievance was not distance so much as it was the impossibility of extracting any help from Goderich, but the citizens feared this might seem pretty niggling to the government.

Goderich — which *had* shamefully ignored and neglected Stratford as long as it had been content to remain quiet — now was irate. So, too, was Blanshard Township, for it had close ties with Woodstock and London, and planned to keep them. They called a meeting in the township, and one man rose to his feet to describe Stratford as "a locality nearly surrounded by swamps" — *clearly* unfit to be a district capital! Besides, there was no passable road east to it from St. Marys.

Nor were Eastern township residents unanimously for the idea of a Stratford-based district. Many were promoting the cause of a new "District of Bruce" with Galt as district center. Out on the Huron Road, they called a secret meeting at Fryfogel's Tavern, and the people were already gathering when Stratford got wind of it. Rounding up the separationists, Daly and Linton whipped up the horses and arrived at Fryfogel's just in time to kill discussion of a District of Bruce.

The time, nevertheless, was right for the elevation of Stratford, and both Daly and Linton were intelligent enough to know it. By the 1840's, all Canada West was entering an era of progressive self-government, and Stratford, already chafing at the absentee rule from Goderich, was all for it.

By 1846, the village had 200 people, with a post office (run by J. C. W. Daly) and post three times a week on the Galt-to-Goderich route. There were two doctors, grist and saw mills, various hotels, a tannery, three stores, a brewery, a distillery, a couple of taverns, two blacksmiths, a saddler, a couple of wheelwrights, three shoemakers, two tailors, and an ashery for soap making.

St. Marys, 12 miles away, still had only 120 people, although it was growing fast; Mitchell was not even listed in W. H. Smith's *Canadian Gazetteer* of that year. Stratford did not yet have a curling rink — like Galt (pop. 1,000). Or a fine

The unlikely allies — J. J. E. Linton (left) and J. C. W. Daly (right)

port — like Goderich (pop. 659). Or even a newspaper, as did its closest neighbor to the east, Berlin, which had begun printing *The German Canadian*. It didn't even have an undertaker, whereas Guelph had two. It wouldn't have a cemetery for over a quarter of a century, when Avondale would be set aside.

Nevertheless, its children were receiving basic schooling; its people were holding religious services. The Huron Tract was changing and Little Thames was all but forgotten. An aging "Tiger" Dunlop, once the flamboyant and beloved backwoodsman hacking his way through the woods with traveling bar and brawling good humor, now was more politician than woodsman, and many said he was taking on, without a scruple, more appointments than he could efficiently handle.

The time was ripe, indeed!

The Daly-Linton political machine went into high gear, and the opponents of separation were too late with too little.

Montreal, where parliament was sitting, was a long and expensive trip away, and it was not easy to scrape up enough money to allow John Linton to journey there to present the county cause. Some did not even think he should go. There was a story that the secretary-treasurer of the Mechanics' Institute, S. L. Roberts, advanced him $30 out of the Institute's funds. Roberts' father-in-law — who was W. F. McCulloch, the richest man in town — had him sued.

Twice John Linton went to Montreal, and it was largely thanks to his eloquent arguments that the area centering on Stratford separated from Huron. He helped draft the bill whereby the eastern section of Huron became Perth County and he named it, honoring the birthplace of the earliest settlers of North Easthope, Perthshire, Scotland — which, by happy coincidence, he, too, knew well.

That same year, 1848, Dr. William Dunlop died in Lachine, Quebec, and the exuberance of separation was dampened. In January, his body was brought home. The funeral procession came through the village and the "Tiger's" body lay throughout one long night in a hotel stable on Ontario Street. Then his devoted sister-in-law, Louisa, took it on for burial at Goderich.

On January 1, 1850, Perth County was a reality, although still a provisional county until county buildings could be erected. John Linton was the hero of the hour, although it was some time before he collected his out-of-pocket expenses. It was a time of change in the monetary system, too. Eventually, when Linton was awarded $100, they paid it to him as 25 pounds, at the legal exchange rate for the pound, as set at Halifax.

The first meeting of the provisional council was called by William Smith, reeve of Downie Township, and by young Tom Daly, just barely 21 but now reeve of North Easthope. John Linton immediately became the first clerk of the provisional council; shortly, his old rival, John Daly, was appointed first treasurer — as soon as there were finances to manage.

Landowner W. F. McCulloch, perhaps embarrassed by his abandonment of Daly and the separation issue, donated land he owned north of the river, and here the first county buildings were built on McCulloch's Hill. Perth, in 1853, was officially a full county, and Stratford was its heart.

To the new county court house on McCulloch's Hill, came the first judge, Read Burritt from Sarnia, sworn in by J. J. E. Linton as clerk of the peace. He left before the year was out, exchanging places with Judge Charles Robinson of the new County of Lambton.

For Judge Robinson, the change did not work out and, after two years, he moved out of his house on the north bank of the Avon River and took himself home with a fanciful excuse for leaving.

Sitting on his porch of an evening, and having his wee nip from the bottle (he said), he found that the frogs along the river got on his nerves with their incessant chorus —

"The Judge is dronk! The Judge is drrrrronk!"

Actually, the Judge was *not* drunk — he was a very temperate man — but it was as good an excuse as any. Judge Burritt returned and, for the next nine years, dispensed justice at Stratford. The next county judge would be the astute crown attorney, Daniel Home Lizars, who would serve for 22 years and become a power in the community.

Although the first county court house would be used until well into the 1880's, the men of the law who dispensed justice in Stratford were never particularly enamoured of their quarters up on McCulloch's hill. The courtroom was small ·and stuffy, the offices cramped and unventilated. Finally, at a spring assizes, the Chief Justice angrily marched his court across the dam and into the airy and spacious concert hall of the Market Building. The town indignantly sent the county a bill.

However, with the establishment of the County of Perth and the raising of the county buildings in Stratford, John Daly and John Linton, those unlikely partners, had, together, assured their hamlet's future, and they certainly should have jarred it out of the doldrums of the thirties and forties.

But Stratford on the Avon was an inland settlement, still cut off from the upbeat life of a Goderich or a York. If the townspeople were quietly gratified with their new status as County Town, they realized only dimly where it could lead. They went back to their businesses.

W. H. Smith traveled through Stratford again in 1852, an itinerent surgeon-dentist, who was also collecting material for his monumental two-volume *Canada, Past Present and Future.* He took note of the excellent river location and of the increasing population, but his profile of the Perth County seat was a sad picture of apathy.

> Stratford is pleasantly and well situated, but has not made the progress it should have done, considering its natural advantages. It has increased considerably in size since we first visited it seven years ago, but the buildings generally are of an inferior description, and appear to indicate a want either of spirit or of means amongst the inhabitants; this, however, is not surprising, as an inland place, surrounded by bad roads for a large portion of the year, is scarcely likely to partake largely of a cheerful character; the inhabitants, no matter how enterprising they may be by nature, most frequently, when subjected to the depressing influences of local drawbacks, find their natural animal spirits lowered to that peculiar level, known in some sections of the old country by the significant and expressive term of 'deadly lively'.
>
> The population of Stratford is said to be about nine hundred. There is a grist mill containing two runs of stones, with a distillery and saw mill attached, and a larger grist mill is now in course of preparation; an oat and barley mill, a foundry, a steam saw mill with carding and fulling mill attached, two tanneries, a brewery, and post office; two asheries, one of which is on a large scale, and six churches: Episcopal, Church of Scotland, Free Church, Congregational, Wesleyan Methodist, and Roman Catholic.
>
> The Upper Canada Bank, Canada Life Assurance Company, Provincial Mutual and Equitable Fire Insurance Companies, and the Canada Company have agents here.

From among the 900 inhabitants, he mentioned a selected group, with their occupations. Notably among them were:

> T. M. Daly, miller; U. C. Lee, merchant and potash manufacturer; W. F. McCulloch, miller, distiller, lumber merchant; A. B. Orr, iron foundry; W. Rischmiller, lumber merchant; J. J. E. Linton, coroner, notary public and commissioner of the court of the Queen's Bench; D. H. Lizars, attorney.

Around the stove, they argued
incorporation, separation, and the price of wheat.
These were uppermost in Stratford minds.

These were men coming up in Stratford's business world. They were also subscribers to Smith's book, which probably accounted for some omissions — such as the name of the elder Daly.

Three years after being chosen the County Seat of the provisional County of Perth, and the same year Perth became a full county, Stratford became an incorporated village. Its application was approved by William Rowan, administrator of the government of the Province of Canada, on September 23, 1853, to become effective January 1, 1854.

To create the village, 2,700 acres were detached from the converging townships: approximately 800 acres from the square block of Downie; 450 acres from the Gore of Downie; 400 from South Easthope, 550 from North Easthope and 500 from Ellice. The boundaries were the river, Front Street on the east, John Street on the west, and West Gore Street on the south.

Up the hill and into the County Court House, where County Sheriff Robert Moderwell was presiding as returning officer, the villagers trooped to elect their first representatives, along with three inspectors of "houses of public entertainment" — hotels and taverns.

Alexander Barrington Orr topped the polls with 77 votes, followed by Peter Reid, 75 votes; John Polkingham Vivian, 71; William Frederick McCulloch, 65; Revenius Hooker Lee, 64. McCulloch, elected reeve of the five-man council, represented the new village on County Council. The new village government, proud as punch, was headquartered for the time being in the county building, up on McCulloch's Hill.

Like any new business, the new council set about appointing officials, making rules (with a spate of bylaws) and studying ways of raising money.

It set up an official police force, consisting, in its entirety, of George Larkworthy, hired on a trial basis at 80 pounds a year. Council dropped him next year, when it found another man who would police the village for free, but eventually reverted to paid employees. However, Stratford still was, as Daniel Lizars, Clerk of the Peace, pointed out just before villagehood, blessedly free of crimes.

". . . And really," he wrote in a piece of Canada Company literature, "the peccadilloes committed . . . do not deserve so high a title . . ." He hastened to point an accusing finger at Toronto that had had 1,608 arrests in 1850, while only 120 persons had been convicted in the whole Huron Tract. Thanks be to Providence "that prosperity is in the ascendant and that crime is on the decline!"

There were village chores that were arbitrarily farmed out. Council divided the village into five areas for statute labor, and began to call up the citizenry to open roads, build sidewalks, dig ditches, cut weeds, or anything that came to mind.

Under the Statute Labor Act, in the 1850's municipalities were entitled to such services. Days worked were tied to the assessment of a person's property. An assessment of $300, for instance, called for two days' labor, and refusal to work brought a fine of $10.

Meanwhile, the meeting place around the town pump was becoming inadequate for the dissemination of news. The rising status of Stratford gave impetus to a flurry of local weekly newspapers, starting with the short-lived *Perth County News* in 1849, followed by the *Examiner* founded by the energetic Tom Daly in 1852; then, the year Stratford became a village, the first issue of the *Stratford Beacon* came rolling off the press on December 29, 1854.

From then on, the citizens had not only regular news, in an increasing number of papers but, also, outspoken comment on the actions of the men they had elected. The Press took its duties seriously. When, in 1855, members of the village council moved from a room in the Perth County offices to the Albion Hotel, the *Beacon* castigated them roundly for meeting in a tavern. Council retreated to the new common school and met there, while waiting for a permanent home to be built.

At this point, a shadowy figure that had been flitting about the edge of Stratford affairs ever since early survey days, now appeared again, and Donald McDonald, the surveyor's cousin, sold the village an acre of land on which to put up a market building.

On all fronts, these were heady times in the mid-1850's — the new market building in the offing, the railway coming, and plans for the gravel road to be built north. As council tackled new problems, the press took note of the increasing financial flounderings of the new and still inexperienced village councilors.

For some time, the village had been embarrassingly short of funds, and had been having difficulty borrowing money. The 1854 council had turned to the Municipal Loan Fund and asked to borrow 6,000 pounds, with which to build a school, a market house and sidewalks — all badly needed, all legitimate requests.

The Fund, set up by Act of Parliament in 1852, enabled hard-pressed municipalities of Canada West to use their joint credit to secure loans at lower rates of interest than had been available previously. Initially, no restrictions were placed on the amount borrowed and Stratford, like some other municipalities, soon borrowed beyond its means.

A loan for school, market and sidewalks was one thing. But, two years later, with the railway age upon it, Stratford was puffed up with confidence, eager to dabble in higher finances, and still lacking in the experience to handle Big League debts. When, in 1857, the village got $100,000 from the Municipal Loan Fund to help bail out the ailing Buffalo and Lake Huron Railway, it borrowed trouble as well, for the city was left with a shaky financial basis that would unsettle council for years.

A worsening financial situation in the village was inherited by the town, as J. C. W. Daly took office January 1, the first mayor of the Town of Stratford. Six months was enough, and he resigned, leaving Reeve William Smith to finish the term.

The year after incorporation, the town still had heavy financial liabilities. The greatly worried treasurer warned, "They ought to be met at once to save the sheriff from taking over the assessment roll."

To make matters worse, the community, like others, was in the midst of a recession, with many out of work and 33 families on relief. The town was giving men jobs at 50 cents a day, and John Linton was running a soup kitchen to feed the needy.

With council able to make only token payments to the Municipal Loan Fund, the Stratford situation worsened, as Sheriff Moderwell served a writ on the town for non-payment of nearly $3,000. Stratford managed to scrape up $1,000 to ward off immediate disaster, but the debt still rose. By 1873, the town owed the fund $208,812 in principal and interest.

It was small comfort that other municipalities were floundering in the same bog of over-borrowing. However, with the situation country-wide, the Provincial Government amended the Act, forgiving much of the debt and reducing interest rates. Stratford came out of it owing $53,408 and a debt that was not wiped out until 1893, long after Stratford had become a city.

While the civic leaders worked their way through the snarls of separation and incorporation and high finances, the character of the community had been changing. The rough camaraderie of pioneer building bees was ending, the

N. B.—All letters to be post-paid.
Stratford, August 7, 1856.   84-tf

Opening of the Grand Trunk Railway to Stratford.

PUBLIC NOTICE.

Messrs. Arnold & Robinson,

PROPRIETORS of the Property adjoining the Grand Trunk Railway Buildings at Stratford, (known as the Lynch Estate) have APPOINTED the subscriber their *AGENT* in Stratford, for the disposal of the remainder of the property.

Plans of the property may be seen, and particulars obtained on application to

JOHN W. MARLING,
Land and Estate Agent, Auctioneer, &c.

P. S.—Lots for sale at £20 and upwards.
Stratford, July, 1856.   84-tf

AMERICAN EXPRESS CO.

Grand Trunk Railway Route.

WE have appointed Mr. J. E. LEE our Agent at Stratford. He will in future transact any business connected with our company at this town. Every description of Express matter received and despatched daily to all parts of Canada East and West and United States.

J. H. TALBOT,
Superintendent.

American Express Co.'s)
Office, Stratford, Oct. 9)   94 4t

NEW AND SPLENDID

Patent Buggy for Sale

FOR SALE, on reasonable terms, a Splendid Patent, Covered (Leather-top) BUGGY, never used. Half cash required down. Time will be given for the remainder. The Buggy, which was made expressly to order for a private gentleman, can be seen by application at the *Beacon* office, to

W. MOWAT.
Stratford, 20th Aug. 1856.   80-tf

Front page classified ads for November 7, 1857, in The Stratford Beacon reflected the railway's coming; and "a private gentleman" offered his buggy for sale.

shanties and early log homes coming down. There were the more complex interrelations of civic development. The town council added to the Shakespearean theme with five Shakespearean wards: Avon, Falstaff, Hamlet, Romeo and Shakespeare, their boundaries fanned out like spokes from a wheel with its hub in the center of town. The names appeared on the assessment roll for the first time in 1862.

At dinner, in the increasingly fine homes of the early 1850's, the talk turned to matters beyond the townline, of the need for improved communication, and of transportation. These were the derricks that would hoist Stratford out of its agricultural age and set it down at the beginning of the industrial era.

Railway fever was in the air not just in Stratford but all through the Huron Tract. Up in Goderich, Commissioner Thomas Mercer Jones, now an established resident, found his interests increasingly those of the local Colborne Clique. He shared their alarm at the waning of Goderich as a center of importance, while places like Stratford and Guelph were going ahead. A railway terminating at the lake would do much to mend matters.

He knew that Frederick Widder, the new commissioner in Toronto, along with the Court of Directors of the Canada Company in London, favored a route from Toronto to a terminus at Sarnia, a better port, in their opinion. With either route, Stratford would be on the main line and would benefit enormously. Fearful of such rival growth, Jones arbitrarily announced Canada Company support for the Buffalo Brantford and Goderich Line. The Company, and the indignant Court of Directors, did not back him up. In 1852, Jones was dismissed as co-commissioner of the Canada Company.

The line to Goderich did make some headway. A railway survey was completed through Stratford to Goderich early in the 1850's, with a station planned a mile out of town. First sod was turned in the summer of 1853 for "The B.B.G." — the Buffalo, Brantford and Goderich Line, originally the Buffalo and Brantford. But the site of the sod turning at the corner of Erie and St. David Streets soon became an embarrassment to the citizens, as financial problems on the railway brought track-laying to a shuddering halt, and there was no money for rolling stock.

It was 1856 before the Railway Age finally opened in Stratford, but when it came it brought with it, as anticipated, a new era.

BEACON HERALD

The importance of Stratford's primary industry was stated in a steaming locomotive carved on the back of the mayor's chair, made at the turn of the century for the new city hall.

4

The Biggest Business In Town

QUITE AN EXCITEMENT prevailed in town Friday last," the *Beacon* informed its readers with great understatement of fact in the issue of September 1, 1856.

Grand Trunk Railway construction men, working near Nile Street, had come upon the idle rails of the rival Buffalo, Brantford and Goderich Railway blocking the route they were extending to St. Marys. They tore them up and went through.

Mr. Fountain, agent of the B.B. & G, telegraphed the line's manager, got his orders, and quickly rounded up a crew of his own. They started tearing up the Grand Trunk track. *However* . . .

> . . . before they had accomplished much the iron-horse of the Grand Trunk hove in sight, having in tow a couple of carloads of navvies, who, it was reported, were all drunk and armed to the teeth, the former a circumstance which seems likely to be true, from the fact that two rather large-sized demijohns, which were on the cars, seemed to be the special object of care. Mr. Fountain and his men, deeming prudence the better part of valor, retreated, leaving the Grand Trunk men in possession of the field, which they still hold. Of course the lawyers will settle the matter.

"Quite an excitement" occurred at regular intervals during the 19th century railway boom, while two companies were constructing lines into Stratford and a third railroad was under discussion by local businessmen. The two building toward Stratford were the Grand Trunk Railway and the Buffalo, Brantford and Goderich. The healthy young Grand Trunk Railway, a true pioneering road with ambitions to link the Atlantic coast with Sarnia, was approaching from the east, by way of Berlin. The rival Buffalo, Brantford and Goderich road, which earlier had turned the first sod and laid the first rails in the village, was coming up from the southeast through Galt, and would build on through Stratford to Goderich.

51

Stratford viewed this race with deep satisfaction. In Canada West, there was not a man, woman or child who would not immediately be affected by the coming of the iron horse, and it would prove doubly important here, where the railway would eventually monopolize the city and become the biggest business in town.

The village was humming with anticipation a year before the trains arrived. William Mowat, the new editor of the *Beacon,* was fully aware of this as he set out, one fine September day in 1855, on a business trip to Toronto. For his readers, he detailed this pre-railway journey: first by stage coach to Berlin; by a second stage coach to the railhead at Galt; on the Great Western Railway to Hamilton, where the station was two miles out of town; by horse-drawn cab into town to await departure of the scheduled boat; finally, by paddle-wheeler down the lake to Toronto. The journey that took him 26 hours he soon would be able to do in four, when the rails reached Stratford.

The race of the trains was not an even one. The B. B. & G. from its infancy had been beset by financial problems. Both Stratford and Perth County had loaned the line money, hoping to acquire two competing railways, but the B. B. & G. was in deep trouble. Finally, the owners had put the floundering railway up for sale. With no takers, the company then had gone after refinancing in England and, out of the eventual shake-up in management, had emerged three new directors to serve with four in England — William Smith, A. B. Orr and W. F. McCulloch, shrewd Stratford area businessmen all! The new president was John Galt Jr. of Goderich, and the new name of the line was the Buffalo and Lake Huron.

Many shareholders in the bankrupt old company lost their shirts — Perth County among them. Stratford came out better, when the restructured Buffalo and Lake Huron company honored the bonds that had been given by its predecessor as security for Stratford's loan. The line began building again. There were construction crews out before the new arrangement was even ratified by a meeting of shareholders at the Albion Hotel, but neither the new money from England, nor the sweating endeavors of the road gangs, could get the Buffalo and Lake Huron Railway into town first.

A Grand Trunk locomotive from Toronto, pulling a single coach, hove into sight on September 3, 1856. It shunted to a stop at a tiny depot on Regent Street and, with the coming of this train, the Railway Age opened in Stratford . . . *not* with fanfare, *not* with trumpets and welcoming crowds, but with stunned surprise. The official opening had been set for six weeks later.

Sir Casimir Gzowski, a former Polish count who was now a partner in the group that had the contract for building the line from Toronto to Sarnia, had become impatient to inspect the work, and had arrived. He missed the bucolic skirmish at Nile Street by a few days. Next month, the Grand Trunk Railway rolled the ''first'' train into Stratford, officially.

It was October 8, 1856, and a milestone date for Stratford.

Although a director of the rival road, A. B. Orr, as reeve of Stratford, was eager to organize a welcoming ceremony for the official Grand Trunk train. When he

At Downie and Guelph Streets
was the third station for the Grand Trunk Railway.

asked for a special coach from Toronto with dignitaries on board, Grand Trunk officials brusquely suggested he wait.

In about three weeks, he was told, the railway planned celebrations of its own, inaugurating regular service between Montreal and Toronto with festivities in every little stop along the way. Following this, in November, Montreal would host a gala two-day "Railway Celebration" to mark the achievement of the whole Grand Trunk which, by the time the railway had been opened to Stratford, had become the longest railway in the 19th century world. Stratford still wanted its own festivities, and pushed the matter.

Between the frantically busy Grand Trunk headquarters and the Stratford Town Hall, there was a colossal mix-up, in dates and in plans, all stirred in with some purely local arguments about who should be on what committees. Council, divided in opinion, could not agree to spend any money at all on the celebration, and finally $120 had to be collected privately for dinner and a brass band.

The village turned out in force around midday to see the train arrive. On board were the dignitaries Reeve Orr had wanted — the mayors of Toronto and Guelph, the western superintendent of the Grand Trunk, various reeves, the sheriff of Waterloo County, and the Perth County warden. Guest of honor, a man who had worked on preliminary agreements which led to the building of the Grand Trunk, and the only real celebrity along, was Hon. E. B. Chandler of New Brunswick — later one of the Fathers of Confederation.

The dinner was a disaster. Only 200-odd persons sat down to the meal served in the freight shed. Somehow, invitations had not been sent to prominent persons in St. Marys, Mitchell and Shakespeare.

However, the line officially was open. Freight and passenger service were inaugurated. Shipments by rail soon were arriving. Express service in 1856 was provided by the year-old British and North American Express Company which evolved, eventually, into the Canadian National Express Company.

Meanwhile, on December 8, 1856, the first train of the rival Buffalo and Lake Huron Railway came rolling into Stratford, noted by the *Beacon* in one inch of column space. Regular service between Buffalo and Stratford was inaugurated before Christmas. Stratford had its two competing railways (with a criss-cross junction to ward off further confrontations), and the businessmen in town, anticipating reasonable freight rates, were delighted.

Stratford remained for a time the "end of steel". Those going on into the northern townships and without stage coach connections could hire "freighters", wagons drawn by teams of oxen or horses, to transport them less comfortably by road. Most main roads were bad. The side roads were impossible. When the spring rains came, the road to Blyth would give out altogether. An abortive attempt to link St. Marys with Stratford in the late 1840's had petered out into mud slides, washouts and crumbling bridges under the onslaught of heavy rains. The Canada Company had been out of the roadbuilding business since 1844, and now the job fell squarely on local shoulders.

The railways had their own problems. Blizzards would come sweeping down the snow belt, and engines would wallow in snow up to their smokestacks, sometimes being halted altogether. Service was often suspended in winter. If a locomotive ran out of wood between stations, the conductor would break out a supply of axes, which he would hand to male passengers with orders to get out and start cutting down some trees.

Nevertheless, the Grand Trunk thrived. At one time, 14,000 men and 2,000 horses were working on the railway in Canada West, and navvies from England were brought in when the local labor supply was insufficient. At the same time, the Buffalo and Lake Huron Railway, like its predecessor, was in trouble, and Stratford ran itself deep in debt, borrowing heavily from the Municipal Loan Fund rather than risk losing its second railway. The road was beyond help. The Grand Trunk gained control, and the old railway that had laid the first rails in Stratford village became the Buffalo and Goderich division of the G.T.R.

Meanwhile, another line that would end up in the Grand Trunk system had been gaining support among the Ontario Street merchants. Two years before the Grand Trunk reached Stratford, while railway fever was running high in the village, a group of local businessmen had been tinkering with the idea of a line to be called the Stratford and Saugeen Railway.

It was planned to link Lakes Erie and Huron through Stratford and, among the names of promoters were some that were becoming increasingly familiar in the growing business community: Orr . . . Smith . . . McCulloch . . . Lee . . . Lizars . . . Moderwell . . . Reid . . . Monteith. . . .

John Daly and John Linton, although keenly interested, stayed a little aloof, with mixed feelings about a railway that would be good for Stratford but, perhaps, burden with debt the new County of Perth they had worked to achieve.

Council not only approved the local idea for the line, but also endorsed the efforts of another company, also with north-south plans, the Woodstock and Lake Erie Railway, which hoped to bring in a line from the south.

Both ventures stalled, and nothing more was done for nearly two decades. It was November, 1871, before town council asked parliament to renew the charter of the Stratford and Saugeen and paid the $60 expenses. It was renamed the Stratford and Huron.

The following spring, a charter was given for a railway to run from Port Dover on Lake Erie to Stratford, over the abandoned roadbed of the old Woodstock and Lake Erie road.

This "Port Dover and Lake Huron Railway" got a $124,000 government grant and augmented it with a system of bonuses collected from municipalities along the route. Stratford kicked in with $30,000 and, a few months later, the County of Perth granted $120,000 — two thirds of which was earmarked for the building of a line north to Wiarton, via Listowel.

It ended up with one line possessing a charter to build, but no money and no tangible assets. The other had the cash. The result was the Port Dover and Lake Huron Railway, a complicated cohabitation of two lines, one entering from the south, one leaving Stratford for the north. They were separate — and yet they were not, for they had an intricate system of overlapping directorates.

To economize, they bought two second-hand engines virtually off a junk pile, the "No. 1" and the "Black Crook". These two began lumbering and wheezing through Stratford with the Crook's engineer stoking her up with bran all night before a run to plug her leaky flues. Wire virtually held her together.

Arrival of the first train from Port Dover sparked a three-way celebration, as two new Stratford industries, the Thomson and Williams Foundry and the Stratford Gas Company, timed their own openings to share in the festivities. As the train came through the yards on the way to the depot, whistles on Grand Trunk engines blew in salute. There was a huge parade, a tour of the town, and a banquet in the town hall with the proprietor of the Robertson House catering and the mayor presiding.

By December, 1877, trains were running to Listowel, although the proposed end of steel at Wiarton on the Bruce Peninsula remained a pipe dream. On March 4, 1881, the line became part of the Grand Trunk.

While the shunting of railways was going on around Stratford, a 16-year-old boy came to town in 1863, to take his first job away from home, that of night telegrapher on the Grand Trunk. He was Thomas Alva Edison, from Port Huron, Michigan, a round-faced, blue-eyed lad who dreamed great dreams. His stay in Stratford was brief and his departure abrupt.

From the beginning, young Edison was an experimenter. Over the protests of his parents, who were well off, he got a job as a newsboy in Port Huron to finance his projects, and he soon wangled the concession to sell papers on the

The young newsboy from Port Huron, Thomas Edison, arrived in Stratford Junction to be night operator for the railway — with disastrous results.

U.S. DEPT. OF THE INTERIOR, EDISON NATIONAL HISTORIC SITE

Grand Trunk trains on the run from Port Huron to Detroit. In his spare time, he and a chum would hang around the local telegraph offices, where he picked up a working knowledge of Morse Code, and, as he did, became forever hooked on the possibilities of electricity.

One day, the young son of the station agent wandered onto the track. Edison dashed after the youngster, pulling him from the path of the oncoming train. The father, in turn, taught the eager Edison train telegraphy, which paved the way for his application for the job of night operator at Stratford Junction, at a salary of $25 a month. For this magnificent amount, he would also work at St. Marys Junction a few miles down the line.

His parents, once again, were less than overjoyed. However, he was only 40 miles from home, and he had a suitable place to board, with William Winter, the operator of the express and telegraph service.

The 7 p.m. to 7 a.m. shift suited Tom beautifully, giving him long, daylight hours for his experimenting and allied projects. Because of his nighthawk shift, he was able, one day, to take the day train to Goderich to get the platinum electrodes from over 80 cells of old, broken-up batteries. This platinum he still would be using in his laboratory 40 years later. Meanwhile, he was a 16-year-old and he needed sleep — which was not easy to include in his duty hours, with the precautionary system of signals the Grand Trunk had set up!

To show that he was on duty, the young night operator was required to send the signal "6" every hour to the train dispatcher. To take care of that, Edison rigged a wheel with notches cut in the circumference and attached it to a clock in such a way that the night watchman could start it. Each hour, the turning wheel dutifully sent out the Morse Code for the "sixing", while Edison blissfully cat-napped. However, it finally occurred to the central control office that there was something very strange indeed going on, since "Sf" could not be roused even when the central dispatcher called back immediately after the sixing signal had come through. They soon investigated. There was a reprimand — not taken too seriously, for Edison then modified his arrangement so that the night yardman knew his call and would awaken him at once if Stratford Junction was called.

One night, a message came through from the dispatcher to hold a freight train until the arrival of another. Edison acknowledged receipt of the message, then ran from his office to tell the signalman. It was probably not his fault, but he was too late. The train was already pulling past him. Horrified, he dashed back to report he couldn't stop it.

He never forgot that awful night. He recalled it later for his biographers:

". . . The reply was: 'Hell!' The train dispatcher, on the strength of my message that I would hold the train, had permitted another to leave the last station in the opposite direction. There was a lower station near the junction where the day operator slept. I started for it on foot. The night was dark, and I fell into a culvert and was knocked senseless."

Luckily, the line between Stratford and St. Marys was a straight one. The engineers of the opposing trains saw one another in time to stop.

The incident was, of course, reported and P. H. Carter, the company's agent in Stratford, and Tom Edison were summoned to Toronto. Superintendent Spicer, explaining the gravity of the situation, was distracted by the arrival of two English businessmen. Edison put on his hat, and nudged Carter:

"I'm not going to wait here!"

He took off for home in Port Huron on the first freight train out of Stratford. The Grand Trunk still owed him some wages, but he never came back for them. He collected only his clothes — and his precious hoard of platinum.

Later, Edison referred to his first job when he applied for membership in the Telegraph Historical Society. The application, in Edison's own handwriting, dated December 5, 1904, came, finally, to the Perth County Archives. He also held an honorary membership in the Stratford branch of the Canadian National Veterans' Association.

Stratford officially marked the inventor's stay on April 1, 1940, with "Edison Day", to coincide with the Canadian premiere of the moving picture "Young Tom Edison" in the Majestic Theatre, with Mickey Rooney playing the young inventor.

Three Toronto telegraphers operated old telegraph keys in a department store on Downie Street; other businesses displayed mementos of the Edison era in Stratford, and a special train brought officials and visitors from virtually every community on the line between Goderich and Stratford. Aboard the train was

93-year-old J. W. Browning, an Exeter physician and oldest living telegrapher on the North American continent, who had known Edison and had "talked" to him frequently on the key.

In the waiting room of the C.N.R. station, was unveiled a simple bronze plaque, "in commemoration of Thomas A. Edison, employed in this city as a telegraph operator by the Grand Trunk Railway, 1863-4." The inventor with Stratford connections had died in 1931.

The railways facilitated travel as nothing else could. They moved passengers, freight and militia, and sometimes runaway slaves. Both Stratford and St. Marys were considered strategic points on the Grand Trunk line in the uneasy era following the American Civil War, when there was talk of an invasion of Canada by the Irish Fenian Brotherhood, a hot-headed organization of revolutionaries dedicated to Ireland's independence.

The Grand Trunk Railway Brigade — an unusual defence force set up to keep the trains rolling — had one company at each place. At the time of the Fenian Raids in 1866, a detachment of the Queen's Own Rifles of Toronto also was posted at Stratford, awaiting an invasion that never came.

Adventurous young men in town enlisted eagerly when the call came, and boarded the wood-burning trains bound for Windsor where they received their military training. However there were not enough of them. Within the county by the 1860's, the local "Sedentary Militia" had become pretty much a paper army of paper tigers when the alarmed Canadian government decided to call up more men than the militia had in readiness. In Stratford, call-ups were decided by drawing lots among the local able-bodied — if unwilling — bachelors. As the *Beacon* noted drily, the procedure brought on a sudden rash of marriages.

The Fenian scare was soon forgotten, but sometimes violence and tragedy flared on the Grand Trunk's own doorstep.

One of the worst disasters in Stratford's railway history happened on May 5, 1879, when a boxcar containing vigorite powder, surcharged with nitroglycerine, was being moved. Unnoticed, it had been leaking its deadly load onto the rails, and, as the wheels passed over it, it blew, and the car ignited. The explosion hurled axles, wheels and rails hundreds of yards and buried them in the earth. The end of the freight shed was blown out like an egg shell. Nearby buildings were completely wrecked. Twenty-three freight cars were totally destroyed, 100 others damaged. Windows in homes were shattered, as occupants fled the flying glass. In the downtown core, the Town Hall and Market Building was damaged, and the 211-foot steeple of Knox Church was knocked three feet out of line. The shock waves fanned out into neighboring communities.

Property damage climbed to $100,000, and three men were killed: Francis Pigeon, Thomas Dolan and George Hawkins. In one family, the five orphaned Dolan boys were offered jobs with the railway as they grew up.

In 1904, Stratford, a city since 1885, considered itself happily in the hub of the Grand Trunk System — 80 miles from Sarnia tunnel, 88 miles from Toronto, 106 miles from Wiarton, 70 from Port Dover. It did not necessarily mean efficient service, though! Passengers laughed at the timetable. Merchants fumed at delays in freight arrivals. Particularly irked was the firm of Walsh Brothers who got an invoice for a barrel of whisky from Seagrams of Waterloo on December 29 — and still hadn't laid eyes on the order two weeks later. When it came, it was broken open, which may have accounted for its delay.

In this same era, the Canadian Pacific Railway was casting interested eyes toward Stratford, and the *Herald* was urging a union station for the C.P.R. and the Grand Trunk — worrying as early as January, 1905, about ruining the Avon waterfront with a second incoming set of tracks. The Canadian Pacific Railway's attempt to move into Stratford was aborted, finally.

That railway never came, nor did the electric street railways that many municipalities were considering at the turn of the century, although Stratford was interested enough in the "radials" to leave a center strip of bricks loose when the first pavement was being laid on Ontario Street in 1906.

Surveys were actually made for the "Stratford and St. Joseph Railway", but the scheme collapsed. So did the People's Railway, which envisioned an electric railway running on a triangular route, Guelph, Woodstock and Stratford.

More aggressive was the Stratford Railway Company, chartered as a street railway, with plans to connect eventually with Grand Bend, via Exeter. Within the city, the new railroad was to serve as a streetcar line on a wide urban loop.

On July 29, 1910, ratepayers approved the project, and there it stalled, defeated by a conflict of interests between two financing concerns, the Canadian Northern Railway and the Hydro Electric Power Commission of Ontario. The radial line to the lake never was built.

The London, Grand Bend and Stratford Railway Company did not get beyond the planning stage either; nor did a proposed radial on a Toronto-Berlin-Stratford-London route. Stratford emerged from its welter of railways with just one: the Canadian National, which took over the Grand Trunk in 1923. It continued virtually to control Stratford's economy until the 1950's, and the reason was simple: the locomotive repair shops.

In taking over the Buffalo and Lake Huron Railway, the Grand Trunk Railway had also gained the repair facilities at Brantford. These eventually came to Stratford, where a delighted town council granted tax exemptions for five years and closed off part of Victoria Street. Meanwhile, an engine shed and small workshops were brought over from St. Marys. A large woodshed went up and was stocked with fuel for early locomotives. The first main building, which was occupied in 1871, had 38,700 feet of floor space, and there was a roundhouse that could hold 27 locomotives at one time.

In 1873, the Grand Trunk switched to standard gauge tracks, reducing the width between the rails from 5 feet, 6 inches to 4 feet, 8½ inches. The change-over of its main line between Stratford and Montreal was completed in 20 hours, between October 3 and 5, with only 16 hours of traffic interruption.

The whole country soon was using standard gauge, and old equipment was lining up at the motive power shops of Stratford for conversion. Besides prosperity, the shops also brought hundreds of skilled craftsmen who came looking for work, stayed, and began building beautiful homes.

Lifeline for Stratford was the arrival of the locomotive
repair shops in 1871. Eventually they were taken over by the C.N.R.

After 15 years, the original repair shops became too small, and other centers tried to entice the Grand Trunk operation away. Council countered by voting an attractive bonus of $120,000 to help pay for enlarging the shops, half to go for locomotive repair shops, the other half for car repairs.

Romance may have tipped the scales for Stratford. T. H. Roberts, superintendent of the Grand Trunk Railway, met the daughter of mayor T. M. Daly on a trip to Stratford, was entranced, and later married her. The repair shops for the engines came to Stratford, the lesser car repairs went to London, and the bonus happily cost the town only $60,000.

The Grand Trunk closed its Hamilton facilities and in 1889 brought the machinery to Stratford, along with 400 more families, in another tremendous boost in population. The payroll of the railway now was enormous for so small a community — over $1,000 a day.

The shops started to develop their own electric power in 1901, using a small generator mounted on the floor and driven by a belt from the machine shop line shaft. A year later, steam-driven generators were installed. By 1909, there were pits for 28 locomotives and an 85-foot turntable. As the size of locomotives increased, longer pits were added, and an overhead crane was installed which could lift a locomotive like a child's toy. By 1949, the buildings spread over 313,020 square feet, the most modern of their kind on the continent.

Along the way, a railway school developed within the motive power shops to train likely young apprentices. In 1870, as 12-year-old Michael Dillon of Stratford started as an apprentice in the shops at three cents an hour, he was probably the first student in this "University of the Mechanical World". Later, a 'diploma' from Stratford could open doors to top positions with any railway, and graduates were in constant demand all over the continent wherever mechanically-trained experts were required.

The apprenticeship system probably originated with Frederick Trevithick, superintendent of motive power, and son of the man who perfected the first steam locomotive to run on rails. Brought out from England in 1853, when the Grand Trunk imported 50 steam locomotives, he took an interest in the young men coming up through the ranks, and they were eager for the on-job training he could provide.

In 1883, the apprentices hired Joseph Allison, a machinist, to give them instruction in his own home, entirely separate from the railway. When W. D. Robb became superintendent of motive power for the whole system in 1905, he initiated technical night classes conducted by the company, and these soon became day classes for promising young men. Wages were boosted to eight cents an hour and, when the apprentice finished, he was getting 17 cents.

An apprentice had to be between the ages of 16 and 21 and have an education equivalent to high school entrance. He had to pass an examination and take medical and vision tests. At first, the boys were taught shop mathematics, mechanical drawing, blueprint reading and shops theory. Textbooks were introduced. In later years, there were advanced classes for specific trades: diesel locomotives, safety and first aid, refrigeration, air conditioning. The system also encouraged sports and social life, but there were rules to follow, as the boys learned! One July day in 1904, some 75 apprentices of the Grand Trunk Railway lost their jobs because they left to watch the circus.

A series of railway stations came and went in Stratford. It was largely thanks to the Grand Trunk engineers that the early depots were located a good mile away from the river. English railroading experience had taught these foresighted men that railways normally destroyed the centers of towns, and they so informed Stratford. The village fathers listened. And thus the original tiny Grand Trunk building was on Regent Street, on the outskirts. Business soon was drawn out Downie Street in the direction of the station and the "new" market square was relocated on Downie too, while the riverfront was left unscathed.

The next station, probably erected in 1861, east of Nile Street, became part of a union station with the Buffalo and Lake Huron Railway — but not without protest.

When they chose to move part of the B.&L.H. depot building on a Sunday, the church-goers of the community rose up in outrage at "the open desecration". The contractors pleaded that it was a work of necessity. The work went forward and the *Beacon* reported, that June, that the union station was now completed and "presented a very neat and substantial appearance".

Pride of the line, and a challenge to mechanics who put it
back in spit and polish shape, was the new Northern (4-8-4) type locomotive that
the C.N.R. added in 1927.

When the Grand Trunk built its third station, at Downie and Guelph Streets, it, too, raised tempers. Hoping to have an official opening of the new main building, Mayor Tom Daly invited C. J. Brydges, general manager of the railway, to participate. But Mr. Brydges turned down flat a formal inauguration, and arbitrarily ordered the station opened on July 11 — sending a uniformed policeman up from Toronto to guard the property. This high-handed action infuriated the people — and their militant newspaper, the *Beacon:*

> The railway authorities have inaugurated the new station . . . [with] a set of rules almost Draconian in their severity and a vigilant officer to see them enforced. Those without visible means of support have to 'step around pretty lively' on their approach, as was evidenced last Saturday when a live alderman, two real justices of the peace, an actual chief constable, an ex-alderman, an ex-editor and a corporation contractor, assembled at the corner of the station to discuss the Prussian War or the quality of Dean's beer, and were gruffly informed that no loafing was allowed. They were ordered to 'move on' which they did with the best grace they were able, on such short notice.

While company officials vetoed a formal opening, the employees made their own plans and threw a dinner in the Grand Trunk Hotel. Three days later, the old union depot was tumbled by a yard engine and a block and tackle. This was

not the end of the explosive sequence of the stations, however. Stratford railroading, forever dogged by inaugural problems, ran true to form with the opening of the Grand Trunk's fourth and final depot in 1913.

Details had been carefully worked out for the ceremony on December 13, complete with special trains and visiting dignitaries. Orders went out that no train was to enter the station before the official one. Somebody forgot. One day early, the Port Dover train pulled into the yard. The yardman threw the switch. The engineer eased open the throttle. The train glided grandly to the platform and out stepped R. Thomas Orr, a prominent businessman returning home. Instead of the official party, Stratford got one passenger, one superintendent, one engineer, and the conductor. Some said the yardman, an Irishman named Flanagan, did it as a joke, and he was fired. However, he was later reinstated and, his career undamaged, rose to the rank of conductor.

As for Mr. Orr, it was fitting that he who gathered and collected history would, on this occasion, make it.

The old station of the Port Dover and Lake Huron Railway was little used, after the Grand Trunk took over the line, although it stood until 1922, when it was razed to make way for a coal yard. One last section of track, between Downie and Front Streets, survived until 1972.

Stratford expected to be a railway town forever.

Then came the diesels. Like a chill wind, was the prediction: *the shops will close.* Old timers thought it wouldn't happen. The railway had been the lifeblood of this community for too long. But they were wrong. The work force dwindled to about 300, as no more steam locomotives came for repairs. At the beginning of 1953, the C.N.R. had 2,417 steam locomotives and 395 diesels on its inventory as a railway spokesman announced the first diesel switcher for Stratford would arrive in April.

That same spring, the trains were bringing a new industry to Stratford with the players for the first Shakespearean Festival.

In December, 1959, it was announced that the Cooper-Bessemer Corporation of Mount Vernon, Ohio, manufacturers of heavy diesel and natural gas engines, would lease 60,000 square feet of floor space in the repair shops for five years, with the option of increasing its occupancy or buying.

In November, 1963, when Cooper-Bessemer bought the entire property, the C.N. staff was down to 180. Some men were absorbed, some went to other C.N. facilities, some took early pensions and some went to other jobs.

With the closing of the shops, the 175-foot smokestack, a landmark for years, was razed. No longer did the sound of the steam whistle call the men to work. Gone was the first blast that came punctually at 20 minutes before morning starting time and could be heard throughout the city. Gone the whistle that sent the workers home at noon, brought them back an hour later, and dismissed them in the evening. Many set their timepieces by it. On Remembrance days, it had been the signal for two minutes silence.

Stratford had been a divisional point since February 1, 1913, when radical reorganization in the operating department of the Grand Trunk had created

The University Company of the Queen's Own Rifles
arrived in Stratford in 1866, when the town was considered a strategic point on the
railway during the Fenian raids.

smaller divisions. Its territory had included a network of lines linking Stratford with Sarnia, London, Owen Sound, Southampton, Goderich and other centers of Southern Ontario. It had 659 miles of rail under its jurisdiction at the time the division ceased to exist in 1961, and Stratford became part of the Southwestern Ontario Region with headquarters at London.

Around the turn of the century, the rail yards hummed with 44 passenger trains in and out of Stratford in a day. By 1979, there were ten. Only a handful of men did the work that five yard crews had done a quarter century before. Once, the railways employed more than 2,000 persons. By the beginning of 1880, around 100 employees were drawing railway pay in Stratford, classified by then, in railway language, as headquarters for the trainmasters' terminal.

Amalgamations, which eventually created the Canadian National Railway, the proliferation of automobiles, trucks, buses, airplanes and the extension of paved highways changed the whole transportation pattern. The transition from steam to diesel locomotive power was the final blow to the Stratford railway shops.

Today, the trains thread a countryside gentled and calmed by settlement and development. The trip from Toronto to Stratford takes a little over two hours. The Stratford coach rolls along with its contingent of businessmen, tourists, townspeople returning home, and, in spring, actors and actresses bound for Stratford and discussing plays. It approaches John Galt's Guelph through rolling lands and attractive fields spotted with stands of evergreen and deciduous trees, with cedars still in the hollows, as they were in the days of ''Tiger'' Dunlop's ''dry swamps''.

The railway boom is long past, but the twin ribbons of steel are still there in Stratford . . . crossing the Avon high above McLagan and T. J. Dolan Drives . . . lying alongside the little station out from the center of town.

A steam locomotive ended up carved on the back of the mayor's chair, and another on an early city seal. As for the bonds of the old, bankrupt "B.B.&G.", they were cashed and, with considerable daring, used for the financing of two new endeavors that would bring down even greater problems upon the head of council: a town hall that, legally, should have been a market building only, and the controversial Northern Gravel Road.

The Port Dover & Lake Huron Ry. Coy.
Of the Province of Ontario.

SCRIP.

SHARES $100 EACH.

THIS CERTIFICATE CANCELS ALL RECEIPTS AND CERTIFICATES PREVIOUSLY GIVEN.

Woodstock, *Nov 30th 1875*

2 **Shares.** $ *200*   **No.** *167*

This is to Certify that _*Thomas Orr*_

of _*Stratford*_ holds at this date _*Two*_ Shares of the Capital Stock of "**THE PORT DOVER & LAKE HURON RAIL-WAY COMPANY.**" of the Province of Ontario, of the Value of One Hundred Dollars per Share, the full amount of which, viz.: _*Two*_ _*Hundred*_ Dollars, is hereby acknowledged to have been received, the said Shares being transferable in the Books of the said Company only by him or his Attorney, lawfully appointed in this behalf.

G. Moore
President.

R. W. Sawtell
Secretary and Treasurer.

[Woodstock Sentinel Job Print.]

5

Growth By The Bridge
And A Scandalous Road

WITHIN EARSHOT of the wooden bridge that spanned the Avon, Stratford village was going about its business.

Along with the clip-clop of horses' hooves and the stagecoach traffic to Goderich, along with the rumbling of heavy wagons coming from the Easthopes to Market Square, and the bawling of a stray heifer pursued by the police constable, there were the sounds of commerce, the blows of hammers, the shouts of merchants directing the loading and unloading of wares.

There were grist and sawmills at work along the Avon River and its tributaries, Erie and Romeo Creeks, and Mill Street was exactly that. The village had started around the bridge, at first just a log span thrown across the Little Thames by the Van Egmonds. As settlement increased, business overflowed westward along Huron Street, eastward along Ontario to Erie, down Market Street and out along the Downie Road.

Perhaps a buried yearning for navigable water had led surveyor John McDonald, laying out the streets in the 1830's, to name three of them for the Great Lakes to which they led — Ontario, Huron and Erie. For a time, Erie had seemed destined to become the main street. But a greedy landowner asked $60 a foot for his property, and the merchants went elsewhere. With unpaved streets and wooden sidewalks, this was "muddy Stratford" to residents and travelers alike in the 1850's. The wooden stores, most of them with verandas and steps, fronted on sidewalk or street. On rainy days, women customers trailed the Avon mud indoors on the hems of their long skirts, and the men gossiped around the pot-bellied stoves.

Most were general stores, stocking everything from bulk cereals and booze to long johns for the blustery winters of a Stratford in the snow belt. As new needs became apparent, they were served.

The "Great Eastern" advertised: "100 barrels of whisky on hand." And Alfred

Haines, druggist, opened up with a flourish in 1853 "At the Sign of the Golden Mortar".

In the front page advertisements of the 1850's, sometimes a merchant noted "Country Produce Taken in Exchange", for this was the era of barter, before the establishment of a sound banking system. J. C. W. Daly, agent for the Bank of Upper Canada, was not, in himself, a sound system for Stratford, much as he enjoyed the monopoly. Well into the nineteenth century, barter persisted, with J. L. Bradshaw still exchanging his furniture for chicken and goose feathers, which he then sold to pillow manufacturers for cash.

Stratford grew slowly during its early years. The swampy site, and the sting of its mosquitos, discouraged some, but there were external things, too, that militated against its progress: political unrest in the Canadas; recurrent cholera epidemics; the greater attraction of Goderich and Guelph and, (until it exhausted its agricultural potential) a rival St. Marys to the west. After two decades, the pace began to pick up.

By the time Stratford became a village, the old frame landmark by the river, The Shakespeare Hotel, was gone and, on that site, by 1854, James Corcoran, of County Derry, Ireland, had built a store that would do business until 1890.

To replace the Shakespeare, there were several hotels, one of the first being the Farmers' Inn, built by John Sharman, the blacksmith, at the corner of Mornington and Huron Streets. The Rob Roy stood south of the river on Ontario Street, as did the Union. Robert Johnson arrived to open his fine wooden Queen's Arms. Before long, Peter Woods had the Albion. They were the vanguard of a rash of hotels the little community shortly would have!

Enterprising shopkeepers came, offering new services: saddlers, soap and candle makers, a boot and shoe store, a tailor, a hardware merchant. The Commercial Bank opened in 1856, to give Daly's Bank of Upper Canada competition. By then, there were two meat merchants, George Larkworthy and Christian Ubelacker, planning soon to rent stalls in a new market building.

One day, a talented Italian carver by the name of Texter arrived in the village, but in 1857 Stratford was still too close to pioneer days to need the services of this artist in stone, or to want the lovely marble carvings he could make for the gravestones. He and his family were too proud or too shy to ask for help, when they found no work to do. Finally, the baby died, then the older child, and only then did the neighbors realize the plight of the unobtrusive family.

The grocer, John Scott, ran to his shop, calling out to his wife to fill a basket with food for the stricken family.

"If you had come sooner, my children might be alive," wept the mother. "You are too late."

"Why did you not *tell* us!" Mrs. Scott cried, horrified that people could die of starvation in the village.

To help, she bought a piece of carving done in the young Italian's all-too-free time, a life-size wooden Indian carved from a single basswood log found on the market building site.

The money helped pay the family's debts. The father left an exquisite marble headstone on the graves of his children, and then the Texters left. The wooden Indian stood before the Scott store on Market Street for years, and the building was called the "Indian Block".

Stratford, as it prospered, paid more attention to dress and to appearance, and to fill the new needs there came a runaway slave with the first barber shop, first dry cleaning place, and a new business that was to last more than a hundred years.

Joseph Christopher Hemingway had been a tall, thin and handsome child, born on the Hemingway plantation in the southern States in 1814. As was usual, he took the name of his owner. The other children called him "Uncle Joe", teasing the boy for his longing for freedom.

Joe ran away when he was 14, escaped to Boston, and changed his name to Joseph C. Harrison. He learned to read and to write and, in the next 13 years, he learned barbering, hair dying, clothes cleaning — always dreaming of one day opening a business of his own. He pursued his dream to Canada; later, he married his childhood sweetheart, Emma, bought a farm in Waterloo County, raised a family, and moved on to Stratford around 1855.

Here, Joseph Harrison built for a prominent local family what may have been the village's first brick house. And when the children were older, he accomplished his dream. He opened a shop and hung out a sign at 106 Downie Street: "J. C. Harrison, Prop."

In one part of his shop, his son Harvey became the "tonsorial artist and barber". In another room, his daughter Harriet ran the "Human Hair Emporium" with its ladies' curls and switches. J. C. Harrison died in 1890, a happy and fulfilled man. His business became a permanent fixture in Stratford.

Following a normal pattern for Upper Canada development, early industry in Stratford clung to the first source of energy, the river. By the Avon, were the wagon makers and blacksmiths, Jacob Seegmiller's Stratford Tannery, A. B. Orr's iron foundry and, of course, the mills.

The Canada Company mills, bought by J. C. W. Daly, frequently changed hands. Daly sold out to W. F. McCulloch, who, before long, added a distillery. A doctor ran them for a time, before he departed abruptly for the States and wrote a cheerful letter of apology to his furious but helpless creditors. Later, the local bankers would take over and run them, until the mills burned in 1881 and, with them, a rich slice of village history.

Other mills worked busily in the village. There was Rischmiller's steam-powered sawmill on Romeo Creek; there was another sawmill on West Gore Street run by Isaac Rigg and, biggest of all, was the early sawmill that belonged to William "Boss" Easson, a Perthshire contractor who also put up many of the early buildings and became the biggest employer of labor in town.

In this era of local expansion and growth, often a father and son, or sometimes the whole family, would run an operation to serve the needs of a strictly local market. With the arrival of the railways, and the expansion of the roads, this situation soon would change but, meanwhile, life in Stratford was pleasant and unhurried and — more to the point — becoming quite lucrative.

At 106 Downie Street, a former slave,
Joseph Christopher Harrison, started the first barber shop
and dry cleaning establishment in Stratford.

The school inspector in 1855 was complaining bitterly to Egerton Ryerson that three quarters of the children weren't attending and that their elders apparently didn't care as people of all classes were "so busy getting rich that they had no time for visiting schools or troubling much about them".

The village, which had had a population of around 1,400 people when it was incorporated, was growing rapidly. And it was seeing the rise of a group of remarkable, hard-driving men, the like of which Stratford would probably never see gathered together again.

If John Galt of the Canada Company had set out to attract the better classes and the capitalists to the Tract, by the early 1850's, he had succeeded superbly.

In the developing community, some businessmen involved themselves in a civic project or two. But there was a group of ambition-driven men who were into everything.

The same names appeared over and over again on boards of directors of the proliferation of railways that Stratford attracted. They were listed as officers of the road companies, and they were on the slates for the elections. They joined the boating clubs and they were on the school board. Many, at some time or other, sat in council — village, town or county.

They tended to use initials, rather than first names in the public reports. They acted swiftly, sometimes without due deliberations — more willing to take chances than those who would come after them and deliberate more cautiously over each new project.

From the money that rewarded their public endeavors and their businesses, they built gracious homes for their families, and they overshadowed their wives completely. Little is recorded of the doings of Mrs. Daly, Mrs. McCulloch or Mrs. Lizars, even by the news-hungry *Beacon*, which never pilloried these well-bred ladies as it pilloried their husbands.

This surfacing in-group was never so clearly-defined as was the Colborne Clique that manipulated the affairs of Goderich, but it was just as elite. In the hands of this Stratford Coterie of Capitalists, to a large extent, was the future of a city, and the unofficial roster of its members contained some impressive names:

—John Corry Wilson Daly, first mayor, still the Little Dictator, even after Stratford became too big for one man's rule.

—Thomas Mayne Daly, his son, operator of a stage coach line before he was 22; a man who had started a newspaper, been reeve of North Easthope, run for parliament — and won — all before he was 26.

—There was W. F. McCulloch, whose name had been written clear and black on the mill property in the Canada Company map of 1834, and who now was the village's wealthiest landowner.

—Add A. B. Orr, the foundry owner, and once reeve of Stratford and warden of Perth County at the same time. . . . Daniel Home Lizars, son of a Goderich pioneer, who moved his wife and children to Stratford and became crown attorney and then county judge. . . . William Smith, vocal, level-headed, the highly respected reeve of Downie Township, and warden of his county five times. . . .

And there were the astute merchants . . . Uzzial Clark Lee, potash manufacturer, and also manager of the new Commercial Bank, ambitious, and on the way up. . . . Andrew Monteith, the Ulster Irishman, deep into civic, provincial and federal politics. . . . Peter Reid, the pioneer merchant west of the bridge, who had sat on the first village council. . . . Sheriff Robert Moderwell, the county's first sheriff. Only important name usually missing from the power group was that of J. J. E. Linton, still the driving individualist, still in single-minded pursuit of his own numerous private interests.

There would be other strong and influential men but never again would so much of the real power in the community be concentrated in such a small group of men.

To the growing community also were coming the professional men, most of them overburdened with their chosen work. Doctors, replacing the itinerants that had served the pioneers, attended not only to the needs of the hamlet but also to the whole surrounding area. Setting up their offices, sometimes they worked from their homes, sometimes established themselves downtown. The first practising doctor, Dr. J. H. Moore, was working away in the mid-30's in the upper storey of his small log shack on Downie Street. Patients who could not pay could clear trees off another lot the doctor owned — or could offer a little nip of whisky, which could sometimes settle the bill.

W. H. Smith's *Gazetteer* of 1844-45 noted that two physicians were working in Stratford by that time. Soon after that, there arrived Irish-born Dr. John Hyde, whose classmate at Glasgow University, Scotland, had been the explorer Dr. David Livingstone. Dr. Hyde proved to be much more than a curer of ills. He ran for council (but lost); he became the village's first coroner, its first medical officer of health and the first county jail surgeon. Later, he was first school superintendent and first chairman of the Mechanics' Institute. In addition, he instigated the formation of Stratford's first Medical Society around 1872, and helped draw up a schedule of fees.

Before the founding of the Royal College of Dental Surgeons of Ontario, anyone could pull teeth if he had a few instruments — mainly a drill and pliers, and perhaps some pain killing drugs for the rich. Dentists established later than doctors, but two of the first Stratford dentists, Dr. C. Cartwright and Dr. J. G. Yemens were instrumental in the founding of the College in 1868.

Stratford was beginning to feel the repercussions of world events in the early 1850's. Remote North American hamlet that it was, it could not forever retain its pioneer isolation.

In 1853 there was a crop failure in the major European wheat producing areas, notably the Danube basin. The following year, the Crimean War broke out, disrupting shipping and shutting off the major Russian supply from the Black Sea ports, thus further increasing the demand for wheat. In Ontario, wheat prices rose to more than $2.00 a bushel, a figure not reached again until the First World War. About the same time, a reciprocity treaty was signed with the United States and brought prosperity to rural Canada.

These were exciting days, internally and externally, for the business men of

Stratford. With the news that two railways were coming and would pass through Stratford, there was a scramble for choice land and an escalation of property values. The wheat boom brought a thousand wagons a day into the Stratford market from the neighboring farms. Grain merchants moved among the wagons bidding against each other for the crop, and waiting farmers whiled away the time in the hotels. In addition, the village passed a bylaw to invest in the Northern Gravel Road, thus opening the markets and stores of Stratford to the rich farmlands of Mornington Township

Downtown, the burned-out Rischmiller property had, through some round-about negotiations, been acquired by the village and, thanks to the availability of the old railway bonds, plans were under way for a market building that would also be a town hall. The trains would be rolling by fall, the village was sitting pretty, its affairs, apparently, in good hands.

This was the situation in Stratford in 1856, two years after villagehood, when all hell broke loose.

The Northern Gravel Road was a basically sound idea, aimed at linking Stratford with Mornington Township, less than 20 miles to the north. The northern townships had long been complaining about the lack of communication with the rest of the county and precious little help it had got them. Stratford, alone of the communities in the south — and mindful of her own trade in-terests — was in sympathy with their plight.

Road-building was high priority in the mid 1850's, not only within settled communities, but between municipalities as well. The Huron Road, which had been dumped in the laps of local residents in 1844, when the Canada Company had bowed out, now, at last, was in pretty good shape. By January, 1856, Perth County had completed 56 miles of gravel roads within the area. Communications, however, were still bad for the three townships north of Stratford, and the complaints of the people there were often, and bitterly, presented to the county council.

Stratford took the initiative, launching into a road-building project that would lose some $100,000, discredit a reeve and bring down recriminations on the heads of some very prominent citizens. Alexander Barrington Orr, reeve of Stratford, worked out a plan for construction, and most of the local merchants supported him. The ratepayers endorsed a plan allowing the town to invest up to 16,000 pounds and to raise the money by selling some of its Buffalo, Brantford and Goderich railway bonds.

In the fall of 1856, the Stratford Northern Gravel Road Company was organized, drawing its first directors from the village's power group: William Smith, Andrew Monteith, U. C. Lee, Peter Reid, D. H. Lizars and, of course, A. B. Orr. They proposed to build north, through Poole and Millbank, and the road was to operate as a pay-as-you-use road — a tollroad. Some 30 Stratford businessmen subscribed for 245 shares at five pounds a share; the town invested 14,000 pounds, giving the company, altogether, over 15,000 pounds ($60,000) of working capital, as a starter.

To the surprise of everyone, the Canada Company, which had been none too

The "Coterie of Capitalists"

The 19th century saw the rise of a group of influential men in Stratford. There were some familiar faces among them.

Daniel H. Lizars . . . county judge.

W. F. McCulloch . . . land baron.

Thomas Mayne Daly . . . a scapegoat?

cooperative with Stratford, loaned a further 2,000 pounds against the security of B.B.&G. bonds. The road seemed off to a good start financially, although the press was skeptical.

The *Beacon* predicted the hoped-for revenue from tolls would fall far short of what was needed, and it flayed town council for undertaking this "road through the bottomless swamp" of survey days. "Stratford would be better advised to spend its money on sidewalks or on grading streets," it admonished, not without some reason.

Reeve Orr, undaunted, ordered work to begin at once, with contracts awarded to — among others — a company headed by his friend and associate, Thomas Mayne Daly.

Within a year, the road was in trouble. The Canada Company, magnanimously, and once again to everyone's surprise, surrendered its claim to the 2,000 pound loan and returned the bonds so that Stratford could re-borrow on them.

Much more money than that, however, had been lost as construction struggled on, and the circumstances surrounding the financing were questionable. By December, 1858, D. H. Lizars, as secretary of the Northern Gravel Road Company, was asking for an investigation and, within the week, Reeve Orr, the president of the company, called a public meeting to explain finances — and, incidentally, to involve the N.G.R.C. treasurer, Uzzial Clark Lee. Reeve Orr claimed that the town had paid over the sum of 14,000 pounds, but the only accounting he could get from Lee was a statement showing a balance of $159.33. It wasn't much.

With currency in Canada at the time switching from pounds to dollars, the double-talking in currencies did nothing to clarify a situation already muddled by dealings in a shaky bond market and by ill-kept books.

A committee, appointed to examine the books, found some damning figures. Paid over by the town to the company: 14,000 pounds, or about $56,000. Paid out by the company: $44,222.90. Balance: $11,777.10.

What happened? Treasurer U. C. Lee ignored several requests for an accounting, and the directors asked for his resignation.

What Lee said in a statement later was quite different from the findings of the investigating committee. One questionable item, he claimed, was paid out on Orr's orders alone, although company rules clearly stipulated that every payment authorization had to be signed by the president, countersigned by the secretary and have the corporate seal affixed. Yes, Orr acknowledged, he *had* exceeded his authority, but only because he was zealous for the progress of the work. He hadn't felt he was doing wrong.

Said Lee, if an error had been made, it was because he, *too*, was endeavoring to "hurry on the road". However, he allowed he should have kept a regular set of books for the company, which would have avoided an unfortunate mixing of town bank accounts and gravel road accounts. The confusion was not just in the accounts — the whole situation was by now extremely murky, and getting worse.

How, said an exasperated John A. Scott, a member of the investigating committee, could some of the town's best businessmen make such a mess of things! The shareholders shortly dumped Messrs. Lee, Orr, Reid and Lizars, and replaced them on the directorate with W. F. McCulloch, P. R. Jarvis, and J. A. Scott. R. S. Service became the new secretary-treasurer.

As the old year ended, Orr was out as county warden and, in Stratford, where he had been reeve of the village, he was replaced by J. C. W. Daly, the bristly Canada Company Agent who had become mayor of the newly elevated town.

Daly's boisterous election campaign had provided a diversion from the road scandal, but it had irked many of the gentler citizens; they were even more appalled by the victory scene, and one resident complained of it in a Letter to the Editor:

> Candor compels me to admit that Mr. Daly's friends exceeded those of the other candidates in the rowdyism of their acts, the large portions of strong drink they imbibed and in the general violence of their proceedings. . . . Mr. Daly, it is true, may deplore the excess of his friends and supporters, and charity would oblige us to think so, had he not suffered himself to be borne aloft on a chair on the shoulders of the most furious and depraved of his partisans. Such an exhibition with the yelling, hooting and swearing of the dissolute mob that formed the procession, to the great scandal of the sober and virtuous citizens, betrays a weak judgment, the love of applause and a very limited measure of common sense.

Undeterred — or, perhaps, in need of a break from the road scandal, and the muddled village accounts which he had inherited with his office — John Daly set about renovating the council chamber in the new market building, for which the *Beacon* berated him roundly in the issue of January 28, 1859. Mayor Daly had run the town into $90 of expenses, the paper complained pettishly.

This was only a byplay, a letting off of steam, in the major concern of the scandal.

That March, 1859, the N.G.R.C. brought a Supreme Court action against Lee for approximately $12,000, but the jury could not agree and was discharged. The presiding judge described the accounts of Stratford as in a sad jumble, and counsel for both sides agreed with him. The matter was referred to arbitration, and was not heard again for another year.

Meanwhile, besides being president of the road company and reeve of Stratford in 1858, A. B. Orr had also been warden of the County of Perth and now it came out that, apparently, he had extended his manipulations to that body.

The *Beacon* had a bonanza of juicy and fast-breaking news.

June 24, 1859: County Council was considering laying charges of embezzlement of County funds against former Warden Orr, and shortly did so. . . .

July 1, 1859: A letter arrived from Orr from Mishananko, Indiana, asking for an extension of the time for payment. The ex-warden had fled. . . .

July 15: The plot thickened. Other Stratford people were allegedly involved.

Embezzlement, fradulent embezzlement! cried the Hon. J. H. Cameron, when asked for a legal opinion. Mayor J. C. W. Daly and John Sharman, blacksmith and hotel keeper, offered land as security for the repayment of the money. And the editor of the *Beacon* got off a stinging and libelous editorial — which involved the mayor's son, Tom, now a member of Parliament.

WHO GOT THE PLUNDER?

> We feel that Mr. Orr, after all, has only been made the scapegoat in the matter for which he has forfeited his position in society, for previous to leaving Stratford he told a gentleman that T. M. Daly MPP got possession of the greater part of the missing money and had not paid it over to him (Orr). A lady, a relative of Mr. Orr, gives it as her belief that no one else could have got the money, as the 'puppy' (Daly) is living in splendor in Toronto, whilst Mr. Orr hadn't a dollar to give his mother when he left.

In spite of everything, the Northern Gravel Road was opened as far as Millbank in 1860. The villagers there were so delighted that they threw a banquet in Cather's Hotel where, as the press reported, they spent the evening "honoring the Corporation of Stratford and the directors of the N.G.R.C. and acknowledging the liberality of the town in the construction of the road, bringing Stratford within three hours of Millbank".

The year following the road's opening, a tri-weekly mail service by stage coach was inaugurated between the two points. Stratford became the hub of the area. And, encircling it, strategically placed between market town and the farms, on both the Huron Road and the Northern Gravel Road, stood the tollgates. By 1866, there were 15 tollgates in Perth County — seven on the Huron Road, two on the St. Marys Road, and three on the Northern Gravel Road. Incoming farmers, and all others on business, soon learned to circumvent them by way of side roads and trails. Some came to town free; others paid the whole shot every time. In early days, the 10¢ toll was a princely sum, the price, in fact, of a pound of butter or five pints of whisky.

Some clergy always passed unchallenged, some only on Sunday or at the whim of the keeper. One fervent gatekeeper issued a pass to one minister — the minister of his *own* faith.

The tollgates were unpopular and they were unfair, for the settlers canny enough to avoid them benefited most. One tollgate lasted on the Northern Gravel Road until 1876, then was taken down because, as one councilor said, it had "become a perfect nuisance". Rail communications had made the tollgates ineffective anyway.

Several times, between 1861 and 1866, the town tried to sell the Northern Gravel Road to the county and the latter was on the verge of buying it for $5,000 when Sheriff Robert Moderwell stepped in and seized the road for the benefit of creditors who were becoming increasingly clamorous. When it went on the auction block, the county got it anyway for $4,850. The *Beacon,* in its issue of

PERTH COUNTY ARCHIVES

*Grading Ontario Street before 1913. It proceeded
without the scandal of the Northern Gravel Road affair, half a century before.*

July 6, 1866, recorded the drawn-out proceedings in detail, and with what
sounded suspiciously like relish:

> The sheriff did the town a good deed last Tuesday in ridding it of
> the Northern Gravel Road. Of the $100,000 thereabouts which,
> with interest, it has cost the town we could not receive back as
> many mills. As readers are aware, the sale took place to satisfy
> recently acknowledged claims long outstanding. . . . There are left
> to the company the magnificent sum of four dollars, to enable it to
> wind up with an oyster supper and the town got for its cool
> hundred thousand the most delirious of old songs. . . . This is the
> account of its exit: Mayor P. R. Jarvis, president of the company,
> offered $2,000; James Trow upped it $50. The warden, who was
> authorized to bid as high as $5,000, offered $2,500. Jarvis came up
> with $4,000. An outsider went up $800. The warden pledged
> another $50 and got it for $4,850. Mayor Jarvis jocularly remarked
> that he wasn't the first man to be relieved of the cares of public
> office by the due process of law.

So ended the Northern Gravel Road scandal, with nobody a winner except, maybe, the people of Millbank and, possibly, Thomas Mayne Daly who went on to a highly colorful career in politics.

There had been intrigue within intrigue so that, in the end, probably no one could say, for sure, what had happened or who had actually been involved. Just as the judge had said, Stratford's affairs *were* in a sad jumble! And all over 17 miles of gravel road.

Although expensively bought both with money and with reputations, the Northern Gravel Road brought the rewards of communication, of commerce and of growth. Traffic now would come increasingly down from Mornington, in along Mornington Street and over the Waterloo Street Bridge on a road that became Number 19 Highway.

BEACON HERALD

The wooden Indian, made by a young Italian carver who could not make a living in early Stratford, stood for years before the "Indian Block" on Market Street and came, eventually, into the care of the Perth County Historical Society. With shopping bag in hand he proved useful among the storage files.

PERTH COUNTY ARCHIVES

Blacksmiths were essential to early development,
and even to the railway. This crew worked for the Grand Trunk in 1874.

6

Stoking Up The Economy

NOT SURPRISINGLY, 1856 was a turning point for Stratford's fortunes. In spite of tangled finances and previous bunglings, the community found itself in excellent shape in midcentury. It had railways and a north-south road, whose headaches the county soon would take over. The coterie of capitalists was mellowing with experience, under the eye of a watchful press; most citizens were content with the arrangement. Younger industrialists, some from distant towns, were being attracted into the economic community, bringing growing payrolls and new ideas.

The first Board of Trade was formed in 1860, at first largely to assist the farmers. The town was encouraging new business by ingenious means: not by out-and-out cash grants (which were, naturally, hard to push through a council so recently embarrassed financially), but by guaranteeing bonds and taking back first mortgages on a firm's property. It was a fairly sound policy, the start of a long history of offering practical inducements to industry.

Between villagehood on January 1, 1854, and the establishment of the town on January 1, 1859, the population increased an astonishing 150%, from around 1,400 to 3,500. In 1874, with a population of 6,101, the assessment for the first time exceeded the million dollar mark.

The very look of the town was different. The log shanties and cabins, one by one, were coming down, and frame, stone and brick buildings were going up until, in 1863, council passed a bylaw banning frame buildings as fire hazards on the main street. It was Stratford's first sally into downtown redevelopment, and a measure of its progress. Meanwhile, there lingered the odd reminder that the pioneer era was not far past as an advertisement appeared in the paper: "WANTED IMMEDIATELY FOR THE ENGLISH MARKET A LARGE QUANTITY OF GOOD BEAVER AND BEAR SKINS."

Over a span of three decades, Stratford got rid of its wooden buildings downtown and rebuilt its center core in brick. Probably the last significant building of that era was built by Mayor William Gordon in the mid 1880's — the

Gordon Block, occupying the prestigious apex of the triangle of Ontario, Erie and Downie Streets. Here, many doctors, lawyers, dentists and other professional men liked to have their offices, overlooking the river in the elegantly simple, beautifully sturdy and, for the era, eminently suitable downtown business block.

What Stratford accomplished in the golden decades before the end of the century was due not so much to a location given it by the Canada Company, or to any other physical advantage, as to the industry and initiative — often the plain guts, faith and an ability to dream splendidly — on the part of most of its own citizens. At the turn of the century, even after the city had amply demonstrated an appetite for achievement, there were still some doubters.

Jeremiah Augustus Duggan surveyed the grand opening of "the big store" in 1900, with its counters brimming with fine millinery, furnishings, rugs, curtains and wallpapers. A friend approached as he stood by the door, accepting congratulations.

"Jerry," he said, "you've got a wonderful store, but I'm afraid it's too large for this city. I'd hate to be investing in the future of Stratford the way you are!"

J. A. Duggan was not the first of the new merchants, but he was typical of the men who began to arrive in the second half of the nineteenth century and put their money where their faith was, in Stratford. The Irish-born Duggan had thrown up a good job in Dundas to go searching through western Ontario for a place in which to establish a business of his own. One could see him driving around the countryside with his hired horse and buggy, stopping here, pondering there, and the rich farm areas around Stratford appealed to him.

He bought out a local business, J. M. Struthers and Company, in 1883 and, for good luck, he opened his own store on St. Patrick's Day. Seventeen years later, when he built his big new store, the *Herald* called it the biggest store west of Toronto. It prospered even after "J. A." died, coming eventually, by 1976, under the British ownership of Marks and Spencer.

Except for some reflections of a general, country-wide economic sluggishness in the 1890's, Stratford, with its Jerry Duggans and men like him, did better than many other small cities, right to the end of the century. It began manufacturing a number of things: windmills, grain grinders, farm pumps, buggy whips, carriages, candy, soap and candles. There was rich variety in the small operations that set up in town, and some were providing little luxuries.

The Misses Torney had a "millinery showroom" in the village (a convenient place, in the spring of 1855, for the Ladies' Aid Society of the Wesleyan Church to hold their first bazaar, four days in a row.) There were some makers of soft drinks and soda waters, and, of course, the cigar makers, outdoing each other in naming their brands.

Late in the nineteenth century, before the small individual entrepreneur had been swallowed up by the larger operations, cigar-making was a highly skilled small town trade. The first cigar manufacturer in Stratford was probably James G. Brown in 1874, manufacturing two brands: *Star of Avon* and *Mine is Better*. George Levett began competing with: *The Belle, Ocean Signal, All Stock and No Style, Importer* and *Leona*.

During slack times, there was the presence of the Grand Trunk locomotive power shops to cushion the little businesses. With an economy no longer tied primarily to the surrounding agricultural community, Stratford overtook neighboring St. Marys, surpassed her and never looked back.

Early in the post-1856 period, the main banks were established (and, in a few cases, failed). William Mowat, a Toronto printer, arrived in 1855, published the *Beacon* for a time, and then, with a son, launched a private banking and loan business with farmers and traders, providing a service which chartered banks were prohibited from undertaking.

Other financial institutions rooted well in Stratford. The Perth Mutual Fire Insurance Company got an early start in 1863, geared primarily to doing business on farm property. That year, it issued 262 policies; its fortunes rose sharply later, when it expanded to take on commercial risks as well.

The British Mortgage and Loan Company was organized in London, Ontario, in 1877, then removed itself and its head office to Stratford the next year. Victoria and Grey Trust eventually succeeded it at One Ontario Street.

It was a time when general merchants began to specialize, announcing their wares in extravagant advertising. There appeared fancy names for humdrum businesses: "At the Sign of the Mammoth Gold Watch" (R. F. Barnett, jeweller); "At the Sign of the Golden Beaver" (J. A. Duggan's first little store on Ontario Street); "The Sign of the Golden Mortar" (Alfred Haines, the druggist). A. Williamson, merchant and tailor, had his "Sign of the Golden Fleece"; W. H. Mitchell's hardware, its "Sign of the Circular Saw"; McLennan's General Store, its "Sign of the Red Flag". Mr. Morris, the grocer, promised bounty with his "Sign of the Barge Cask".

It was the era both of temperance societies and of fierce political partisanship; a time of strangers coming in to make their fortunes, and staying to become solid citizens, and of adventurous natives leaving town for "The Northwest". A time of the farm wagons, too. All that activity required outlets. A hard day's work begged sociability afterwards, and the answer was at hand. Booze, bountiful booze!

Was ever a place more bountifully supplied with liquid refreshment than Stratford! Whisky could be bought for 15 cents per gallon and it was the very best. James Kennedy claimed his liquors were so pure that the gallon jug he used as a measure never needed to be washed.

It was also the heyday of the hotel. In 1856, there were, in Stratford, eleven hotels, a brewery and a distillery, and the weekly *Stratford Beacon and Perth County General Intelligencer* ($2 per annum in advance) had a standing head for a classified ad column: "Hotels, Saloons, Etc." By 1871, there were 25 hotels and taverns, four saloons and five liquor shops. It was said that you could walk the four blocks from the corner of Huron and John Streets to Erie Street and pass (or fail to pass) fourteen places where you could get a drink.

There were even more before the century was over, with as many as 38 hotels in existence at one time, some old-timers said. With names and owners changing regularly, an exact tally soon was lost, although the list was awesome.

*The great hotel boom
produced, among early inns, the impressive New Albion.*

There was the American Hotel (which became the Avon), also the Crown and the Ontario House, the old Queen's Arms with stabling for 100 horses, and then another Avon. At one time or another there flourished: the Central, the Arlington, Browning's Hotel, the Commercial, the Dog and Gun, the Falstaff, the Gladstone, the Glasgow and the Golden Inn; the G.T.R. Station Hotel, and the Junction Hotel; King's on Wellington Street, the Lake Huron Hotel — later McCauley's Tavern — near the railway overpass.

There were: the Market Hotel and the Mathews; the New Found Out on the Huron Road at the outskirts of town; the Palmerston, the Robertson House, the Rose, the Royal, Shipman's near the station; the Stratford on Ontario Street; the Terrapin (which had the best food in town, they said); Toronto House, the Victoria, the Waverley, the Wilson House and Herron's.

Pethick's Hotel near the station advertised: "Express trains stop long enough for passengers to take refreshments." Getschell's Hotel on Erie street was a favorite haunt of immigrants from Yorkshire. Charles Duperow operated a hotel for a while on Erie Street, and there were two at the Embro Road corner — Chowen's and McPhee's. Another two small hostelries appeared at the junction

The Mansion House
was a durable hostelry, surviving into a new century.

of Guelph and Nile Streets. Succeeding with his first venture, which was Browning's Hotel on Market Square, owner Charles Browning then opened up another, the Balmoral. It, in turn, became the Mansion House, after 1876.

Even after business blocks replaced the inns, the skyline of Wellington Street, three stories up, reminded the people hurrying along the road below that four hotels had once been there: the Cabinet, the City, the Worth and the Corn Exchange, which became the Royal Exchange and then just the Royal.

Most famous hotel after the old Shakespeare was probably the Albion, built in 1855 by James and Peter Woods on Ontario Street, across the square from the burned-out site of the Sargints' original inn. It pulled in the farmers from the townships and the citizens from the village, and the commercial travelers en route to Goderich. Ben Douro, the colored man, drove for it with a fine team of grey horses and a wagon. Adjoining the hotel, were Corey's Livery Stables which operated the Albion Hotel Omnibus to and from the station.

Like the coffee houses of the eighteenth century, some hotels had their own special clienteles. For a while, the Queen's Arms was the special headquarters of the county councilors and their friends. The Albion was considered a "Tory hang-out''. The Mansion House at Wellington and St. Patrick, with large stables across the street, attracted the farmers, as did the Farmers' Inn, across from the blacksmith shop. Farmers were welcome at all the establishments, of course, and the hundreds of them that hauled their wagonloads of wheat into Stratford had a lot to do with the mushrooming of the hotels.

The thirsty wayfarer did not have to go to a hotel, of course, although he might have trouble avoiding one. There were also the saloons. Most popular was Ben Sleet's Market Refreshment Hall near the market house, where this astute colored man advertised ''oysters, fried and pickled pigs' feet, tripe and other refreshments'' as well as ''the Best of Wines and Liquors''.

In 1857, the village council asked the ratepayers to vote on a bylaw to close the saloons. Although the ''yes'' *vote* was 82-2, the bylaw was defeated because it did not win, as required, a majority of the *ratepayers* — who numbered 280.

As if this weren't enough of booze for one community, Stratford also *made* whisky and beer — and had been catering to its citizens' thirst since the earliest days of settlement, when W. H. McCulloch had added a distillery to his mills. Later, Vivian's Brewery opened on St. Patrick Street, and continued, off and on, to operate under different proprietors and various names for more than a hundred years. Its product resembled British ales, using no artificial carbonation, and, for years, Vivian's was the only brewer of ale in Perth County. It became the Formosa Springs and Perth Breweries, and was the last independent left in Ontario in 1949, before it was acquired by Canadian Breweries, and closed down. Much later and less famous was the Empire Brewery on Erie Street.

And meanwhile, somewhat lost in the array of watering holes, there existed, determinedly, in Stratford the Temperance Hotel and Boarding House, which had opened in 1857.

When the hotels began closing, Stratford acquired business blocks. The historic Albion, after 1875, was replaced by three stores — a grocery, known as the Italian Warehouse, a jewellery store (Goldsmith's Hall), and George Klein's drygoods and ready-to-wear clothing. The New Albion, on the other side of Ontario Street, one block east, had originally been the Waverley House; it too, eventually was converted into a business block.

Only a few hotels made it into the 20th century in recognizeable form: the Dominion House (1870) and the Windsor (1881) were still in business under their original names in the 1970's. The Avon on Downie Street had once been the American. The Mansion House was starting its second century in 1976. The Queen's Arms, early established on the main road from Hamilton to Goderich for commercial travelers and boarders, retained mementos of the old hotel when it rebuilt around 1906. The Queen's Hotel today still has a few of the tiny old rooms, equipped with their small taps and basins.

As time passed, the pioneer industries began branching out. For some, like the first blacksmith, John Sharman, it was an easy and natural progression. From the hammering out of ox shoes, the business expanded predictably. It became a family-owned foundry, then began the manufacture of agricultural machines.

Like many others, this family acquired some choice lands, among them a farm on the outskirts. The son, Joseph Sharman, a rising young industrialist in town, also became interested in a breed of cattle just beginning to attract attention in Ontario — the white-faced Herefords of England. At Guelph, the pioneer F. W. Stone had imported the first Herefords into Canada in 1861. They were doing well, and Joseph despatched to England his young son, Harry, a recent graduate of the Agricultural College at Guelph, with orders to select stock. Soon, "Joseph Sharman and Son" were among the country's pioneer Hereford breeders. They registered their first imported bull, "President Grant", on July 29, 1885; their first local one, "Tom Wilton", on October 24 of that year.

In 1885, the family moved west. Joseph Sharman went into partnership with a brother in the cattle business, and Harry went on to found the Student Christian Movement. In Stratford, the Sharman farm later became part of the city's agricultural grounds. The £100 the pioneer blacksmith had brought to Upper Canada had provided an excellent return on the investment.

Similar changes occurred, in varying degrees with the other blacksmiths. In the long winters, with less to do, they became makers of farm implements, of wagons and of carriages. The mills, too, were changing, and out of this evolution came the furniture industry of Stratford, internationally famous, second in importance only to its railway shops.

Stratford was superlatively situated to become a furniture center, set within reach of early, magnificent tracts of trees . . . oaks and pines several feet through . . . maples, birches, black walnuts and basswoods. It had been built by a river suitable for sawmills, with good rail and road connections soon developing. Skilled Swiss and German craftsmen from Pennsylvania had already sifted north into Waterloo County, where Jacob Hoffman's furniture factory, the first established in Berlin, in 1830, had been turning out work while the first settlers were making their way to Little Thames.

In the furniture tract of Upper Canada — Waterloo, Perth, Oxford and surrounding counties — furniture plants usually originated in one of two predictable ways: a sawmill and planing mill would expand into the manufacture of window and door frames — as did the Scrimgeours — or a cabinet maker would diversify and increase production. Alexander Scrimgeour and his two sons, David and Alexander Jr., also built many of the fine homes and buildings of early Stratford. George Porteous joined the firm and developed the furniture wing.

One day, in September 1886, a small and seemingly insignificant news item appeared in the paper:

> Messrs. McLagan and Porteous, two enterprising and industrious
> young men, have leased the furniture manufacturing shops from
> Scrimgeour Brothers.

And so arrived in Stratford perhaps the most influential industrialist in the city's history.

Canadian-born, and skilled in cabinet work from his "learning years" in the furniture mecca of Grand Rapids, Michigan, the young McLagan arrived in town full of plans and enthusiasm. Canadian furniture still was, for the most part, heavy, unoriginal, often with ugly proportions and overpowering lacings of "gingerbread" decoration. Into this scene came the young George McLagan, hating the ornate and the fussy, possessing a finely-tuned knowledge of how to make furniture strong and substantial, yet graceful in proportions, and both simple and dignified.

Soon, he was sole owner of the business, designing all his own furniture, as he would continue to do for over 20 years. After 1910, he still designed 50% of it.

McLagan integrated himself happily into Stratford life, investing both his money and his time. The Parks Board, the Baptist Church, the Y.M.C.A., even

George McLagan became a leader in the Canadian furniture industry. When his Stratford factory burned, he rebuilt.

the temperance movement drew his support and, like everyone in town, he became a sports enthusiast. On the night of March 1, 1900, he and most of Stratford were packed into the old ice rink where the junior hockey team was playing Peterborough in the second game of a home-and-home O.H.A. playoff series. The Stratford team had a deficit of several goals to make up and tension was mounting. Midway through the game, word raced through the rink.

"The Easson mill is burning! McLagan's is on fire too!"

In minutes, the rink was emptied of a third of the spectators. George McLagan stood on the crowded Huron Street bridge with his fellow citizens and watched his factory burn. The fire department was helpless to put out the blaze.

Afterwards, there were rumors McLagan would move to London. It was no secret that that city was wooing him with attractive concessions. Instead, he told city council he was no bonus-hunter and he was staying. He asked that his bonds be guaranteed for his proposed new, $35,000 four-storey factory on Trinity Street. The ratepayers agreed, and McLagan in 1901 built the first major plant in the east end, the area which would become the city's factory district.

A number of enterprises came under McLagan's wing, or thrived with his backing. Other factories were attracted because of his reputation and the city's annual furniture show. Some came to share carload lots of furniture going to an expanding and eager market in western Canada, which had no suitable hardwoods of its own.

The other important early mill that developed into a furniture factory in the 19th century was Thomas Orr's Stratford Planing Mill that operated above the dam. It became the first Stratford furniture factory to have significant nation-wide sales, and was first also to compete in the markets of Europe, before being absorbed, finally, by Canada Furniture Manufacturers Ltd., which, around the turn of the century, was amalgamating many small furniture plants.

George McLagan, with his love of fine furniture, died, as he would have wanted, suddenly, at work in his factory, in 1918. As the Toronto press said, he "probably contributed more to the industry than any other man in Canada".

The last two decades of the 19th century were dampened by a depression affecting the whole of Canada, and the furniture industry, especially, was sensitive to changes in the economy. It was not until the beginning of a new century, and the early 1900's, as Stratford shared the first real boom of the young country, that furniture achieved its full international potential for the city.

At the height of prosperity, there were around 20 furniture factories in Stratford, including subsidiaries: Kroehler . . . Imperial Rattan . . . Farquharson-Gifford . . . the Stratford Manufacturing Company (popularly called "The Ladder Factory"). There were others, mostly short-lived: Avon Chests . . . Colonial Player Piano Company . . . Diebel . . . Stratford Brass Bed Company.

By 1978, the number had dropped to three: Kroehler's, Imperial and Flexsteel. McLagan's plant went through changes in name and management, and finally closed in 1952. The reason for the decline was complex. McLagan's death perhaps was the start. Then, also, there was the exhaustion of the hardwood forests, the slowing down of western expansion, growing competition from

"Composites" once were popular, picturing, usually, leading
citizens. This one also showed off the fine Stratford furniture, which was becoming
internationally famous.

plants in Quebec and United States and, finally, the depression of the 1930's, the rise of the unions and the aging of top executives.

The third industry to rise to importance in Stratford, after furniture and the railways, was textiles.

E. T. Dufton was a Yorkshireman, who came to Canada as a small boy, and eventually got into the wool business in St. Marys. In 1877, he bought the Stratford Woollen Mills for $9,000. Under his name, then as "Dufton and Sons", finally "Dufton's Ltd.", the firm built an enviable reputation in the Canadian textile industry.

Twice fire destroyed the mills, first on April 4, 1910; a second time, on July 28, 1922, which spelled the end of the business by the bridge. The plant was especially busy at the time. The staff was working overtime and there were large stocks of raw material and partially finished goods on hand. The loss was set at $157,000. A rebuilding program did not materialize and, in January, 1925, the Parks Board bought the property. All they could salvage from the wreckage was the 65-foot chimney and on top of this, inspiredly, they placed a bird house, and around the mill property they planted a Shakespearean Garden.

Clothing companies, upholsterers and tailors all were springing up in the 19th century, along with other textile establishments such as the Stratford Wool Stock Mill and the Shoddy Mill. Large flax mills were established in the 1860's, dressing 100 tons of scutched (pulled) flax a year. In the season of pulling and rotting, the staff of 40 swelled to 200 people at work at the Stratford scutching mills.

There were at least three tanneries in the last half of the century, the Avon, the Stratford and John Scholtz's Tannery and Whip Factory on Erie Street; farm-oriented industries were on the increase.

The Hon. Thomas Ballantyne, both a politician and a businessman, contributed much to the Canadian farmers. He built the early Black Creek Cheese Factory in Downie Township in 1867, and he was a founder of the cheese industry of Ontario. When he died, his will included a couple of touching legacies: to his son, James, "the chair and foot rest which I received as Speaker of the Ontario Legislature"; to his grandson, Thomas, "my gold watch and chain".

For a while, the most important industry in town was the Thompson Williams Manufacturing Company, employing 200 men and shipping farm machinery around the world — to Great Britain, France, Russia, Australia, the Canadian Northwest. . . . In their enormous shops, where one ladle could handle five tons of molten iron, they turned out their specialties the Johnston wrought-iron reapers and mowers, along with sulkies, ploughs and other equipment. In their Stratford office they hung medals won at the World's Fair in Sydney in 1877, and the Paris Exhibition of 1878. Ratepayers had been interested enough in this enormously successful business to vote a $10,000 bonus to bring it from Mitchell, and town citizens were among its directors when it set up in Stratford in 1875.

Another farm implement business was Macdonald, Macpherson and Company, which later became the Macdonald Thresher Company. So successful was it that Alex Macpherson was subsequently able to retire with, as the *Beacon* put it, "a comfortable fortune". This firm's specialty, the Decker Threshing Machine, also was a leader in its field, marketed from Ontario to British Columbia. The Stratford Agricultural Works, a more general foundry business, had a specialty in the "Little Giant" separator, which also found good markets in the west.

There was a short-lived fanning mill factory manufacturing the "King of the West" under a patent taken out by a Stratford tinsmith. Also short lived was the Anchor Wire Fence Company.

There were, however, more success stories than failures. The innovative sons of a German immigrant, George and Henry Kalbfleisch, turned their machine shop into the Emperor Cycle Works located in a frame building on Erie Street. Here they turned out bicycles built with two wooden rimmed, chain-driven wheels, and, when they began making the "Little Emperor" for children, they announced its arrival in the birth columns of the daily newspapers.

There was some talk of adding the manufacture of automobiles to their line of "Emperor" bicycles, which, at one time, sold for $100 each. But this venture did not materialize; Kalbfleisch Brothers instead turned to car sales and service.

The "Baby Emperor" Bicycle was built at
the Emperor Cycle Works on Erie Street around 1900.

Before it became a city, the growing town of Stratford already was possessed of an old and honorable city-maker — A Board of Trade, incorporated in 1868. Ancient towns and cities of the old world recorded the existence of such voluntary organizations promoting numerous facets of community life: civic, commercial, industrial, agricultural, social, even local beautification. Marseilles, France, formed the first actual Board of Trade — a *chambre de commerce* — in 1599. The idea spread to Britain and the new world, reaching Halifax in 1750 and Montreal in 1822. Its westward march got it to Stratford in 1860, with cityhood still a quarter of a century away.

Here, in a little town of a bit over 3,500 in population, and with W. F. McCulloch as first president, it was formed, initially, to receive daily telegrams and reports on the grain markets in Montreal and Buffalo, and the sailings of ocean steamers. It hoped to regulate the price of wheat locally so that area farmers would be paid a fair price for their grain. Out in the townships, however, many farmers saw the formation of the board as an attempt to keep prices down, and early development of this first little board of trade was often beset by problems.

At one point, there were widespread suspicions of unfair dealings at Stratford, talk of frauds and light weighings in the wheat market. Around 1866-7, so many rumors were flying that Buffalo buyers would not buy from Stratford unless the weights were guaranteed. Stratford was urged by the local trade committee to install a public weigh scales in the market.

In the midst of all its economic blooming, the town was determinedly on its way to becoming the Corporation of the City of Stratford. No longer was it situated in Upper Canada or in Canada West, but in Ontario. There was a huge, new, self-governing country, the Dominion of Canada, and the townspeople observed Confederation in 1867 with celebrations in Queen's Park, speeches by the mayor, the clergy and many others, and with general rejoicing.

The next great celebration year would be 1885, when Stratford became a city. The years between had brought changes in the social as well as the business community. Both John Corry Wilson Daly and John James Edmonstoune Linton were dead; John Linton in 1869 at the age of 64, John Daly in 1878. The venerable, respected William Smith, too, was gone. Young Dan Lizars from Goderich had become Judge Lizars, and his daughters, Kathleen and Robina, who had been schooled in Stratford, Toronto and Scotland, were becoming authors. A. B. Orr never recovered from the Northern Gravel Road scandal. But Thomas Mayne Daly's career had been little diminished by the insinuations of his involvement. His progress had been as news-worthy and as colorful as that of his father, and Stratford had followed his rise in politics with interest and often misgivings — but never with boredom.

There had been biased press reports at first, for Daly owned the *Examiner,* only paper in town. With the appearance of the *Beacon* in 1855, readers had more meticulous accounts of the doings of the member of parliament for the United Provinces of Canada meeting in Quebec.

In his 1872 campaign for the Conservatives, too tired, or too uninspired to write out his own address to the electors, Daly cribbed from a speech that had been delivered during the Confederation debates by George Brown. William Buckingham, the owner of the *Beacon,* had heard the speech live, as a reporter, recognized it at once — and promptly headlined it.

T. M. DALY IN GEORGE BROWN'S OLD CLOTHES
THE GREATEST PLAGIARISM OF THE AGE.

Area editors gleefully reprinted it. In spite of it all, Daly won, partly thanks to the votes of the Grand Trunk employees in Stratford. Sir John A. Macdonald appointed him party whip.

Other, more urgent business began to edge Tom Daly off the front page. There were grumblings over taxation by the county, and concern for the future of the hotel business should the whole area go "dry". The cityhood question had been simmering for two decades and finally showed signs of coming to the boil, while Daly's political star was beginning to set. He retired, and his name rarely again appeared in the *Beacon.*

Thomas Mayne Daly died of a paralytic stroke on March 4, 1885.

It was the same day the people went to the polls for the referendum that would determine whether or not Stratford would become a city before its time.

GRAND

GALA DAY

ON THE OCCASION OF THE

Inauguration *of the* City of Stratford

WEDNESDAY, JULY 22, 1885,

IN THE

AGRICULTURAL PARK.

$2000.00 in Prizes and Entertainment !

Grand Trades and Firemen's Procession.

LACROSSE MATCH, BRANTFORDS VS. ONTARIOS.

Band Contest, Bicycle Races, Indian War
Dance, Firemen's Races, Fancy Drill
Competition, Benevolent Societies
and Firemen, Testing the New
Water-works System, &c

**The Celebrated Ladies' Gold Cornet Band,
from Fenton, Mich., has been secured for the
Occasion.**

WM. GORDON, Mayor,   JNO. WELSH,
Chairman.   Secretary.

M. F. GOODWIN, Treasurer.

(BEACON PRESS.)

7

"1885"

THE REFERENDUM of March 4, 1885, was a necessary prelude to cityhood. But it was a particularly uncomfortable voting day for the clergy of the non-drinking churches and for some others with a conflict of interest. All wanted to see their community prosper but, at the same time, some couldn't, in all conscience, vote for cityhood. A vote for cityhood was a vote for booze and the unfortunate ministers found themselves in a political bind, allied with the temperance societies.

Agitation for cityhood had been going on for some time without much to show for it. To begin with, Stratford did not have the required 10,000 in population for it to become, automatically, a city. However, if the town *could* somehow swing it, the elevation to cityhood automatically would bring separation from its county under the terms of the Municipal Act. And this many in Stratford sorely wanted: to be free of Perth once and for all, and as speedily as possible. For *this* — besides some hoped-for improvement in taxation — would mean Stratford would continue to operate its hotels and saloons even if the county went dry, as many thought it shortly would do.

The Canada Temperance Act of 1878 — the Scott Act — provided that a county should have the say regarding the sale of liquor throughout its entire area. This legislation differed from previous liquor control laws in that, if any part of a county went "dry", the whole county became a prohibited area for the sale of all alcoholic beverage. Perth County could close every bar and tavern in Stratford, along with three liquor stores. Many townspeople lived in daily fear that it would do so, for the prohibitionists' voting strength in 1885 was much greater in the rural areas than in the towns. This in spite of the fact that the farmers, bringing produce to town, were some of the best customers of the hotels!

The see-saw progress toward "Home Rule" for Stratford had been stumbling along for over 20 years. Besides the prohibition question, there was also the matter of unfair assessment by the county — and there was iniquity in the assessment arrangement to be sure. The farm majority argued, simply and

95

Many citizens tucked away into safekeeping the silver commemorative
medal struck by the city to mark the 1885 inauguration. On one side was the new
corporate seal, the fourth seal Stratford had used since 1854. The reverse showed
the city hall.

reasonably, that Stratford was bigger, therefore should pay more toward county costs. But there was also one system for assessing rural municipalities, another for assessing urban municipalities, and it had been in use for many years. The county fixed a rate per acre for each of the townships, based on the supposed quality of rural lands. For the towns and villages, it applied an arbitrary percentage to the assessment reported by the town or village assessor. It was a system that allowed for abuse, and protests through county council got nowhere.

In 1876, a vote on separation was defeated by 168 votes; another in 1881 had whittled down the opposition, but still it was defeated by 41. Mayor William Gordon, in his inaugural address in 1884, called Stratford "the largest unincorporated city in the Dominion of Canada", and his listeners were well aware of the overtones. The whole furor over prohibition was actually three decades ahead of its time for, although Perth County did, as expected, vote itself dry, it was not until the 20th century.

In an effort to assess a situation in which it had no experience, town council wrote to five small Ontario cities, Guelph, St. Thomas, St. Catharines, Brantford and Belleville, inquiring about the advantages and pitfalls of cityhood, as they saw them. The replies were encouraging.

Next step was to have the town's assessment appealed to the courts. The appeal was dismissed without costs and solicitor John Idington promptly sent in his bill for $25. Council meanwhile set up a special committee headed by the retired headmaster of the grammar school, who was now 3rd deputy reeve, and, on August 26, 1884, received an historic report, which was probably worded by C. J. Macgregor himself.

> Our relations with the county are so strained that if Stratford remains in connection with the county it may expect the present high rate to be continuously increased. The present rate is $2,709 but under the ruling of the court of appeal on the equalization of the county at its late sitting we may expect the rate next year to approach, if it does not exceed, $4,000.
>
> We recommend that the necessary steps be taken to apply to the Legislature of Ontario at its next session for an act to incorporate the City of Stratford and that the solicitor see that the proper notices are given.

The referendum was called a little more than six months later. The town was short more than 900 citizens that day in 1885. The population stood at 9,068, including the 1,000 or so employed by the Grand Trunk Railway shops. And so the citizens went to the polls to vote on whether or not the town should apply for a special Act of Parliament to allow incorporation as a city — *now.*

This time, the vote was decisive: 1,162 in favor, 322 opposed.

When the results were announced that evening, according to the *Beacon* the front of the city hall was illuminated, a large bonfire was kindled in the market square and "an immense concourse speedily assembled". A procession was headed by the Grand Trunk Railway band and followed by members of council and other citizens in sleighs, the rear being brought up by several hundred people bearing torches.

After the shouting died, the liquor issue still rankled with some, along with normal grumblings about an unnecessary election. An editorial in the *Beacon* in its next issue following the referendum commented.

> As might have been expected, the voting on the question of city incorporation on Wednesday excited a good deal of interest, the number of votes polled being within a few of as many as at the municipal election in January. . . . It was expected all along that the majority would be in favor of independence, but we hardly looked for such a crashing rebuke to the impertinence of the little clique of officials who, to gratify their own selfish ends and love of intrigue and notoriety, put the town to a heavy expense and involved a number of citizens in the worry and turmoil of an election contest. Of course, without the influence and active assistance of the promoters of the Scott Act, the efforts of the little clique wouldn't have amounted to much. The leaders of the temperance movement allowed themselves, foolishly as they no doubt realize, to be dragged into the fight, and their Sunday evening orators appealed strongly to their audience to vote against incorporation.

A special provincial statute was passed and on March 30, 1885, Stratford was a city. Council took care of formalities the next day.

After the jubilation died, there still remained some settling of accounts with the county, and it was done in an atmosphere of extreme hostility. It was ironic that Stratford, which once had fought tooth and nail for the establishment of

Perth County, now considered that same Perth County to be the threatening overlord.

Up on McCulloch's Hill, north of the river, sat the county buildings, sadly outdated, with jail cells bigger than the county offices, but still the very heart of Perth County. Already, the architect was at work on plans for the new county building at the head of Ontario Street, where land had been acquired from the Daly estate. But, even when county council moved, all county operations would still be located in a "county town" that was no longer within the county. Stratford was not absolved from paying its share of the bills.

The county debt was $225,652, at the time Stratford separated. The county wanted Stratford to pay $17,358, about one-thirteenth. The new city said no, and went to arbitration, which was a mistake, for it then was ordered to pay more. Stratford's adjusted share of the debt became $19,000. An appeal got it somewhat reduced, but Stratford still ended up paying approximately $1,000 more than if it had accepted Perth County's offer in the first place.

There was also a matter of paying for the administration of justice, the operation of the county courts and the expenses of the county legal offices. Stratford's share was set at 15 per cent, St. Marys' at six per cent, and the remaining 79% remained with the county. The city kept up its contributions until 1968, when the Province of Ontario assumed the cost of such administration in municipalities and, in Stratford, rented the second floor of the Justice Building.

It took more than three months to get ready for cityhood celebration and an inauguration on July 22, 1885. It took more than six columns of type in Stratford's *Times* to describe it, in all its color and exuberance.

"Such painting, dusting, cleaning and scouring had never before been witnessed in Stratford!" the paper said. The city was as bright and clean as a new pin. Arches were erected at different points in the principal streets; evergreen decorations, flags, banners, streamers, lanterns and other decorations "were displayed in profusion".

Scarcely a house could be pointed out which did not display at least a flag, while stores, hotels, and public buildings were literally covered with them. The gas illuminations of city hall, Odd Fellows' Hall, the post office and customs building, Foresters' Hall, Albion Hotel and other buildings were splendid.

At daylight, the rumbling of conveyances was heard on every street. Before the special trains arrived, streets were crowded and, as the paper said, "a severe jam was felt, but when the railways unloaded some 8,000 to 10,000 visitors, the word jam was useless."

Almost every fire department in Western Ontario turned out for the day, firemen in their shiny steel helmets, red coats and trappings, the chief carrying a shining trumpet filled with flowers and the fire apparatus loaded with bouquets. Some 30 manufacturers and businessmen produced floats for the parade.

There were speeches. The city's progressiveness was praised. The pioneers were lauded. There were band competitions, and races, and fancy drills for the firemen, and Indian war dances and bicycle races, and a lacrosse game between

Brantford and Toronto teams, *and* selections enthusiastically played by the celebrated Ladies' Gold Cornet Band from Fenton, Michigan! (Not to mention "Testing the New Water-Works System, Etc.", as the program for the Gala Celebration noted.)

The visiting firemen went off to be entertained in the various hotel dining rooms, and over 100 special guests sat down to dinner at city hall. There were some pioneers at dinner who had seen over half a century in Little Thames and Stratford; John A. McCarthy (1832); William and John Cashin (1834); William Dunn (1835); Robert Ballantyne (1839); Robert Johnson (1841); James Woods (1842); William Fraser (1843); Peter Leitch (1844) and P. R. Jarvis (1847).

Throughout the day, delegations had been arriving from 40 or more municipalities in Ontario, and from the states of Michigan and Illinois. It was a fine occasion for the light-fingered, too, as an epidemic of pickpocketing broke out. Among the victims was Mayor Scarffe of Brantford who, the *Times* reported, "was relieved of a valuable gold ticker".

The celebrations swelled as the sun settled toward the Avon willows. Shortly after 8 p.m., more than 500 torches blazed in the streets and a jubilant procession formed. Fireworks were set off in a vacant lot behind the Victoria Hotel in a noisy inauguration for the new city.

Smiling at the success of the celebration were three men, John Gibson, Johnston Abraham and John Payne, who first promoted the marvelous and joyous affair and, for their pains, had been, said the press, "set upon at a public meeting and snubbed by some of the councilors". The three had persisted, circulating a petition, and getting 70 signatures "asking Council to give a grant of $1,000 and squeezing $600 out of that tight-fisted body". In addition, $300 was raised by public subscription and more than $2,000 was taken in as gate receipts. Without the three determined Stratfordites, it would have been a skimpy inauguration indeed!

There had been hurt feelings and angry words in the days leading up to the inauguration, but, now that cityhood was an accomplished fact, it was time to let loose the suppressed and long-delayed emotions of civic pride. A groundswell of public opinion was building up, demanding a suitable title for the new city, filling the Letters columns of the newspapers with suggestions, raising heated argument at evening gatherings.

Prominent merchant James Corcoran came up with a suggestion: "What about 'The Classic City'?"

After that, there was little further discussion. The Classic City it became.

The Corporation of the City of Stratford in 1885 (population well under 10,000) still had wooden sidewalks, and occasionally livestock roamed the unpaved roads. It had been only a year since a bylaw had prohibited cows from running at large at some seasons of the year. But it had a telephone directory that boasted 30 telephones — all of them very, very busy that cityhood year!

Stratford's romance with the telephone went back long before that, however. It had been involved with the development of Alexander Graham Bell's invention as early as 1877, the year the Canadian patent rights were issued to the inventor.

Stratford Agency.

Central Office :—Market Street.

Office open from 8 a. m. to 8 p. m. Week Days, 2 to 4 p. m. Sundays, and 10 to 12 a. m., and 2 to 4 p. m. Holidays.

G. A. JACKSON, Agent.

Rules relating to Messages, &c., will be found on inside of Cover.

SUBSCRIBERS.

American & Canadian Express Co.'s, G.T.R. Station
Ballantyne, T., Cheese Factory Erie St
Ballantyne, T., Residence, Front St
Beacon Printing Co., Ontario St
Boys' Home, Avon St
Commercial Hotel, Downie Road
Corrie, John, Residence, Mornington St
Court House, Sheriff's Office, Hamilton St
Fire Hall, Market Buildings
Forbes, J. & R., Livery, Ontario St
Fraser, Dr. D. B., Ontario St
Fraser, Dr. D. M., Downie St
Gas Works, Wellington St
Grand Trunk Railway, Freight Sheds
Grand Trunk Railway, Round House
Grand Trunk Railway, Station
Great North-Western Telegraph Co., Market St
Herald Printing Office, Ontario St
Hodd & Cullen, Flour Mill, Railway Ave
Hossie, John, Res'dence, Norman St
Jackson. G. A., Express Agent, Market St
Marshall, W. R., Commission Merchant, Market Buildings
McDonald, McPherson & Co., Foundry, Railway Ave
Royal Hotel, Wellington St
Smith, G. T. & Co., Foundry, Erie St
Smith & Gearing, Barristers, Albert St
Times Printing Co., Erie St
Water Works Hamlet St
Windsor Hotel, Albert St
Woods, Fisher & McPherson, Barristers, Albert St

Complaints, relating either to the Instruments or to unsatisfactory service, should be made to the Local Agent personally, by mail or by Telephone

The telephone company had 30 subscribers in cityhood year.

For a demonstration of long distance operation, Stratford sent forth a fine, rousing chorus of "Scots wha hae!" over the telegraph circuit to Guelph. Guelph warbled back, "Hold the forks, the knives are coming!" to the tune of the revival hymn "Hold the Fort!" — and to the outrage of proper Stratford people who approved this parody not at all.

In 1880, the Bell Telephone Company of Canada was incorporated, and the next year Stratford was asking for an exchange. By 1883, it had it, housed in the Trow Building at the corner of Downie and Albert Street, and, by cityhood year, 1885, there were long distance connections not only with Guelph, but also with London and Listowel — and 30 busy telephones.

The first subscribers included the cheese factory of Thomas Ballantyne, the Sheriff's Office, the Gas Works, the Boys' Home, the Fire Hall, several hotels, and Dr. Donald Blair Fraser who was considered very progressive as first doctor in town to order a telephone.

Sometimes, operators had to break in on conversations to relay messages over the crackling lines. Under an agreement between Bell and the City, fire calls were handled by the operators who then notified the fire department of emergencies and, occasionally, acted as messengers as well. Before 1896, while the fire department was still in the old city hall, the caretaker would receive the calls, sound the bell on the hall and keep up steam in the fire engine until it was needed. The telephone poles were handy places for the fire alarm boxes and for public notices, until Bell began putting the wires underground.

In 1887, the city's 100th telephone went in; three years later, telephone numbers finally were assigned and, by 1898, the thriving young exchange was ready to move to larger quarters. The quarters were, alas, at Number 47 Downie Street, previously a fish store. Long-departed fish had left behind an overpowering stench embedded in the very grain of the wooden floors, and Bell's first president, Charles Fleetford Sise, personally advised carbolic acid. Apparently it worked, for the telephone company didn't move again for over a decade.

From the first 30 phones in 1885, Stratford would have 18,968 of them by New Year's Eve, 1977-78. It would send greetings over transatlantic circuits in 1934 to Stratford-upon-Avon in England, and be the first community in southwestern Ontario to have the new "melodic touch-tone" service.

Meanwhile, the early telephones speeded the news of Stratford's incorporation as a city and then facilitated the carrying out of the city's business.

As a brand-new village, Stratford, in 1854, had had no seal of its own, nor had the new County of Perth yet acquired one. However, the first clerk of the county was also the clerk-treasurer of Ellice Township and he now became first clerk of Stratford. He was the Scotsman Stewart Campbell, and it was his seal the village first used. By spring, however, Stratford began using the personal seal of its own first officer, Reeve W. F. McCulloch, with its crest containing an upraised arm and arrow, and the motto *"Vi et animo"* — "By strength and courage".

This "temporary" seal served for three years, until 1857, when Stratford finally ordered its own corporate seal, designed by John Ellis of Toronto.

The Seals of Stratford

The new village used the county clerk's seal; then adopted the crest of Reeve W. F. McCulloch, above.

The corporate seal of Stratford since May 17, 1965, designed by Stratford's own citizens, and drawn by Adam Zimmerman.

It borrowed the locomotive and beehive from the new Perth seal, reversed the locomotive and added the inscriptions "Industry" and "Enterprise".

The seal was changed after cityhood, and two supporters were added alongside the shield: a man in knee britches, on the left, and a classically-gowned lady carrying a harp, on the right. The piece of equipment that arrived at city hall from the firm of Ralph Smith and Company, Toronto, was itself impressive — gold and black and with the massive head of a lion rounding out the base. When this old stamp was finally retired, its replacement was more streamlined, the garb of its figures more modern.

Meanwhile, in the growing city, an increasing number of official letters were going out of city hall, and from an increasing number of departments — the city clerk's office, the engineering department, the water commissioners' office. Further variations of the civic seal began turning up on letterheads as early department heads exerted their time-honored Stratfordian individuality.

A bylaw setting forth polling places carried the faint imprint of the first corporate seal (1857-1885). It has been retouched in the document above.

The first Town Hall and Market Building drew the farmers.
In the foreground are the market weigh scales.

The final coat of arms for the Corporation of the City of Stratford, adopted on May 17, 1965, was unlike any that had gone before.

The Shakespearean Festival, by then, had been in existence for more than a decade, and was much in the minds of the citizens as a public contest was held to draw ideas for the design. From the suggestions received, a committee of council prepared a sketch, and the actual drawing was done by Adam Zimmerman of the city engineer's staff.

The distinctive line of the Festival Theatre was shown at the top, with, beneath it, the spears from the coat of arms of Stratford-upon-Avon, England, and a golden maple leaf in the upper left corner to distinguish this as the seal of the Canadian Stratford. Three cogwheels in the upper right signified that Stratford had become a most industrious city. The distinctive "S" swan, in the lower portion, was adapted from the Stratford Festival trademark. The circlet enclosing the crest stipulated a city, and the motto was "Industry and Arts". The colors were: the red of the spears for the blood shed by Stratford citizens in two world wars; a blue background for the waters of Lake Victoria; green in the circlet for Stratford's famous parkland. The gold was symbolic of the golden maple leaves in autumn.

A city had taken stock of itself. Stratford had come of age.

8

The Old Queen Of The Square

THE NEW CORPORATION of the City of Stratford had a council chamber in which to meet—which was more than the village council of 1854 had had. Stratford's council started out in the Perth County building on McCulloch's Hill, moved to a hotel, moved out when the *Banner* criticized it for meeting in a tavern, met then in a school and finally, just after it officially became a town, settled down in its own council chambers — if somewhat illegally.

The first official offices for the perambulating council of Stratford occupied a piece of the land that had been squeezed into the triangular apex of Downie and Wellington Streets. It came into Stratford's possession in the summer of 1855, and, at ten o'clock in the morning of the 11th of September, 1855, the sale to the village of one acre of land was registered at Stratford.

For two hundred pounds (around a thousand dollars), the village was "to have and to hold the said land and premises and appurtenances . . . in trust to use the same for the purpose of erecting and maintaining thereon a Market House and the buildings incident thereto as aforesaid for ever."

Nothing about erecting thereon a town hall.

Nothing, whatsoever.

Those strings to the sale would haunt the municipality, and the man who laid down the stipulation was one quite familiar, by now, with Stratford — Donald McDonald.

He was no stranger to the area, and he had learned much about the country while working with his tall, brawny cousin, John McDonald, the surveyor.

Their fathers — two ambitious Invernesshire brothers, Alexander and Evan — had emigrated together from Scotland, joining a group bound for New York State. There, Donald had been born. Later, both families moved to what would become Waterloo County and, with their arrival in Canada in 1823, John McDonald qualified as a Deputy Provincial Surveyor. Five years later, he was working along the Huron Road with his young cousin Donald at his heels.

Donald McDonald became an engineer and surveyor in his own right, and worked on some early Canada Company maps of the Huron Tract, including the 1839 copy of John McDonald's plan of Stratford, envisioning a city of 35,000.

When, in the early 1840's, rheumatism forced him to give up active surveying, Donald McDonald was transferred to the clerical staff of the Canada Company, based first at Goderich, then at Toronto. He became, finally, assistant commissioner.

Often, his life and his cousin's ran parallel. One day "Stout Mac" went boldly riding south from Goderich to select a wife. He married Elizabeth Amelia, the elder daughter of Judge James Mitchell of the London District Court, and took her back with him the next day. About a decade or so later, with more decorum, Donald married the younger sister, Frances. The girls were also nieces of Egerton Ryerson.

Donald McDonald became a very wealthy man, partly due to astute land deals, and, in Confederation year, 1867, he became a senator of Canada. At his death, he left an estate of $141,800. He also owned a 2,000 acre ranch in Kansas, and had been speculating in land in Michigan; he still held interests in Stratford, which passed to his wife.

Such was the man who tied up the Stratford city hall. At the time he was negotiating with council, he was 44 years of age. McDonald had the canniness to grasp opportunities and, from involvement with the surveys, he also had a sound knowledge of the area and a good idea of its future prospects. When the little triangular property became available, he was interested. He may even have taken some pains to track down its owner.

City hall was not, originally, supposed to occupy that triangle of land. Surveyor John McDonald, Stratford's first town planner, had, apparently, intended the town square to be from Ontario Street north toward the river — and the open land there was an integral part of his 1834 plan.

But business began moving away from the river, drawn toward the new railway station. By the time the villagers could afford the luxury of a town hall, shops and little industries were establishing farther out and the town hall went with them.

Ownership of the land in question had changed frequently, since the Canada Company had sold its original lots in the Wellington-Downie-George triangle. A number of lots had been surveyed there: lots 51, 252 and 253 in the apex of the triangle, others south of them. However, they usually changed hands in blocks. The wedge straddling the meandering Romeo Creek came, finally, into the possession of William Rischmiller, who built a small sawmill there in the 1840's.

In the heart of the growing village, Rischmiller's steam-powered sawmill worked away, strewing the area with logs, slabs, stripped bark and brush, until the village council began complaining — much to the distress of the schoolboys from the nearby Grammar School who used the marvelous, primitive jungle for their games. The mill turned little Romeo Creek into a moving belt of sawdust that went sluggishly downstream into Erie Creek and, eventually, into the Avon.

After a few years, the mill property changed hands again and, at this point, ownership of the site of the future Stratford city hall went briefly across the border as William Rischmiller (or *Rueschmiller*) sold his mill property in two pieces, in 1851 and 1852, to Dr. Morris Lee Wolf of New York City.

In 1853 Dr. Wolf resold. The buyers were Donald McDonald "of Toronto in the Province of Canada, gentleman", and Frances, his wife. In August of 1855, the McDonalds sold to the Municipal Council of the Village of Stratford, and, that fall, it was duly registered.

The stipulation in the sale was an attempt to preserve the character of the downtown core — although it was probably not altruistic. The McDonalds had vested interests in the triangular square, for they owned other land in the vicinity, all of which could appreciate in value. Donald's father, Alexander McDonald, also, apparently, had some vested interests in local land. It was much to the McDonalds' advantage to maintain a healthy commerce in market square. The calculated gamble — which certainly it was — could pay rich dividends.

Meanwhile, the village took over the old logs, slabs and debris of the abandoned sawmill, as well as the little creek that wandered along by the proposed building site.

The property was surveyed that year; then money ran out. This did not defeat the town fathers, however, and their financing of an enormous building for such a small community was bold and adventurous. The money that had been loaned earlier to the railway, once again became available. Late in 1856, with the first trains arriving, the village sold some of its Buffalo, Brantford and Goderich bonds and invited building plans, offering a bonus of 50 pounds for the best. The contract went to William Thomas and Sons of Toronto, who also undertook to supervise construction of what the town fathers were careful to call "The Market Building".

The slabs and refuse were finally cleared away, the land was levelled, and the work progressed. The city did partially live up to the spirit of the sale in that the first town hall was a compromise building, half of it a town hall for government and half of it a market building to supplement the weekly outdoor market — a practical arrangement in the 1850's, but also one legally required.

The plans called for white brick, with stone cut facings, for a building two storeys high with an attic above. It would have a dome-shaped belfry rising from the middle of the roof, and would contain four stores, a market house, council chambers and offices, a concert hall, fire hall, police quarters and jail cells. Eleven contractors bid. The tender of Oliver & Sewell, of Stratford, was accepted for 5,490 pounds, a figure too low for all that was required.

The work was under way in 1857-58. The building that began to take shape faced northeast, with the market section at the back and the weigh scales nearby. Romeo Creek still meandered through the square and, on a quiet day, wild ducks would come gliding down on the water. At the creek's edge, a little grocery store prospered, with Mrs. Patterson, always in a gay, bright apron, waiting on a dozen people at once on market day. It was a folksy setting for a grand building.

This first official municipal building was impressive. Wrote historian William Johnston: "With its cupola and extended flag staff it was for years the pride of

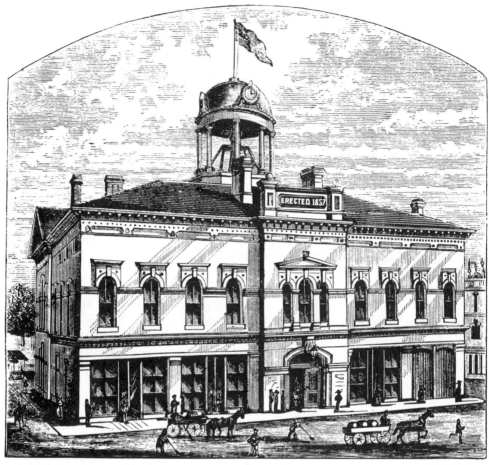

The old market building, Stratford, housed also the council chambers.

the citizens, exciting wonder and admiration in backwoods youths who came from the northern townships with their oxen, to trade in this great metropolis.''

Council held its first meeting in the new chamber on May 10, 1858, sitting grandly around a table covered by a green cloth, with Reeve Alexander B. Orr presiding and with matters pertaining to railways and the Northern Gravel Road still high on the agenda — along with the ongoing problem of extracting money from reluctant ratepayers. It was another year, and the village was a town, before the market building was fully completed.

Although his was not the lowest tender, Walter Oliver got the contract for stores and stalls for $1,425 because, as he said, he and his partner, Sewell, ''had lost so much on the original building''. The four stores were built, flanking the main entrance. The butcher stalls went on the south, facing onto the market square, and there was space, also, for the farm folk who brought their produce to market. The fire fighting equipment was housed in the northwest corner of the building; the horses were billeted at a nearby livery stable. The police department moved into the southwest corner. Coal oil lamps and candles were used until gas lighting was available.

George Scrimgeour built the platform for the huge concert hall in a market building; Isaac Rigg built the seats ($1.55 each with backs, 90 cents without backs), and Jacob Imlach made the chairs for the council room.

Mayor J. C. W. Daly's attempt to have the council chamber spruced up drew the ire of the *Beacon:*

> The mayor has run the town into $90 expenses in getting the council room fitted up on the exact plan of the hurricane deck of a Mississippi flat boat with elevated wheelhouse, in which the captain sits and gives his orders. One of his hands named Watson (Councillor Joseph Watson) seems to be training himself for the position of 'first mate'. A wink from the wheelhouse is all that is required. The ratepayers ought not to neglect to go and see the craft at the first opportunity.

To offset all the expense of building, furnishing and decorating, the town was able to collect some revenue. The concert hall rented for $12 a night to strangers, $5 to citizens, and that included cordwood for heating. With something going on almost every night, the town had a steady income.

The stores and butcher stalls were rented by auction, with bidding starting for stores at $120 per annum, and for stalls at $32 per annum. Council's outlay included a salary for Michael "General" Brown, the first caretaker, who was paid $7 a month in the winter, $4 in the summer, to keep the hall clean, saw wood and light the fires. A. G. Cameron, the first market clerk, received a magnificent $24 a month.

The first occupants moved in, among them, John McCrea operating a flour and feed store, and selling fish fresh from Lake Huron; also W. M. Clark with his drygoods and grocery business. Other tenants were listed in the assessment roll as "merchants" or "tradesmen".

The butchers were quick to complain that there were no toilet facilities and no means of heating. And so, for $40, an outdoor privy was erected, and two wood-burning stoves were bought for the market building. Council, retaliating, complained about the butchers, and the "vile practice of dragging filthy hides through the front hall, making the rooms upstairs redolent with a not very pleasant perfume". The village constable was ordered to stop the practice.

Before the end of 1859, the town hall was also providing accommodation for band practices in the mayor's room; for the Stratford Debating Society and the Music Club, in the police rooms; for the Stratford Reading Room Association and the Mechanics' Institute, upstairs.

Nearby, in 1859, the first monthly fair was held on the McDonald-owned land adjoining market square, under the auspices of the Perth County Agricultural Society, which was allowed use of the idle but appreciating property for the payment of taxes.

*Donald McDonald — the Senator
hedged his bets when he parted with
market square!*

For more than four years after the building was occupied no sound came from the belfry, the town being too poor to buy a bell. Two members of the fire brigade opened a public subscription list. More than $200 was raised. Council added another $17 and purchased a 700-pound bell from the Troy, New York, Bell Foundry for $217. "Big Mack", as they called the bell, was installed on November 14, 1862, and "General" Brown, the caretaker, was appointed bellringer, with an 8-day clock to help him keep track of the time.

In 1866, during the Fenian Raids, the market building became a barracks for troops of the second battalion of the Queen's Own Regiment, the York Rifles and the Caledonia Rifles, who had seen service in the battle of Ridgeway. The Queen's Own had lost their regimental drum in that encounter, and in Stratford they replaced it, with a drum bought from the Orange Lodge with money raised by public subscription. Their commander in Stratford was a famous and distinguished soldier, Colonel Garnet Wolseley — later Viscount Wolseley, who became commander-in-chief of the British Army, and after whom Wolseley Barracks at London, Ontario, was named.

Council already was discussing renovations to the Town Hall and Market Building in 1876, proposing to raise the walls about five feet to provide another storey; also, they planned to extend market square. They approached the owner of the desired extra land.

Donald McDonald had prospered in the two decades that had passed. In the late 1850's, as the Reform candidate, he had successfully challenged his former superior, the Canada Company commissioner, Thomas Mercer Jones, for the new seat in the Legislative Council representing the constituency of Tecumseh, which took in 33 municipalities in Huron, Perth and Middlesex counties. In Confederation Year, 1867, he had been appointed to the senate, and it was now with Senator Donald McDonald that Stratford dealt.

He offered to sell his land south of the municipally-owned property for $20,000. Council made a counter-proposal of $15,000, in debentures, bearing interest at 6 per cent. McDonald rejected the offer, and gave instructions to subdivide and sell.

The price of land had escalated beyond his rosiest hopes over two decades, and in January, 1877, Senator Donald McDonald, who had sold the city an acre for about $1,000 in 1855, now sold a little over two acres south of the market place for $50,000, to a new purchaser: "Her Majesty Queen Victoria", as represented by the Minister of Public Works of Canada.

Once more, council turned its attention to interior renovations, replacing the original long table with a new semi-circular one, adding lock drawers for each member and putting in a separate desk for the clerk. However, when councilor John Gibson suggested that a new type gas burner be installed in the council room, Mayor T. M. Daly retorted that he thought the council members generated sufficient gas without artificial aid.

The vacant space at the rear was graded and a platform and sheds erected, as shelter for vendors and buyers. Thoughtfully, the market committee also provided accommodation for the English sparrows that were beginning to arrive in Stratford at that time. Two "tenements" for their use were erected near the market.

The market square area was eventually extended southward in 1887 when the widowed Frances McDonald, by then living in Los Angeles, California, conveyed, for the sum of $1, a 30-foot strip of land between Wellington and Downie Streets, to the municipality, again contingent on its being used only as a market place. The city was required to replace with pavement the wooden sidewalk fronting the business places on the square, and to remove the existing eyesore of a wooden railing.

That, they thought, was the end of the troublesome McDonald proviso, and, for the next ten years, council settled down to business in its city hall.

About 1 a.m. in the early morning of November 24, 1897, Police Constable George Robertson looked up to see an unnatural red glow on the windows of the market building. A Scottish concert had been held there the evening before, and the Hibernian Ball was to take place that night. But, at that hour in the morning, the Scots had gone home. The building was empty, except for three tramps who had been given shelter for the night in the cells.

The constable turned in the alarm, then ran to liberate the men, still sound asleep on their mattresses.

"Get the hell out of town as fast as possible!" he shouted.

beginning so as to comprise one acre of land. —
To have and to hold the said land and premises and
appurtenances to the said parties of the third part the.
successors and assigns in trust to use the same for
the purpose of erecting and maintaining thereon a
Market House and the buildings incident thereto as
aforesaid for ever. — — —
And which said Indenture is witnessed as to the.
execution thereof by the said Donald McDonald —
and Frances McDonald by D Mitchell McDonald
And this Memorial thereof is hereby required to be
registered by me the said grantor. — — —
As witness my hand and seal this Twenty ninth
day of August 1855.

Donald McDonald.

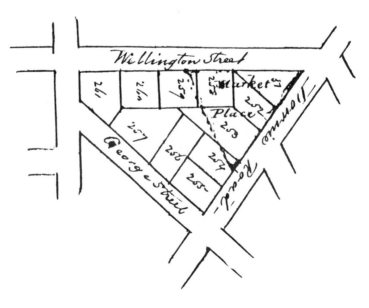

The words that ordered a "Market House", and the drawing
of the site. From a Memorial of the Indenture in the Registry Office at Stratford.

The fire department had moved out of the building a couple of years before, and now the fire hall was at Albert and Waterloo Streets, a block or so away. It still relied heavily on volunteers, and a city hall in flames was beyond its ability to cope. The blaze, already well established, was quickly out of hand. The belfry crashed during the early stages of the fire. The prized town bell, "Big Mack", fell into the fire, where it was reduced to molten metal. Butchers and feed merchants watched helplessly as stock and equipment burned.

By daybreak, the building was gutted, and charred walls rose gauntly in the ruin of market square. A stunned Stratford assessed the damage, and debated what to do next.

Losses were substantial. The public library lost books valued at $4,000, as well as library furniture and the Mechanics' Institute records. A piano, moved in for the Scottish concert, was destroyed, along with stage fittings, owned by Albert Brandenberger. Chairs and a curtain borrowed from R. S. Porteous, the furniture manufacturer, had gone up in flames, and even the hall custodian lost some personal belongings.

There escaped a few city documents locked in a vault . . . the first two bylaws of the Board of Police Commissioners . . . the Canada Company grant, of 1855, to the school trustees of the Village of Stratford . . . "By Law No. 74" of December 1863, for appointing returning officers and fixing five polling places located in the Common School, in two shoe shops, an office and the Council Chamber . . . "By law 77", for the appointing of a Pound Keeper for the year 1864 . . . the 1843 indenture by which W. F. McCulloch acquired the debt-ridden Mitchell land. Luckily, assessment rolls and some other vital records were saved.

The real cause of the fire was never determined, and only the library had adequate insurance, as it moved, with its salvaged books, to temporary quarters in the Macklin Block on Ontario Street. The City had only $5,000 insurance on the building, and $1,000 on the contents.

Council found quarters in the Worth Block on Wellington Street, which it rented from the owner, Charles L. Worth, for $60 a month. There, Mayor John O'Donoghue hastily called his council into special session. Some citizens wanted to rebuild inside the old walls; others wanted a complete new job. Before the meeting adjourned, the market and police committee had been instructed to have two plans prepared, one showing the old structure restored, one for a completely new building, to be used for municipal purposes only. In the urgency of the need to rebuild, the old McDonald proviso received scant attention.

The princely sum of $100 was offered in prizes for plans and a local architect, H. J. Powell, was the winner. Council decided to go for a new building. The Powell plans called for Credit Valley brown stone for the foundation and the trimmings, No. 1 buff pressed brick for the outside walls, a balcony in the council chamber and a public hall to accommodate 500 people as before.

Reading of the plans and specifications droned on, and on. And *on.* Council minutes recorded that "as the reading proceeded, a number of aldermen retired and as there was no quorum the mayor declared the meeting adjourned". Next meeting, council rejected the balcony idea, as well as the use of white pressed brick, and, much pleased with their work, sent a $30,000 debenture bylaw to the ratepayers. The ratepayers, not at all impressed, promptly turned it down by 74 votes. Council had to pay the architect and start all over again, this time with a Toronto firm.

The building committee that May was feverishly eager to pare costs, with precious little insurance money to help out. It wanted to reduce the size of the public hall and gallery to accommodate no more than 200 persons, with the stage to be from 15 to 20 feet in depth. With a population now of over 10,000, it was not impressive. However, it was a saving.

They then began wrangling over the color of brick. The original plans had called for buff pressed brick. However, the first building had been white, and some councilors nostalgically wanted white again. Red brick then gained a few supporters, but, before long, the majority in council wanted white after all.

Letters to the editor appeared in the paper. A delegation waited on council, urging that red brick be used, because white would become dirty much more quickly. Meanwhile, the men at the brickyard over-fired their white bricks and were having trouble making enough of one batch of uniform color. Council backtracked again. Red brick walls were ordered, along with the cornerstone and a commemorative plaque for the front hall.

A couple of nights before the cornerstone was to be laid, council was discussing a Downie Street sewer. As the meeting droned to its close, a weary Mayor O'Donoghue, shuffling his papers together, made some casual reference to the laying of the cornerstone the coming Wednesday. The aldermen alerted like beagles.

Wednesday — ? This Wednesday?

Some aldermen had heard nothing about it at all, including one on the committee in charge! After they had straightened out the communication foul-up, there was another matter — costs.

In money matters, Stratford council was rapidly building a reputation for penury, and it now was preparing to sweep the ceremony of the cornerstone laying under the carpet, mainly because it didn't want to spend $200 for a banquet that must, inevitably, follow.

It finally shamed itself into a proper ceremony and the *Beacon,* on November 2, 1898, reported it went off very well:

> Mayor O'Donoghue, in the presence of many assembled citizens, declared the stone well and truly laid. Council and the band marched from the Worth Block to the site. A representative of the Crown attended and every vantage point was used, even to the tops of telegraph poles. The children from the various schools were present. Ald. Ingram, chairman of the building committee, handed the trowel to the mayor. The trowel was handsomely engraved.

One of the city's prominent and respected lawyers, John Idington Q.C., said he hoped "the hundreds of little eyes that had witnessed the day's ceremonies would have occasion to look on this structure with pride, even when those little eyes were dimmed with age".

The cornerstone of a new city hall was "well and truly laid" —
with a celebration that very nearly didn't happen. Some climbed on roofs to watch.

Placed in the stone in the lower outside wall was a copper box containing a parchment listing civic representatives and public officials; also names of all the scholars at the collegiate with their autographs; records of the public and separate schools; copies of the city newspapers; the current directory; the city bylaws; the last audit; a copy of *The Stone Cutters Journal;* several insurance papers; a quaint old Roman coin and some specimens of current coins.

The inscription carved on the stone was a model of brevity.

CORNER STONE
Laid by THE MAYOR
November 2nd. 1898

After the ceremony, Messrs. King and Siddall, the architects, took the members of council to dinner at the Windsor Hotel.

A statement of workmen's costs submitted in 1898 itemized some of the smaller touches: "Rope and ball for flag pole, $2.50 . . . Varnishing council chamber rail, $12.75." Total building cost, from an old document at city hall, came to $34,689.46. However, other costs in finishing would, before all was done, bring it above that figure.

As the walls rose, the red-brick theme grew more and more dominant. When it was complete, the whole building was the same reddish-brown, even to the frames of the windows. It looked like nothing so much as an enormous, russet-brown plum pudding squatting in the middle of the square. Much later, white paint appeared as trim, white touches were added to the windows, blinds were bought, and the remarkable, mediaeval castle of a city hall finally assumed its proper appearance.

Council's first shopping was for the bare necessities, including: electric fixtures, on contract with W. T. McGuire, $805; furniture and furnishings from R. White & Company, $796.25; 500 chairs for the auditorium, from the Canadian Office & School Furniture Company, $735. Another $836 was spent for furniture at a later date.

A mayor's chair was ordered, with a steaming locomotive carved on the ornate oak back in tribute to Stratford's primary industry. The tender carried the date 1899. Two smaller chairs to flank it came from Stratford's R. S. Porteous furniture factory. Other furnishings would change, but these three pieces would remain through the years in City Hall.

The first council met with little ceremony in a still-unfinished building on January 8, 1900. Within a month, city officials were in their new offices, the public library was open on the main floor and the police and magistrate's quarters and health department had moved into the basement.

The first outside group to use the new auditorium was the Cheese and Butter Association of Western Ontario, which held its two-day annual meeting there nearly two weeks before the official opening. Organizations were eager to be among the first to use the new hall, or to share in the opening ceremonies for the new building.

Across the ocean, the Boer War was in full swing and Canada was deeply involved, with over 7,000 Canadians already sent out to South Africa to help England maintain her supremacy. The official opening day, January 29, became a patriotic occasion, as the Canadian Club, as part of a nation-wide effort, held a concert to raise funds for the dependents of the men at the front. The Women's Hospital Aid joined forces with them.

The auditorium was decorated in red, white and blue, with Union Jacks flanking a picture of Queen Victoria. The 28th Regiment Band, in full uniform, played. There were patriotic addresses and vocal solos, Mayor James Hodd extending the official welcome, and, as the *Beacon* said next day, "a throbbing mass of humanity surged about the corridors and soon after the auditorium doors were opened every seat was filled."

A tidy sum of $175 was collected at the concert and a public subscription raised the total to more than $2,500 for the war dependents.

The next month, the 1900 council had second thoughts about other organizations using the council chamber when not occupied by themselves, and booted out all three school boards — collegiate, public and separate — sending them to the new board room in the basement. The school boards took exception to council's action and moved out of the building. However, by 1901, council relented and the school boards moved back in.

Meanwhile, council, in buying its furnishings, had forgotten one item — a flag for the mast atop city hall. What reminded them, late that February, was the build-up of the Boer War, with a besieged and starving Ladysmith on the verge of falling, and British fortunes running low. It stirred up patriotic fever, and a flag was ordered forthwith. Then, in a miraculous turn-around of British luck, Ladysmith was relieved that same night. Word reached Stratford the following day. The mayor proclaimed a half-holiday, and touched off a celebration that lasted far into the next morning. That same day, the junior hockey club won the OHA championship over Peterborough, and the McLagan furniture plant and Easson planing mill were destroyed by fire. Probably no one noticed that there was still no flag atop city hall.

And no commemorative plaque in the lobby.

If council had nearly botched the cornerstone laying and forgotten the flag, it managed to lose the commemorative plaque altogether.

In 1898, a marble tablet, 48 by 21 inches, and bearing 21 names, had been ordered for the front entrance of City Hall. But the incoming 1899 council wasn't aware of it until the excellent Stratford stonecutter, James Gadsby, presented his bill for $30.

There were a new mayor and new members of council and now, naturally, all of them wanted their names cut into the stone — possibly on the reverse, turning the 1898 list to the wall.

While the aldermen squabbled, Mr. Siddall, the associate architect, suddenly noticed, to his horror, the abbreviation made of his title. When there was no money available for the very small change he requested, the stone tablet suddenly vanished. And small wonder.

The missing tablet did not show up again for over half a century, and it did a lot of traveling before it finally re-appeared.

Mr. Gadsby eventually collected $25 for his work, and was told to keep the tablet — "The Tombstone", as the citizens were then calling it. He soon sold it to Street Commissioner Alex Easson, who, in turn, was offered $5 for the "tombstone" by a hotelman who intended to put it behind the bar to attract business. Mr. Easson, with notions of sending it to the Paris (France) Exposition, stashed it away in his cellar, for the time being. Later, however, without putting it on exhibit, he parted with it. The tablet continued to travel.

The son of one of the city hall contractors came upon it in 1957 in the attic of the home his father had built 50 years earlier. He donated it to the Perth County Historical Society. However, when a member of council went to retrieve the tablet, the society's president said nothing doing. Where was the proof the city had paid for it in the first place? The plaque went back into hiding.

BEACON HERALD

The new City Hall in wintry finery, for Christmas.
From the ruins of market square rose a truly magnificent building.

Finally, when Stratford City Hall was being renovated in 1974, the newly-formed Perth County Historical Board (which then owned the plaque, as part of the collection it had taken over), presented it to the city. It was some 76 years after it was ordered, when the tablet finally was placed where originally intended, inside the front entrance of City Hall, on the right hand wall.

And there it would stay, for all to see, with the name of the luckless architect at the bottom:

J. W. Siddall, Ass Architect

In building the new city hall, Stratford rather skirted around the McDonalds' provisos of 1855 and 1877.

The Senator, his wife and his heirs could scarcely have helped but know how things were going in Stratford's city core but, apparently, were content to let matters ride. Their intention in making the "Market House" stipulation was, after all, being met nicely. While the butcher stalls might no longer be below the council chamber, the market square still was a thriving meeting place of the citizens, and the land was in no danger of depreciation.

Still, although no protests came from the McDonalds, there were some uneasy moments for the city's solicitors, from time to time!

After the turn of the century, in a city that took increasing pride in itself, a newly-fledged and eager Board of Park Management in the first year of its existence, suggested severing the market entirely from the city hall, planting grass, putting in flower beds and, perhaps, even adding a few benches. The Board was reminded of the conditions of the sale, and the matter dropped.

In a few more years, a market building was erected on Waterloo Street behind the fire hall, and Market Square became a free parking area.

The year 1925 found the council considering a new project and the city solicitor exploring "the legality of erecting upon the market square a comfort station". From the letter of W. G. Owens to the city clerk on November 26th:

"The lands were granted to the City in trust 'to use the same for the purpose of erecting and maintaining thereon a market house and buildings incident thereto as aforesaid, forever'.

"So far as I am aware the City has never carried out the exact terms of its trust. I am informed that at no time did they ever erect a Market House or any buildings incident thereto, unless both the old and new City Hall can be deemed to be the buildings incident to a market.

"Apparently the erection of both the old and the new City Hall might be considered to be breaches of this trust. If any breach has occurred I believe that any ratepayer in the City might bring an action to enforce the terms of this conveyance. As to the probability of such an action being taken, I cannot express any opinion. The members of the Council will have to use their own judgment as to whether such an action is likely. . . ."

Regarding the legality, he could not guarantee that the city would not incur litigation if the washrooms were built.

Had the matter come to court, the fact that the "market house" was now more often called "city hall" would probably not have had much legal significance in itself, but an alert lawyer, aware of the fine distinctions in the use of words, could have made a good case for the defence, after consulting the definitive *Roget's Thesaurus*. There, listed together, are such nouns as: "market-place" . . . "hall" . . . "exchange". . . . And, also: "shop" . . . "stall" . . . "office" . . . "chambers" . . . "establishment". . . . They are often much alike.

It certainly was the *intention* of the original old document that people should congregate for trading purposes and be there for lengthy periods of time — a situation the old market square continued admirably to maintain, even as drygoods replaced poultry and "trading" could sometimes be applied to the verbal transactions of council.

As for the country sellers of vegetables, grain and meat, they would have needed some place to wash their hands and accomplish some other things. Truly a "loo" in the market square could hardly *but* be considered a building "incident thereto"!

The legality of City Hall was never tested in court, as council went on about the city's business.

9

A River In Jeopardy

THE RIVER RAN through the city of Stratford a little north of city hall, where council frequently debated its fate, and it was in a sorry state as it flowed past the turn-of-the-century shops and homes, over the decrepit dam, through Avondale Park, which was part of a cemetery, and out into the country again.

The river had been there before the city. To a large extent, it was the reason *for* the city, whose origins went back to a river crossing on a Canada Company map and the diaries and field notes of the surveyors. There, Stratford had had little choice but to grow.

Now, the river was glutted with weeds and choked with fine, rich silt brought down from farmlands upstream. Because of a leaky dam, the water level had gone down in what once had been the millpond, and gaunt, black skeletons of stumps made an obstacle course for the motorboats still trying to use the expansion called "Lake Victoria".

There had been colorful steamboats once, but they had gone, by the turn of the century. There were rumors of draining the sad little lake altogether, and selling lots on the lake bottom. Judge J. P. Woods, one of the officials of the Syndicate that now controlled the lake, had held out precious little hope that this would not happen.

It had not always been so. Once the millpond and the river had been alive with boats, and music had drifted sweetly over the waters from the bandstand. Boating had been born and bred into the people of this inland community. There were boats on the millpond almost as soon as the first dam was built by the Canada Company in the early 1830's. The first organized club — The Stratford Boat Club — started in 1845. In an old scrapbook that ended up in the Perth County Archives, was pasted the yellowing account of the organization meeting of this remarkable club on May 30 of that year at the Shakespeare Inn, where they named officers and drew up an impressive list of rules and regulations.

There was, apparently, just one boat.

The rules set forth: "that none but members shall be allowed to take the boat; that any wilful damage that shall happen to the boat, the member that took the key shall pay for, or have repaired, said damage; that any member breaking a rule shall forfeit his claim to the boat; that any new member shall pay the sum of 1 pound, 10 shillings currency to become a shareholder."

A second group, the Avon Boat Club, was formed May 27, 1864, at a meeting in the Albion Hotel. Dutifully, members undertook to keep the river clear and free of obstructions, construct suitable landing places on both banks, and stage spring and fall regattas. And what regattas they were!

Of the first one, next year on the Queen's birthday, the *Beacon* reported: "The banks of the lake were completely lined with spectators, whose patience was marvelous considering that many were standing up to their ankles in mud and slush. A number of the more venturesome undertook to get a good dry view by trusting themselves to deceitful logs and stones at the edge and, much to their disgust and discomfort, and the amusement of the multitude, had the misfortune to be submerged."

The little boats came swarming out. Most were oar propelled and had been built by their owners. There were, first of all, the *Mayflower*, the *Jessica*, and the *Merrimac*. In the second division came the London-built *Swan of Avon*, the *Maple Leaf*, the *Thistle*, as well as the *Ironclad*, the *Happy Jack*, and the *Juliet*. Then there were the *Alexandria*, the *Lizzie*, the *Fannie*, and the *Alabama*. Spectators on the banks cheered for every one.

In 1866, the year of the Fenian Raids, the local militia formed a naval board and placed the 20 river craft on a "war footing", with the mayor, P. R. Jarvis, as Commodore and First Lord of the Fleets.

"Commodore" Jarvis was usually first man to have his boat on the river in the spring and took great pride in it. In March, 1868, it was recorded that "the flowing tide enabled him to steer his bark over the tops of stumps and crags, areas almost inaccessible at a later date".

There were regattas every year, both on Victoria Day and on Dominion Day, weather permitting, and they soon were attracting out-of-town competition. One memorable year, there was THE GREAT STEAMBOAT RACE.

The steamboats came to the Avon River about 1877, when William Jeffrey built and launched the 17-foot paddle-wheeler *"Firefly"*, said to be the first steamboat in Perth County. About the same time, another man, D. Nichol produced his 12-footer *"Dreadnaught"*, also a paddle-wheeler.

They decided to stage a race from the dam to the island and back at the annual Victoria Day regatta, an event previously confined to canoes, rowboats and racing shells. Mayor Tom Daly put up a prize for the winner, and the two men readied their boats while trading friendly insults. However, as regatta day approached, there was news of a third boat, a surprise entry. Messrs. Jeffrey and Nichol would have competition.

Over in the little village of Baden in neighboring Waterloo County, lived a young man whose father had founded the place and named it for the family's home in the Grand Duchy of Baden, Germany. And he, too, was building a boat.

Sir Adam Beck, when a boy, won the Great Steamboat Race on the river. Later, Stratford was a pioneer in joining his Hydro Electric Power Commission.

ONTARIO HYDRO

Adam Beck called his steam paddle-wheeler *"Water Lily"*. His arrival at the regatta in Stratford enlivened proceedings considerably.

The audience crowded to watch the race from the long wooden bridge, or stood on lumber piles along the banks at Easson's mill or Orr's. There was great excitement as the three boats churned off upstream.

Early in the race, the Nichol boat broke down. Then, pressure on Jeffrey's *"Firefly"* dropped from 160 to 40 pounds. Beck won handily. A return engagement was held July 1 between the Nichol and Beck boats. Young Beck won again.

Years later, the young winner was to return. He was now Sir Adam Beck, chairman of the Hydro-Electric Power Commission of Ontario, and he was the principal speaker at the official opening of the new power distribution station on York Street on August 29, 1919.

Stratford had been one of the original 12 municipalities between Toronto and London that had pioneered the way for the municipally-owned public power system in Ontario. In 1908, the 12 signed a 30-year contract to use low-cost electricity from Niagara. Most of the municipalities had their first power in 1911.

A year or two after Adam Beck raced on the Avon, a queer double craft was steaming up and down the river, owned by three agile-minded local boatmen. Actually, there were two boats, each 30 feet long, built in Port Dalhousie. Only one of them had steam power; the other was lashed to its side.

In this engineless twin, passengers were carried. With this perfectly legal, if somewhat suspect arrangement, no licensed captain or engineer was required in the passenger craft. The boats ran for a couple of seasons. Then the power boat was sold, and the other, fitted up with a pair of engines, and, with a captain's license acquired at last, became a normal craft on the river.

In winter — Skaters on the river, around 1910,
from an old glass negative, taken by Stratford photographer William Becker.

There was a lull in the 1880's, when the dam was washed out. After it was rebuilt and the channel deepened, once again, by 1887, boating was flourishing at Stratford.

William Jeffrey and W. R. Marshall formed the "Stratford Navigation Company". They purchased a new steamer, *City of Stratford,* and constructed wharfs along the south side where the steamer would call, as well as at Easson's wharf on the north bank.

However, when the *City of Stratford* slid into the millpond in the late 1880's, its smokestack was too high to pass under the Waterloo Street Bridge. The owners convinced the city fathers that the boat was an asset to the lake — and council parted with $220 to raise the bridge.

Another *City of Stratford* was put on the river later, followed by the yacht, *Stella,* probably the last steam craft on the river.

After the steamboats disappeared around the turn of the century, gasoline boats took their place, although, for a dozen years or more, the river was hardly ideal for boating, regattas, or any kind of aquatic activity. No longer was the river alive with the small craft — sailboats, rowboats, racing shells, canoes, even hand-made rafts. The motorboats continued until 1958, when they were banished because they were washing out the banks and disturbing the swans. Even when the glorious heyday was over, veteran boaters discussed boating with nostalgia.

"Thoughts wander back to those lazy summer evenings," mused one newspaperman who had seen it all, "when the band played and canoes, bedecked with Chinese lanterns, drifted aimlessly over the water, paddles dripping trails of silver. Others will admit to romantic moments when they slipped away from the crowd, extinguished lights and went up Idington Creek. Some, even, will not deny that the sparking that went on under the stars, among the willows and reeds, led to life partnerships. . . ."

The youngsters had favorite swimming holes — near the dam, at the "Old Grove", under the railway bridge west of Romeo Street, where the water was usually deep and the bridge girders made fine diving boards. Half of Stratford learned to swim in the Avon, and swimming and diving competitions were held along with boat races on public holidays.

In the glorious days of skinny dipping, Police Chief Jack McCarthy would come — reluctantly, it was said, and only at the urging of citizens of the neighborhood — to issue stern warning to the young swimmers.

"Suits on!!" he'd bellow at the white bottoms disappearing into the river near the dam.

He never stayed long. Off he would go. Off would come the suits.

Swimming regulations became stringent around the turn of the century. In 1896, nine lads were hauled into court and fined $1 each for breaking a curious city bylaw that forbade bathing any day between sunrise and sunset. Another four were fined for swimming on a Sunday. Stratford seemed bent on keeping its bathers invisible that year.

There were various ways of crossing the river, especially for the agile. At its weed-clogged worst, it could be crossed by clambering from stump to half-submerged stump. The Huron Road went across it, first with a log bridge, then a wooden one. Finally, there was a stone bridge of St. Marys quarry stone, built by John Corrie for $11,400 and with the builder's name proudly carved on a column. Once, there were even stepping stones across the Avon, and, at one time, there was a floating bridge at Queen Street.

Ordinarily, the Avon was placid and good-natured, reserving her tantrums — which were considerable — for flood periods. In 1883, she crashed through the mill dam, leaving her bare bottom fully exposed and spending her fury on the farm lands of Downie Township. In the flood of April, 1937, she ripped through the earthwork north of the dam and wrecked a pretty pergola that had been erected in 1931. The dam itself, while damaged, was saved by sandbagging. During Hurricane Hazel, in October, 1954, she overflowed her banks to an unprecedented height, flooding parklands on both sides as well as some houses on Douglas Street, downstream from the dam. Once, two men drowned in the river, and were buried together, under one tombstone on St. James' lawn.

But the Avon was much more a blessing than a scourge. In the early days before electricity, she supplied the power to operate the saw and grist mills and later played a part in the operation of the city's first electric light plant. For years she was the only source of drinking water for many households and the chief source of ice for ice boxes. She helped the railway by supplying water for the steam locomotives. She was an ally of industry before the artesian wells provided water.

Even after the dam broke in 1883, she continued to aid the fire department when the board of works built a platform extending 100 feet into the channel, and ran the fire engine onto it. Group baptisms took place in her waters. She pleasured anglers, boaters and bathers in the summer; skaters, iceboaters and budding young hockey players in the winter. For years, the Stratford Turf Club staged race meets on the ice. She became the summer home of Stratford's famous swans.

House owners downstream from the dam, who lived with the constant threat of floods, periodically complained. But the people of Stratford really loved that capricious old river. The river, they knew, somewhere on levels of awareness deeper than instinct, should always be an integral part of Stratford. The past had proved this right. So would the future.

The Avon River had had a long and honorable history in the 19th century, before it came to its sorry downfall. Surveyors had mapped it and put it on the maps as early as 1827. They defined it further with each survey, until there was little about it that was not known. The Avon River had her source in four farm springs at lot 14, concession 2, in North Easthope Township, east of what became the Amulree Road. It was fed and fattened by other springs, by swamps, surface runoff, open ditches and by the tile drainage on wet farms. Of a total drainage area of approximately 60 square miles, 34 square miles lay above the dam at Stratford. North of the settlement was the natural water storage area, the Gadshill Swamp; to the southwest, the waters flowed away to enter a branch of the Thames River north of St. Marys.

The nature of the river had been documented early and precisely.

"East Branch of the Thames, ½ chain wide and one ft. deep runs swift."

Surveyor John McDonald had noted this on his 1828 map for the Canada Company. Following that, the Avon became the single most unifying force in Stratford, and sometimes a problem.

In the early 1870's, when the town started building the Waterloo Street Bridge, it discovered that the river itself was private property, for the mill owner, Adam Argo, promptly charged the corporation with trespassing. The town bridge piling extended into his water, Mr. Argo complained to council, and it was interfering with his business.

Argo had come from Fergus to establish large flour and grist mills on Water Street. They were three stories high with four run of stone and could dress and pack 140 barrels of flour a day, plus another 100 bushels of custom work. It was a thriving business and Mr. Argo did not want it interfered with!

In vain, did town council try to effect a settlement. Finally it had to pay to take its bridge across the Avon. However, the town was given title to full street width across the pond, whereas, previously, it had had no legal right at all to cross it.

Ownership of the "land under water" had been a fine legal point right from the start. It had not, of course, become an issue with the first owners, the Canada Company, who, in 1832-33, had built the first dam across the watercourse they owned and set up grist and saw mills. In all land sales along the river, the Canada Company had taken care to protect the water rights.

Interestingly, when W. F. McCulloch had acquired the mills, in his deed of sale it was *implied* that the millpond, described as "land under water", was included. But it was spelled out in 1873 when the "land under water" as far as Front Street, having passed through the hands of a number of owners, was conveyed to Mr. Argo. The rest of the millpond, approximately 31 acres, which extended upstream to the railway tracks, was retained by the Canada Company and leased to the dam owner.

After the dam went out in 1883, temporary repairs were made. But, when the grist mill burned, there was little financial incentive to proceed, and the dam became increasingly dilapidated. Mayor William Gordon referred to the "empty river", and urged Stratford to buy it and fix it up; and it would have been a fine, bold project, with cityhood coming.

The boating people of Stratford also wanted that dam and the stretch of river. A citizens' committee, including some of Stratford's most prominent people, pressured a mayor and council already half convinced.

A plan eventually was prepared. It featured a pretty lake in a setting of trees, with a carriage drive alongside. But it was now 1886, with new men in office. The young city was already in debt, and council was cautious. The property was sold to the newly formed Victoria Lake Syndicate, headed by Malcolm Macfarlane and including in its membership influential Judge Woods and others who had joined the citizens' committee. They got the lake for $4,000.

The sale did not sit well with many citizens, who soon were referring to the new owners as the "dam syndicate". The *Beacon,* however, relented, once the sale was accomplished, and supported the new group:

> Notwithstanding the vaporings about the 'grasping tendencies of monopolies' and 'the scooping up by interested parties' of this now desirable acquisition, we are glad that the property fell into the hands of gentlemen of means, enterprise and taste.

The "gentlemen of means, enterprise and taste" could see the potential of the old millpond, all right! They went ahead, even though a tight-fisted council refused to grant them tax concessions. The river became again a lovely sheet of water and the *Beacon,* with truth, if not much originality, called this new Lake Victoria "a thing of beauty and a joy forever".

Private land alongside was willingly made available, free of charge. The driveway was laid out along the north shore, with mounting stones placed here and there to assist persons entering or descending from the carriages. On the south bank, the driveway could not go ahead because the Orr mill property extended 70 feet into the lake. And meanwhile, hostilities mounted around

In summer — the glorious, rip-roaring regattas.

private ownership vs. public use, with the old ogre of over-spending still hanging over city hall.

At one point, the Syndicate's lawyer told council flatly that "the owners of the millpond will not permit Romeo Creek to be drained into the pond", as council tried to devise means of keeping that winding creek away from its back door. Actually, attempting any such diversion of the watercourse would have been nonsense, for Romeo Creek would then have had to flow uphill. Council's eventual solution was to straighten the creek and put it underground, encased in cement.

The fire department was allowed to build a platform out into the lake from the shore. And the youngsters were allowed to swim, until they abused the privilege by much clambering over the dam . . . sometimes minus their clothes. Citizens didn't much like the idea of nude bathing at the dam. And council wouldn't help with money for a "public bath" — pleading that Stratford already had two run-down parks, Avondale and Queen's, that were more deserving of funds — if and when should funds be available for distribution, of course!

The Syndicate went doggedly ahead with development and built a barbed wire fence around its property. It signed a contract with the newly-formed Stratford

Navigation Company, giving the company the monopoly on the passenger traffic on the lake for five years, with the right to build docks. It granted licenses to about 20 boat owners to use the lake and ordered lumber for a gothic style boat house, capable of housing 20 boats.

The Syndicate also agreed to supply water to the Stratford Gas Company for its new electric light plant and sold the company a plot of land on York Street on which to erect the plant. Stratford had its first electric lights in town on July 14, 1887, its first street lights the next year.

The Syndicate frequently needed financing. It required more working capital than it could obtain just by selling boating and ice rights on the river. In 1891, it reorganized as a joint stock company, the Lake Victoria Company (Stratford) Limited, and capitalized at $50,000. It made plans to develop the water power potential, harvest the ice crop and generally make itself self-supporting, while improving the recreational and esthetic aspects of the river. Basically, it was the same old Syndicate and it fared little better, either as this Company or, in a further reorganization later, as "Victoria Lake Limited".

In the council chambers at city hall, almost within earshot of the river when the windows were open, the city fathers talked and argued, turned a deaf ear to the entreaties of the Victoria Lake Company, and steadfastly kept the civic purse closed.

Council still refused tax concessions in return for having the lake thrown open to the general public. Nor was it interested in buying the mill property from the group when, on several occasions, it was offered. The unyielding position of council, along with growing vandalism, started the land-poor owners on a new line of thinking which, in 1899, produced the idea of drying up the lake and selling building lots.

The *Herald* was up in arms at once. It warned of "noisome smells and vapors, detrimental to public health, arising from the river in dry seasons of the year". It described "the torrents of water babbling and bubbling down at flood times".

A *Herald* reporter was sent to interview Judge J. P. Woods, reputedly one of the leading policy-makers of the company. The judge minced no words. The housing-on-the-river-bottom idea was, he said, "under serious contemplation".

The plan hung over the uneasy head of Stratford like a Damocles sword but nothing more happened.

After repeated turn-downs by council, the company soon was trying to sell to anyone who would buy. A Sarnia contractor, formerly of Stratford, took an option, but the deal didn't materialize. The Company hung on, hoping for a buyer, and the City made no move either.

While the city had no control over the water, it got some backwash. When the lake was drained in 1902 in an effort to kill the weeds, the city's fire chief complained, fearing a shortage of water for fire-fighting purposes. City Hall also was having a hard time fending off the boat-loving citizens of Stratford — and that included just about everybody, even Mr. Argo, who had earlier given council a hard time about the Waterloo Street Bridge.

On June 10, 1903, the boathouse was destroyed by fire, believed to have been

ONTARIO MINISTRY OF INDUSTRY AND TOURISM

A black swan guards a fluffy cygnet.

set. It was too expensive to rebuild. More dredging was needed. Weeds waved in the current; little ripples lapped dispiritedly along a dirty shore.

The river was, in a word, a mess.

One who watched the creeping paralysis of the Avon with alarm was a bushy-haired, twinkly-eyed, nature-loving dentist who bore a striking resemblance to King George V of England.

Dr. Edward Henry Eidt was one of nature's gentlemen, a crusader, a conservationist and, to a large extent, a forecaster. The good dentist had his office upstairs in the Gordon Block on Ontario Street, and could scarcely avoid seeing the sorry river every day he went to work. He was a prominent man in town, and had sat on council for a number of years. He knew his city and he loved its river. The *Beacon* truly said, after he died in 1937, that this man had had "a vision of what nature, aided by man's handiwork, could do for his city".

Dr. Eidt's handiwork began with the notion of establishing a parks board. The Ontario Parks Act was still fairly new — a government-backed system to assure preservation of parklands. Park boards were beginning to be set up and, while dependent on local civic councils, they could appeal to the government if there was a dispute about lands placed under their jurisdiction. Thus, while tied to council's coattail, they had a certain amount of clout.

In Stratford, up to this time, the straggle of city parklands (mainly Queen's Park and Avondale) was lumped in with Avondale Cemetery, under the jurisdiction of a committee of council. With frequent goings and comings of personnel, there was no chance for continuity or long-term planning. There had been only sporadic agitation for more land to be set aside, and, from time to time, council had discussed setting up a board of park commissioners, without anything coming of it.

Dr. Eidt began his crusade early in 1903, with letters to Kitchener and Brantford, where parks boards recently had been established. He presented his findings to council. Next, he circulated a petition and gained the 500 signatures needed before council would consent to present a bylaw to the ratepayers. He won the support of the Trades and Labor Council, but, within his own council, the going was often tough.

Two aldermen vehemently opposed the formation of a parks board, one stating flatly, "Taxes are high enough now and Victoria (Queen's) Park is a nice little spot!" This was largely weaseling. The parks were in deplorable state.

Dr. Eidt persisted. He found fault with the way the evergreens were planted in Queen's Park (in an outdated orchard style instead of in clusters), and he dismissed talk of increased taxation as simply scare tactics.

"Putting a little here and a little there, as has been done by city councils, is no good," he insisted. "A system is needed!" He got it.

In the January, 1904, election, when the bylaw he sponsored was approved with a majority of 546, Stratford's Board of Park Management was a reality under the Ontario Parks Act.

Dr. Eidt chose the first board, and for it he assembled men with a wide range of knowledge: John Reed, experienced in municipal matters; Daniel Dempsey, professional nurseryman; H. M. Johnston and Alfred J. Roberts, both fine horticulturalists; George Hess, knowledgeable about government and former member of the Ontario Legislature; R. Thomas Orr of the firm of Orr and Russell, architects, a man who would have much to do with the Parks Board in future. Mayor William Hepburn was an ex-officio member.

They invited to Stratford two of the most outstanding parks architects they could find in America: Frederick G. Todd of Montreal, who designed Winnipeg's Assiniboine Park and also the Ottawa parks, and F. Von Hoffman of New York, assistant landscape architect for the New York Park Commission.

These men came for consultation, and walked along the shore, with the dirty Avon lapping at their feet, and they were impressed and appalled.

"The lake is worth a million dollars to Stratford," Mr. Von Hoffman said. "Some places, if they had it, would spend a million dollars to beautify it."

Frederick Todd got the job, and the Parks Board was ready to move.

ADELAIDE LEITCH

A white swan surveys its personal river; and a swan symbol is now synonymous with Stratford and the Festival.

10

The Magnificent Parks System

STRATFORD LAUNCHED ITS PARKS project with a rag-tag parks system — less than 100 scraggly acres divided between the "Old Grove" (Avondale) and Queen's Park with, between them, the neglected river.

Pioneer Stratford had been conscious of the river potential. The 1862 council had inspected its modest little Shakespeare Square on Ontario Street and set aside $30 "to fix it up and plant trees". Municipal parks had been established relatively early with Avondale, the first, in 1870, and Queen's, 12 years later.

It had also had, since 1876, a triangular scrap of land bounded by Douro, Downie and Waterloo Streets, which was designated as parkland but not actually acquired. It was called Romeo Place, and it had been largely ignored until an enterprising citizen attempted to claim ownership — and produced evidence of his rights. The town hastened to register it as a public plot and park, and fenced it in. It still ended up buying the tiny property for $200.

When Mayor P. R. Jarvis decided, in 1864, that the Stratford young people needed a stimulant to their patriotism, he wrote to the Home Office, requesting a suitable symbol. In due course, he got a cannon captured in the Crimean War. After that, the scrap of land was called Battery Park. Although shrinking in size with each road widening, it was a nice little oasis, and at one time even sported a bandstand, although — as Rev. Dr. Langford pointed out — "the tired pedestrian was obliged to rest upon the Russian cannon".

The city had, over the years, steadfastly refused to sink any money whatsoever into river development. Now, ironically, the Board of Park Management, as soon as it was formed, borrowed $10,000 from the city to do that very thing.

In 1904, it bought Victoria Lake Limited holdings with the city's money and with scarcely a whimper from council. The deal included the dam and water rights as far east as Front Street. From there upstream to the railway tracks, the board assumed the lease on the water rights for property still owned by the Canada Company. The lease was due to expire in 1909.

On the credit side, the river would continue to provide the new trustees with two sources of income — $600 a year from the Gas Company for water power and $400 from ice-cutting operations.

The first riverfront land purchased by the new board was Post Office Square, and, with it, was acquired the appalling mess along the river — the sagging boathouses, warehouses, outhouses, dead cats, garbage and ashes all slithering down to the edge of the water. It was a far cry, in 1904, from the "thing of beauty and joy forever" described by the *Beacon* in the previous century!

They plugged the leaks in the dam, and opened negotiations with the Canada Company for its "land under water". They dynamited the rotting stumps and hauled them away. There were workmen to hire at prices council would underwrite. They engaged surveyors and contractors. They set dredgers working with horse-drawn scoops. In spite of problems in extracting money from the pockets of the taxpayers and their own enthusiastic over-spending, the parks men got the development under way upstream from the dam, before turning their attention downstream, where Douglas Street residents complained of "a dirty creek clogged with rubbish and dirt, the bank impassable with brush and dead trees — a veritable little wilderness".

To further leaden the hearts of the Board of Park Management, the Canadian Pacific Railway had begun making strong overtures to council about entering Stratford and laying railway ties along both sides of the beleaguered river. The Parks Board had enough on its hands in 1905, without the C.P.R. threat. By now, it had started hauling fill from the excavations for the new Armory on Waterloo Street, and bringing more fill from streets being prepared for paving. With this, it began to level the riverfront slope, create flower beds and build a foundation for a stone wall lookout.

Post Office Square, after much hard labor, was beginning to shape up, and the board bought a nearby livery stable property on York Street from Col. William Smith, paying him $1,500, on the understanding that it would be used for park land along the river.

However, there was now a men's furnishing business, Thornton and Douglas, moving to the business block on the corner, and the owners proposed to expand across York Street toward the river, building a clothing factory several stories high. The parks commissioners saw the plans of their illustrious, expensive architect going up in smoke.

Thornton and Douglas was a pioneering, long-established firm, much valued by the city. From a first little building on Market Street in the 1880's it had moved to the Idington Block and begun manufacturing in the upper stories. From a modest start with one foot-powered machine and five workers, it had outgrown its quarters and had also established branch stores in Guelph and Chatham.

Council was loath to antagonize this business, and the board of trade was militantly behind such a commendable attitude. Col. Smith, however, was threatening to issue an injunction, if his old livery didn't end up in the park system.

In May of 1905, Thornton and Douglas tried a little blackmail, and threatened to move to Hamilton if they didn't get the property clear down to the lake. The Parks Board flexed its new muscles, and the city reluctantly backed it. The firm did take its factory away; however, that October, it opened a new store in the Albion Block on Ontario Street.

There was a nice side effect to this particular skirmish. Up on the Northern Gravel Road, at the outskirts of town, Mr. William Battershall had a 100-acre farm, and there he sat on his porch, mulling over — with mounting ire — the utter assininity of buying the Colonel's tiny, dirty livery stable property in the first place, especially since everybody knew that the C.P.R. was going to take over. Mr. B. wrote to council.

"... I have been pondering very much lately on the folly of the city throwing away so much of the toiler's hard-earned money on such a small speck of land, which is only fit for some drover's cattle pen at best. If it should unluckily be made into a pleasure ground and if, some fine day in the month of June when the ladies have on their white toggery, there should come a shower of smut from the soft coal furnaces, which soap will scarce wear off, I fancy I hear the blessings that would be heaped on the heads of them that proposed such an underground smutty hole for a pleasure ground.

"So as to give the people a little more recreation in the pure air that will add to their health, as there is no happiness in the world if that has deserted its citadel, I thought to make up for any disappointment that it might cause if they did not get their lovely spot. I would bestow on the city two acres for a shooting park and football ground. As one acre would be sufficient for both, where the clerks could spend their half holiday and interfere with nobody, the other half could be laid out in flower beds by members of different clubs. ..."

The city accepted the offer of two acres of his farm. When William Battershall died, in 1906, he bequeathed a further 5¾ acres adjoining his original gift, "for the same purpose". And so Stratford got a nice new little park, a gift of sheer annoyance.

While the river was being restored, the threat of total destruction increased. And the name of the threat was the C.P.R.

Railways had been the allies of Stratford, widening economic horizons, then boosting employment with the motive power shops. Now, another railway would spell the end of the parks.

Ownership of the former Lake Victoria Company property had barely passed into the hands of the city, when the parks board faced this proposed entry of the Canadian Pacific Railway, with tracks to flank the river and a station and freight yards within a whistle of the stone bridge.

As negotiations proceeded, various plans for the route were discussed. Under the original C.P.R. plan, the railway was to enter the city from the northeast, its connection being with the C.P.R. extension at Conestoga. It was to run along the north shore of the river as far as Huron Street. Later, the railway intended to build a connecting line in from Thamesford on a route to follow the south side of the river approximately to St. Vincent Street, and cut across the collegiate flats to the north.

The picture that saved the parks system

''If the C.P.R. is run as projected,
all the people in the foreground would be
trespassers on railway property
if they attempted to reach the water's edge.''

—*From the parks fight poster.*

The freight yards were to be east of Mary Street (Waterloo), the station near the corner of Huron and St. Michael (William) Streets, about as visible as it could be. One freight and two passenger trains would run each way daily and the C.P.R. planned to secure running rights over the Grand Trunk tracks to the east end factories, which at least pleased local industry.

The city needed only provide the right-of-way. However, this would mean the purchase and destruction of homes, and the buying of land along the lower Avon right to the city's southwesterly limits. The north bank of the river, from the dam upstream to Waterloo Street, would be filled in by some 60 to 70 feet, to accommodate the tracks. Estimated cost to the city was between $30,000 and $35,000.

Interestingly enough, about the time the railway was looking at the Stratford plan, Scottish-born Sir William Methven Whyte, a one-time Grand Trunk station agent at Stratford, had just become second vice-president of the Canadian Pacific system. Although in the background, he had no direct hand in the negotiations at Stratford.

To work out the project, the board of trade and the city formed a joint railway committee in Stratford. Negotiating for the C.P.R. was W. J. Leonard, president of the Guelph and Goderich Railway, a C.P.R. subsidiary. On December 30, 1904, the parks board was asked to sanction a right-of-way along the north shore of the Avon river. It was no way to end the old year.

Council had its first actual look at the plan a fortnight later. The aldermen were under no illusions: the parks and the river were at stake. On the other hand, Stratford was a one-railway town, and competition from a second line would be enormously healthy for local industry.

South shore development was, of course, the thorny question, with plans for the parks just nicely under way. The railway committee was forced to reject Leonard's wish to bring the railway in by that route.

No one in town was indifferent. There was very plain talking on street corners, in letters to the press and at public meetings. The parks commissioners were, in turn, praised for their stand against the line along the river and damned for impeding the city's progress and depriving it of tax dollars. There was even talk of dissolving the board.

Some citizens had to defend their reputations. One of them, J. D. Barnett, was a strong parklands supporter, but he had been a one-time master mechanic of the Grand Trunk Railway, and was still a shareholder in that company. He was accused of conflict of interest, when he called for a union station, and it was implied he was backing G.T.R. interests, not the interests of the city. Angrily he offered to give his G.T.R. stock to the city, providing some other citizen or citizens would make the city a similar gift. The money was to be used for the parks, the library or the hospital, and be kept as a source of income. He had no takers.

There was a stormy session of council's finance committee in March, when the parks board came with a legitimate request and found itself blackmailed. When the board bought the Victoria Lake Company property, it undertook to honor the company's contracts for water rights and ice-cutting privileges. However, it required passage of a special legislative bill before the board legally could collect fees that amounted to $1,000 a year. Council was asked to take the necessary legal steps.

Council smiled politely and invited the board to sign a resolution, the gist of which was that if the board would surrender the land necessary for the railway, then the city would petition the Legislature for the private bill. The board declined, saying the offer defeated the very purpose for which Stratford's Board of Park Management had been set up.

The C.P.R. continued pressuring for action. Reluctantly, very reluctantly, the board later agreed to cooperate with the city in allowing the line along the north shore, but added provisions: that the line be built within two years and be not more than 50 feet in width; that the board be compensated for any loss of revenue and for damages that it might become liable for; that a strip 20 feet wide be embanked on the north side of the right-of-way and that passage of the special bill before the Legislature be expedited — *at once!*

The next concession to the C.P.R. — which was becoming increasingly vexed with Stratford — was to offer a bonus of $30,000 to be applied toward purchase of property on the north shore, along with some sweeteners regarding city building assistance on approaches to subways.

The C.P.R. was just not interested and, rather than lose the railway altogether, council in desperation turned again to the south shore so vital to the parklands, and dangled it as inducement. A survey was made by C.P.R. engineers, while the railway also reconsidered the offer on the north shore route.

In September, came a bombshell of a letter, and it said: "Should we eventually decide to build to your city, we probably will, when the time comes, ask your citizens to grant us such right-of-way and station grounds as are owned or controlled by the corporation, and we finance the balance of the right-of-way required, without asking the city to contribute towards it." The deal was off.

The railway, in 1906, deposited a plan of the north shore route with the Dominion Railway Commission. In 1909, it sought a five year extension of the plan, which quickly drew opposition from council as well as the parks board. Land values were changing; owners along the river were improving their properties and a lengthy period of indecision would be unfair. The railway withdrew its request.

The river, however, had not really routed the railway, only won a reprieve. In 1911, the C.P.R. again asked for a free right-of-way along the south shore of the river, this time for an Embro-Stratford-London route for its subsidiary, the Tillsonburg, Lake Erie and Pacific Railway. Wanting no repetition of drawn-out negotiations with a recalcitrant Stratford this time, Mr. Leonard stated flatly that "it was the south shore route or nothing".

The plan offered in 1912 differed, somewhat, from the one put forward earlier. En route to a riverside station, the tracks would still cut through the collegiate flats and bisect important riverfront property, including the Dufton Woollen Mill site just rebuilding after the fire of the previous year. It was worse, by far, than the earlier plans and the parks system was now eight years old.

The Board of Park Management was asked to study the plan. It replied: "It would be useless to offer any suggestions, as to make the proposition acceptable to us it would mean cancelling the whole plan."

The railway plans were finalized in August. The 1912 council, now thoroughly uncomfortable, and faced with a growing number of outraged citizens, procrastinated about setting a date for the vote. The battle lines were forming much as they had done eight years before, in three camps: council, industry and parks supporters.

When a voting date was called for the following March, the C.P.R. bylaw was to be presented to the ratepayers together with two money bylaws, one to assist in the establishment of a furniture plant, the other for establishment of a plant for the manufacture of mitts and gloves. Some thought voting on the three bylaws the same day might be detrimental to the two industrial bylaws. The citizens' committee, and later also the board of trade, asked council to set a separate date for the railway bylaw. Council would not.

The citizens and the Parks Board organized to fight. A subscription list was opened to finance the cause, and ward committees were named. Soon, there was a "Boosters for the Bylaw Committee", and the citizens' committee was referring to the "Grab-The-Park Bylaw". Both local papers firmly opposed the river route, although the *Herald,* less outspoken, did not want to see the city lose the C.P.R. connection.

The real catalyst, and what saved the river when it came right down to the vote, was a picture. They blew it up and used it on a parks fight poster, titled simply: "SUMMER SCENE IN RIVERSIDE PARK, THE PEOPLE'S PLAYGROUND".

The citizens' committee wrote a masterly bit of copy to go with that emotional picture: "Try to imagine what the south shore above the 'Long Bridge' will look like when turned into a freight yard." And — "Do not be frightened by threats of the Big Stick. . . . Be on your guard against the roorbachs." The committee was fighting the most powerful railway in the world.

The people voted for the parks, but by a majority of only 127. And, while they had spoken to preserve the parks system, they hated to lose the railway. Immediately following the vote count, there was a public meeting in the city hall auditorium, and a telegram was sent to the C.P.R. president:

> A large mass meeting of citizens of Stratford . . . desire to assure
> you that today's voting is solely to be interpreted as one in defence
> of our unique parks system and not as hostile to the C.P.R.
> entrance. Your great railway, by some route other than by our lake
> or river, would be welcome by our whole body of citizens.

A committee including the mayor and three aldermen, the president of the board of trade and the president of the Retail Merchants Association went to Toronto to see if anything could be salvaged. The C.P.R. thought not.

Meanwhile, work along the river had gone on uneasily, but as usual. The river below the dam and the areas on the north shore were being developed.

The first public bath house on the river was built in 1912. In this frame structure, cubicles cost 10 cents each, suits could be rented for a like sum and towels were a nickel. The poor children of the community were admitted free for one hour in the mornings, and skaters could shelter there in winter. (It was 1923 before a bylaw banned swimming "unless attired in proper bathing suit and, in cases of persons 12 years of age or over, such suit shall be a two-piece suit or combination suit, with skirt of substantial material".)

The Parks Board got into the boat business in 1916, with the gas-powered *Juliet* on a passenger run on the Avon. The one-way fare between any of the Board's docks was five cents, but it cost a dime to ride one way to the Country Club, and a nickel to return.

Boating revived a bit, during gas rationing of the Second World War, but comparatively few people owned their own boats and rental services boomed. By the 1970's, the only motor craft allowed on the river were the *Juliet II*, and a launch, kept at the boathouse, for patrol and lifesaving purposes.

Expropriation of land was required only twice, when it came time to build driveways, and both the collegiate board and the Grand Trunk Railway gave right-of-way over their properties. Thousands of yards of material were hauled out of the river below the dam to make a driveway, and to create a Lilliputian island eventually linked by a bridge to the "mainland" of the Shakespearean Garden.

The river was "opened to navigation" on October 16, 1920, when R. Thomas Orr, long a champion of the parks, launched a canoe below the bridge and paddled clear through to the westerly city limits. Upstream, when the north shore development got under way with the dredging of the north channel, there appeared a tiny "Long Island" and a man-made "Loch Lomond".

For many years after the initial dredging, the Avon continued to be a useful and apparently healthy river, but each year, particularly during the spring floods, tons of silt were being carried down from the farmlands of North Easthope, and debris from drainage ditches and storm sewers was building up.

One parks commissioner feared that the river was becoming so silted "that the waterfowl would tread bottom and break their legs". But council maintained a "hold the line policy" on public spending.

The Upper Thames River Conservation Authority, which had been formed in 1947 in Stratford to aid municipalities in the watershed, was concerned both with conservation and with flood control and also was in a position to help seek financial aid from senior governments. Stratford succeeded in getting a survey done in 1954. Residents, Parks Board and Conservation Authority all were urging a clean-up for the clogged river, but progress was excruciatingly slow. Money problems, inter-governmental negotiations, January storms, a squabble between engineers and contractors, even muskrats, plagued both the dredging operations and the building of a new dam.

The riverside superintendents were out in force each day, and sometimes were rewarded with considerable entertainment. Two drag-lines were out of operation at the same time when they slipped off their timber mats into the mud. Trucks also skidded off the temporary roadways made on the river bottom. In February of 1964, the muskrats bored holes right through the coffer dam. It was reinforced a second time, with sheet steel.

Somehow, workmen had the structure ready to receive the gates by summer. The water rose slowly in the reservoir behind the dam, aided by a supply from the city hydrants, hosed in by the fire department. The lake had to be presentable for the opening of the Shakespearean Festival. But, although the water neared the top of the spillway, it was still well below the old waterline at the boathouse and at the Waterloo Street bridge. An error had been made in calculations. Timbers had to be placed on top of the spillway and, that fall, replaced by an eight inch concrete cap.

Watching it all, were the swans.

The swans arrived on the river in 1918, the gift of a Stratford railwayman, J. C. Garden, who had also worked in the railway's shops in Battle Creek, Michigan. On a visit to Florida, he had seen the birds in that state's beautiful inland lakes and become so fascinated that he bought a pair and presented them to Battle Creek. In due course, they had offspring. After Mr. Garden returned to Stratford as master mechanic of the motive power shops, he arranged with Battle Creek authorities to ship a pair of the young white mute swans to Stratford. They, too, were prolific. And so began the long and mutually-happy association of the corporation and the cygnets.

Unlike the ducks and geese on the Avon, the swans never were wild, or free to roam, but lived pampered lives. While the ducks were flying the long miles south, or paddling about the shrinking ice pans on the Avon River on a bitter early March morning, the Stratford swans were cozily wintering in quarters provided free by the city. In spring, often they would be formally escorted back to the river by a Scottish piper, in full Highland dress, as befitting creatures with royal connections. Veronica Tennant, prima ballerina with the National Ballet, participated in one such swan "launching", and a film of the event was shown later at a world exposition in Osaka, Japan.

However, maintaining wildfowl in controlled surroundings proved difficult. By instinct, the swans tended to roam and nest in unpredictable places. If pinion feathers were not removed early, the birds would take flight and often would not return. Death, disease, vandalism — even 24th of May firecrackers — took their toll of the early Stratford swans. The birds themselves sometimes killed each other during quarrels at hatching time. In 1949, there was one lone swan on the Avon.

The Parks Board explored the possibility of obtaining swans from the royal flock in England, but freight rates were too high. Instead, two pair were bought in New York State.

To further replenish the flock over the years, Stratford received other birds, including a pair of white swans from St. Thomas, and two black swans, native to Australia, which produced two tiny cygnets, to the delight of the entire city and its visitors.

A pair of black-necked swans native to Argentina were brought to the Avon in

1959, but they did not do well in the Canadian habitat, and Stratford's last black-neck was finally given to Guelph University's agricultural college in exchange for a pair of white ones.

The white swans thrived. At times there was a surplus of them on the river. Some were sold, traded for other types of fowl or given as gifts. Most went to public parks, a few to private ponds or sanctuaries. Lady Eaton received a pair from the Canadian Players. Two went to former Governor General Vincent Massey and two to Montreal's mayor Jean Drapeau, as gestures of goodwill.

Stratford did, finally, get its birds with royal lineage. Negotiations were opened with Ottawa, which had received a number of swans from Queen Elizabeth during a Canadian visit and, in July, 1973, the two cities exchanged a pair of white swans.

There have been other species of waterfowl on the Avon: mallard, muscovy and black ducks, Canada Geese and, once, nine Chinese geese. But the swans, the imperious panhandlers of the river, have always been the main attraction. One private citizen, Frank Burnham, became known as the "guardian of the swans". He regularly was on hand when they built their nests and when they hatched their young; he visited the nests almost daily, on the lookout for predators; he studied the habits of the birds, on and off the water, and came up with theories concerning their behavior.

Another Stratford man, Armour Keane, who owned a sanctuary east of Morenz Drive, gave years of volunteer service to caring for the sick and injured birds among the flock, nursing many of them back to health, caring for a few freshly arrived from the swan battles on the Avon.

The Avon swans prospered. A stylized "S" in the shape of a white swan became synonymous with both city and festival. In 1977, as the Stratford Shakespearen Festival celebrated its silver anniversary, the Stratford swans marked their diamond jubilee — their 60th season on the river.

In 1972, the city bought the final scrap of land needed to make the parks chain complete along the river from one end of the city to the other. Quite an assortment of properties had been acquired by then. There was part of McCulloch's pioneer estate . . . old Post Office Square, with the post office still alongside . . . a burned-out woollen mill property with the chimney still standing . . . a tangled, neglected park bordering a cemetery . . . a gas works . . . a junk yard . . . some lakefront property once owned by an American slave.

Across the river on the north side, there had been an old hotel that had burned. At the turn of the century, there were a variety of businesses on the Huron Road: grocers, a tinware merchant, tailor, Chinese laundry, shoemaker, machine shop, monument works, some with apartments over them. A lane led east from Huron Street to give access to a junk yard.

Now, strung along the riverfront like beads in a chain, were the parks: Queen's Park and Centennial, Lakeside, Memorial, the Shakespearean Garden and all the others. They had brought new enterprises — a merry-go-round, for a while, cheerfully operating below the parapet; later, an eight-foot checker board for the senior citizens.

For three winters, in the early '30's, the board provided a toboggan slide behind the post office, with the two runways offering a glorious speedway, 130 feet long and 12 feet high, right to the river. Some wanted more parking space, but the Parks Board delayed adding it, even although council offered to paint the parking space a nice grass green.

The first of the Stratford parks, which existed long before the establishment of the Board of Park Management, was Avondale. When the 1870 council bought 47 acres of land in the old Cawston Farm in the first concession of Downie Township for $3,000, the area south of the river was set aside for a park, the area north for a cemetery.

Avondale Park, the "Old Grove", thrived at first, but a number of factors militated against its development. One was the creation of Queen's Park in 1882, on a site more central. Another was council's willingness to allow pieces to be nibbled away for other purposes. A piece came off the southern boundary for "Hamlet Avenue", an extension of Galt Street (West Gore); five acres more were removed for a hospital site in 1899. The lovely hard maples were cut for firewood, cattle were allowed to graze there, and the west end became the town dump.

Out-of-town visitors, alighting at the Grand Trunk platform at the cemetery, walked between the tombstones and over a footbridge to the Old Grove. Local people used a footpath cut in from John Street. By the turn of the century, Avondale had lost most of its picnics to Queen's Park, and was about as silent as the adjoining cemetery.

Although Avondale was designated as a park in 1904, it was not formally vested in the Parks Board until five years later. The board developed it as a wilderness area, with nature trails projected along the river to the city's limits.

The second river park fared better. Not sharing space with a cemetery, but occupying probably the finest property of early Stratford, Queen's Park had been part of the "Grange" property, William McCulloch's 100-acre estate that straddled the river and millpond. McCulloch's land stretched north to what would become Delamere Avenue and south as far as Ontario Street; to the railway land on the east, and to Front Street on the west.

After the original purchase from the Canada Company in 1843, the land had changed hands a number of times, and had varied in size and shape also. A Stratford lawyer, G. G. McPherson, at one time owned a piece of it, and the town bought 45 acres of prime land from him for $100 an acre — profoundly worrying about acquiring so much land and spending so much money. In 1882, Stratford established its second park, and named it in honor of Queen Victoria. Before long, it became just "Queen's".

Mindful of repeated admonitions that development of the park would be costly, council decided to "sell a barn on the property, rent the grass for pasturage and use the money to plant trees and build a fence". An Avonton drover "rented the grass" and, within a few days, 300 sheep were grazing contentedly on the lush slopes by the river.

By 1884, the public was beginning to use it. The first three group picnics were

Before 1900, cattle grazed near Avondale Cemetery.

held: St. Joseph's Roman Catholic Church and Separate School in June; the Grand Trunk Railway firemen in July, and the Odd Fellows' on Civic Holiday, in August.

But little was being spent on park development.

The Mayor complained of picnicers breaking off the branches of the shade trees in the grove, and kindling fires against the roots to boil their tea and cook their picnic delicacies. Like Avondale, Queen's Park deteriorated.

Council appointed John Barker to make improvements at a salary of $1.25 a day and to act as constable for nothing. Thus he became the city's first park superintendent, or ranger. They gave him a wheelbarrow, rake, scythe, fork and some other small articles, as well as two tons of salt to keep down the weeds.

A successor, ten years later, was also given part-time use of a horse. The rest of the time, the animal worked at the cemetery, and to economize, each year the thrifty city bought a new horse. It cost $20 in 1898 — and they sold it before winter for the same $20. That year, the ranger got a raise from $8 to $9 a week, including Sundays — which wasn't very inflationary over the ten-year period.

Queen's served an assortment of tenants: the Athletic Society, who brought a racetrack . . . a new Normal School . . . a smallpox isolation shack . . . finally, the Stratford Shakespearean Festival which proved to be the happiest choice of tenant of all.

In the first major geographical change, in 1893, the city leased a 330-foot strip of parkland, from Queen east to the railway tracks, to the Stratford Athletic Company Limited, the brainchild of a group of Stratford residents who wanted to provide the city with a suitable recreation park. G. G. McPherson, who later became president, still owned some lots that had been part of the old McCulloch estate, but the area was too small for what the Athletic Company had in mind. The company asked for a strip of park land. The area in question was low and swampy, and the Athletic Company got a 25-year lease at $1 a year. The buyers formed a limited stock company, with capital stock of $10,000 consisting of 1,000 shares, at $10 each, and received an Ontario charter.

They built a seven-foot-high board fence, painted brown, around the property. The grandstand was on the north side and the stables on the east. In three concentric circles were the racetrack, the bicycle track and, in the middle, the playing grounds.

By late May, everything seemed in readiness for the three-day official opening, except for one thing. No provision had been made for a carriage entrance to the grounds.

There was strong suspicion that the omission was deliberate and that the Athletic Company figured on using the Queen's Park drive to give access to the grounds. The suspicion deepened when the park ranger caught the Athletic Company cutting a road between their high brown board fence and the park drive! The Athletic Company made formal application to council to use the park drive during the official opening days only.

Council was not amused, and it was the night before opening day before the aldermen met, and granted the request, begrudgingly, and by a one-vote margin.

The three-day opening drew more than 13,000 people. Visiting horsemen described the racetrack as the best half-mile track in Ontario, but the *Beacon* was critical of "the occupants of 50-odd rigs who drew up along the fence on Ontario Street to view the races for free". The first race ever trotted on the new track was won by a Stratford horse, Axtel, owned by A. Thompson.

By 1889, with picnics on the increase, Queen's Park had a parking problem with the horses and buggies, and the ranger was calling for more tie posts. There was also growing congestion on the Avon, as boaters came ashore, and so the parks commission of council authorized a small dock at a cost of $15, and set out a coal oil lamp to light it. They turned down an electric light as too expensive.

Later, council had a chance to buy the Athletic Company property for $3,500 but muffed it. The property finally went by public auction to the versatile, Welsh-born speculator, James Trow, and the Athletic Company dissolved. The land leased from the Parks Board went back to the park.

The Parks Board and the Board of Health had one clash over the arbitrary location of a smallpox isolation shack on the flats in lower Queen's Park. Next time it was necessary to quarantine a smallpox patient the shack was located in the little-used Old Grove. The Normal School was built in 1908, without fences to detract from the park. For a touch of elegance, two cast iron dogs, once part of a prominent doctor's home, were placed at the ornamental park gates. Later, a hand-crafted English sundial, made in the Cotswold Hills, and sent by the Stratford-upon-Avon Rotary Club, was moved to Queen's Park from its original location near the stone bridge.

One of the most delightful additions was an historic old drinking fountain resurrected by two concerned citizens. Once it had stood in front of city hall, gift of the children — the W. J. Freeland drinking fountain, named for a local humanitarian and first supervisor of music in the public schools. The young members of the Band of Mercy, a junior branch of The Humane Society, had paid for it penny by penny and presented it to their city during city celebrations on Queen Victoria's 60th Jubilee in 1897.

It had cost $200, and was topped by an ethereal and very scantily-clad lady, representing the Goddess of Mercy. After the street was paved, the fountain was moved near the old fire hall on Waterloo Street and, when horses no longer needed it, it was dismantled, and lay neglected until rescued and placed in Queen's Park. By then, the lady had vanished.

The Stratford Shakespearean Festival raised its tent theatre in the gem-like setting of Queen's Park in 1953. A handsome Festival Bridge replaced the old one to the north shore; a new footbridge was built to a tiny nameless island which finally was named Tom Patterson Island in honor of the Festival founder.

Everywhere, the Parks Board erected signs: "Please Enjoy Respectfully."

May 28, 1936, was special for Stratford's park system — the formal opening of the Shakespearean Garden by Lord Tweedsmuir, Governor General of Canada. Out of the vice-regal visit, came gifts of white and red rose bushes for the Garden, sent by King George V, along with oak saplings from England's Windsor Park, contributed by Lord Tweedsmuir, for planting in the parks. Walking with the Governor General, R. Thomas Orr had mentioned that the King had donated rose bushes to the Shakespearean Garden in Stratford, England, and might like to make a similar gift to Stratford, Ontario.

The Parks Board had acquired the old Dufton Mills property in 1925, and it was largely through the initiative of Thomas Orr, that the burned-out site took on the character of an English garden. By 1935, the area had been planted with more than 60 kinds of flowers, bushes and shrubs, many of them mentioned in Shakespeare's plays. Some seeds, such as rosemary, came directly from the garden in Stratford-upon-Avon, England.

A bust of Shakespeare was made possible by donations by the Sons of England Benefit Society from all across Canada, and sculptor Cleeve Horne, in 1949, was commissioned to make the 80-pound head.

With the building of a new post office on Waterloo Street, the Parks Board acquired the old site. The land was worth $200,000 — and council optimistically offered $500, reminding Ottawa that the land on Ontario Street had been a gift from the city in 1882. The city eventually got it for $10,000, demolished the old building, and sold the old post office clock to the Minnie Thomson Museum.

The cenotaph was moved nearer the river, and the sun shone brightly on Remembrance Day, November 11, 1961, for the dedication service of the new Memorial Park. Here, since 1910, had also been two cannons — the old Russian

BEACON HERALD

The old post office came down and the site eventually became
part of the parks. The bandstand, right, also was removed, and a new shell
bandstand sparked yet another citizens' battle.

gun from Battery Park, along with a British relic of the War of 1812, one of two acquired from the Canadian Government in 1899. Its mate went to Queen's Park. A permanent monument to the Perth Regiment, set in flower beds, completed Memorial Park in 1972.

Initial steps to acquire the property for Lakeside Park began in 1909, but it was 1921 before all of it was obtained. There had been a conglomerate of businesses there, near the Waterloo Street Bridge. In the 1870's, George Kerr's tannery extended 70 feet into Lake Victoria. It became the Orr planing mill, then a thriving furniture manufacturing industry. West of Waterloo Street was Ben Sleet's property, with its ice house, stable and cottage. The parcel could have been bought in 1909 for $3,000. Twelve years later, they bought it for $5,000 from James Sleet, the son of the former owner.

The old octagonal bandstand that had stood at Erie and Ontario Streets was carted down to the river, with the whole community loudly advising where it should be located, and then arguing hotly about what design should be chosen for its successor.

Today, the magnificent parks are peaceful,
the railway no longer a threat to the river.

There were also the smaller parks, and properties. Out of the great depression of the 1930's came a relief project to cheer the city for years afterward — the Lions Pool, 105 feet long and 45 feet wide. It later was expanded to 150 feet *and one inch,* making it just a trifle larger than the regulation length required for Olympic Championship trials. The big pool opened in 1953, managed at first by a committee of the Parks Board, later operated by the Lions themselves. When the Lions Club dropped its sponsorship in 1965, the city took over, with its recreation committee.

World War II produced one of the tiniest and most poignant parks in Canada — the Dutch Memorial Garden, with the little statue given by a grateful Netherlands to the city that had welcomed its servicemen. For Canada's Centennial in 1967, was added one of the most beautiful of the "small parks" — Confederation Park, with its rock hill, waterfall and Japanese garden, reached by an arched footbridge over the railway track from Queen's Park. It occupied the old Public Utility Commission property, and the pumping station, built in 1887, was converted into an art gallery. Boy scouts planted a whispering grove of evergreens in 1937, marking the coronation of King George VI.

Neighborhood parks with their local participation, and small, diversified parks distant from the river also benefited from the existence of Stratford's Board of Park Management: Lions Dufferin Park in Shakespeare Ward; Anne Hathaway Park in Romeo Ward, the Optimist Playground — even tiny Gibraltar Point, wedged between West Gore and Inverness Streets, at their convergence near Victoria Street. The board bought this scrap of land — once thought too small for a park — in 1917 for $1,600 ($100 cash). It had been "Gibraltar Point" as far back as 1894 — no one knew why. Two more pieces of land were acquired in 1966 and held for development: eight acres mostly under water, but formerly a brickyard and then a testing pond for a pump company; and 28 acres of the Jarrott property on the lower Avon.

The Stratford parks have always been a people thing . . . north shore residents giving freely a right-of-way for a carriage road . . . Dr. Eidt fighting for the park management system . . . Mrs. Reginald Ranton asking that trees be planted instead of funeral flowers sent on her death . . . the people of Shakespeare and Romeo Wards laboring without pay for their community parks. And the festival-goers picnicing by the Avon.

Four men played exceptional roles in developing the Stratford system of parks: Dr. Eidt, who started it; R. Thomas Orr, one of the founders of the Parks Board in 1904; George McLagan, the furniture manufacturer who gave land and money; T. J. Dolan, who devoted time and talent to the parks for 35 years. T. J. Dolan Drive and McLagan Drive make note of service rendered. So does the R. Thomas Orr dam.

For Dr. Eidt, who started a chain of events in 1904, there emerged an unbroken string of parks from one end of Stratford to the other — 850 magnificent acres framing a river.

A blast from the whistle, and the working men
at the C.N.R. locomotive repair shops head for dinner.

11

"When the Whistle Blows at Stratford . . ."

NINETEEN HUNDRED AND FIVE was a good year for the City of Stratford. The parks system at last was taking shape, and there was a general feeling of prosperity downtown. In the early 1900's, Stratford was sharing in the first real boom the young country of Canada had ever had, following the depressed eras of the 1880's.

City water was about to be introduced, an improvement over the old windmills, and Ontario Street was to be paved with asphalt blocks. There were classes in literature and plain sewing at the Y.M.-Y.W.C.A. quarters in the market square, and council was even getting around to putting blinds on the windows of city hall, after six years.

There were major building projects afoot: for the armories, the Catholic Church, Queen's Hotel and Romeo School, as well as for an extension to the G.T.R. buildings.

Employment could have been better, perhaps, but it was satisfactory enough. The Canada Furniture Company was closing, but Borland Carriage Company was going to open with 50 to 75 employees, and the additions to the Cordage Company would mean employment for 20 more men. McLagan had rebuilt after the fire. Twelve big new factories had been established since the beginning of the 20th century, among them Globe-Wernicke, a furniture factory, the Mooney Biscuit and Candy Factory, and the Kemp Manure Spreader Company, pioneering a new business in Canada and soon to become part of the young and growing agricultural giant, the Massey-Harris Company.

Factory whistles were sweet sounds to the ears of one of the healthiest small cities in Ontario!

Even although some other centers offered greater inducements, Stratford attracted manufacturing firms, notably furniture, for its strategic location midway between large Canadian centers of commerce, for its good shipping facilities, and for its relative freedom from labor troubles.

The *Beacon* took note of such satisfactory progress:

> When the visitor arrives at the G.T.R. station he is pleased with the busy aspect of things and this is heightened by the huge buildings slightly to the west. No matter what part of the city he chooses, he runs across extensive manufacturing establishments . . . Stratford people seem to live by the old proverb, which tells us to work while we ought to, but at other times to do something else. We see well filled bowling greens, tennis courts well occupied, crowds flitting to the park, where the band or other institutions provide healthful entertainment. Stratford people, above all, impress one with the fact that they honestly believe in the present excellence of their city, and in its future.

In an upbeat era, it was, however, natural that the working people should start thinking of further improving their way of life. There were grumblings within the railway's locomotive repair shops, where unionized machinists wanted some bettering of their working conditions, including a 25% pay hike to bring the rates up from 20¢ an hour to 26¢.

The machinists in Stratford finally joined forces with brother machinists at shops and roundhouses elsewhere, insisting it was not a local problem but system-wide. They asked for talks with railway management in Toronto.

The machinists had probably the first union to be formed in Stratford. The charter of The International Association of Machinists, Pioneer Lodge 103, the oldest charter of record with the Stratford and District Labor Council, was dated June 27, 1892. By 1905, the union had 350 members in Stratford, working side by side with non-union men. The local pay range was relatively low, at a time when wages in the system were as high as 29½¢, with apprentices getting 15¢ an hour.

It was general knowledge that the railway was opposed to a closed shop, and so, when it was announced that the repair shops would be shut down temporarily "to clean boilers, repair shafting etc.", it sounded like a move to defeat unionism.

There had been labor troubles in the system before and, at first, scant interest had been paid. In Toronto, the *Globe,* that spring, dismissed the Grand Trunk unrest as "just the annual ripple".

Then, on Monday, April 10, 1905, a notice was posted at the Stratford shops. The men were *"temporarily"* out of work. Robert Patterson, local master mechanic, repeated the company's explanation: that the machinery had been running continuously and overhaul was necessary.

The unionized machinists met with members of other Stratford unions: Apprentices, Amalgamated Society of Engineers (an old country organization), Boilermakers and Pipefitters. Non-union machinists, some of whom had been with the company for up to 30 years, wanted to maintain harmonious relations. They went to Toronto to emphasize that the union which was teetering on the verge of strike action did not speak for them.

Monday, May 8, some 1,400 machinists went out across Canada and United States. All 350 local union members were on strike in Stratford the next day, and master mechanic Patterson was officially notified. Money instantly became an urgent problem for the strikers. Strike pay gave them only $5 a week for a single man, $7 a week for a married man, less than half of what they had been getting.

The shops were the backbone of the city's prosperity. Half the people in town worked for the railway, and the monthly payroll, with overtime, normally was between $45,000 and $50,000. Now, downtown business slowed down, although it was not completely crippled because of the buffer of small, healthy industries and stores that had developed in Stratford.

In Toronto, conciliatory railway officials used a soft approach, saying that, since the shops had been ordered closed for repairs, the men out of work were not in a true sense "strikers". However, the men who had gone out stuck to their claims, refusing to go back until the dispute was settled.

Toronto didn't really believe them.

"When the whistle blows at Stratford," said Mr. W. Kennedy, mechanical superintendent, "the men will come to work. We know the situation."

However, a G.T.R. notice went up in the immigration office at the Toronto Union Station, offering employment to machinists and other skilled workers arriving from overseas. Newcomers were taken to Palmerston, Sarnia and Port Huron, but no strikebreakers went, at first, to Stratford.

By the end of June, however, nearly three months into the strike, the city had received some machinists from Montreal. Nerves were wearing thin, and there was the first whiff of intimidation. The city put on extra police, but the railway's Montreal head office asked for still more protection and said that, if it was not forthcoming, the railway would close the shops.

Railway management tactlessly dispatched its own detectives to Stratford, and Mayor Ferguson and his council reacted to what they considered inexcusable interference in an internal city matter, and considered an injunction.

The strikers in Stratford, on the whole, had acted in an orderly manner, and still had the respect and sympathy of other citizens. Many were their neighbors. The detectives were firmly told to leave.

With repairs finished by the skeleton staff, the shops reopened. On August 4, the whistle blew, a heavenly trumpet that could be heard throughout all five Shakespearean wards. It was the first time in nearly four months — a sound sorely missed in Stratford, where citizens had long set their watches by the siren on the G.T.R. shops. Soon, there were 400 to 500 men back at work — but the striking machinists were not.

The trains still were running on a reduced schedule, but crippled locomotives were beginning to line up at the shops. New arrivals from Quebec began to be intercepted by the pickets, taken to strike headquarters, and threatened with violence if they went to work. Some were provided with passes and sent back where they had come from. The G.T.R. filed an application for an injunction to stop the strikers from molesting those filling their jobs and some charges were laid against machinists.

In Ottawa, Sir Wilfrid Laurier went to the railroad, which assured him most machinists had been taken back — which may or may not have been the case.

*Labor Day was cause for celebration in Stratford. For the
1899 parade, Hodd and Cullen Milling Company decorated even the horses.*

Still not satisfied, the prime minister sent to Stratford an intelligent and
knowledgeable man, William Lyon Mackenzie King, the Deputy Minister of
Labor. Two days later, the strike was called off.

They had talked frankly, men and management, said Mackenzie King. They
had stipulated only that an arrangement similar to theirs be worked out with
other striking shops. Terms of the agreement were not announced but, later,
union officers did visit other shops to discuss the settlement.

On October 30, after seven long months, the strike of the machinists in the
Grand Trunk locomotive power shops was over. The future Prime Minister of
Canada expressed his pleasure and returned to Ottawa.

This was not the first nor the last railway strike to affect Stratford, the city tied
so closely to the trains.

Railways had expanded enormously throughout Canada since the mid-19th
century. In just one decade, they had gone from 50 miles of line in 1850 to 2,000
miles in 1860. They had become essential to a young, growing country; they
were the lifeblood of a young, growing Stratford.

A strike of G.T.R. locomotive engineers on Dec. 29, 1876, left transportation snarled in the snow belt. Some men deserted their engines between stations, and, in the freezing cold, both passengers and shipments of livestock were stranded.

The union responsible, the vigorous young Brotherhood of Locomotive Engineers, had originated in the United States and had come to Canada in 1865, establishing the first divisions in London and Toronto. They had established a lodge around the same time or shortly after at Stratford, with others at Belleville, Montreal, and St. Thomas. With the trains stalled, angry Canadians asked to have troops brought in, and the railway did request some mayors to call out the militia. Stratford's mayor was not to be pressured by the railway. He said he would have special constables sworn in if he was ordered to do so by the Attorney General, but pointed out that the police favored the strikers.

Within the railway, there continued to be clashes over the years. In the spring of 1910, one that got up steam in the States spilled over to affect Canadian centers, among them Stratford.

In a strike-bound Philadelphia that year, they were waiting out an impasse between that city's Rapid Transit Company and the street car employees union. Stratford, far removed from the scene, remained only mildly interested, as the local press became increasingly full of it. Elsewhere, strike fever was spreading and, in some places, had erupted into violence. In New York, a strikebreaker had been stabbed. Then, on July 18, 1910, the Montreal Grand Trunk trainmen went out, and Stratford woke up next day in the midst of it.

Suddenly, there were 2,000 men idle in the city — quiet, waiting men, aware that this strike was to test the strength of unions. They did not panic. There were no riots, as in Brockville.

With no freight moving through the Stratford yards, the mayor wrote the president of the Grand Trunk Railway, an action that may have helped bring about a final settlement. By August, passenger and freight service resumed, but many men had lost their jobs and some were still out of work a year later, when the local press was still calling it "the great settlement that didn't settle".

There was a minor spat in 1911, when local G.T.R. yardmen refused to work with the non-union switchmen; and there were other strikes of various origins over the years, for Stratford would always be vulnerable to labor troubles affecting the railway, its biggest employer.

Stratford, in the first half of the 20th century, was a paradox — both a working man's town and a cultural society; a product of John Galt's policy of hand-picked settlers, and a city that depended for its life on the railway.

Both city council and the board of trade were aware of the need for a balance wheel for the benevolent but overpowering monopoly of the railway, and, to the best of their ability, they encouraged the healthy small businesses that were growing up. Relations between management and labor generally were more stable and friendlier than in most other small cities. One major employer, E. T. Dufton, bragged to the day he died that he had never had a strike or a lockout at his woollen mills. Two weeks before his death in 1919 he reduced the work week to 50 hours but left the workers' pay at the 60-hour amount.

In 1914, when World War I broke out, the prevailing mood downtown was still one of optimism and "business as usual". The board of trade immediately informed the proper authorities of Stratford's ability to fill war orders. Extensive orders rolled in for knitted and woollen goods, as the local knitting companies became the first to feel the effects of war.

Lights burned late in the three city plants of Ballantyne, Williams-Trow and Avon Knit, working overtime to turn out gloves for the troops. Soon, heavy industries, including the G.T.R. shops, Canadian Allis-Chalmers, Macdonald Thresher and Stratford Brass, were gearing up for the production of munitions. The furniture factories produced shell and rifle boxes and furnishings for the barracks. Women replaced the men as they went to war, and factory output, instead of decreasing, increased.

The 28th Regiment opened a recruiting office in the armory, and armed night guards appeared at the water pumping station. In the old Central School on the corner of Church and Andrew Streets, were billeted the first of the men recruited for the new Perth County Battalion — "the 110th", the Pride of Perth.

In the spring of 1914, the ratepayers refused to replace the fire horses with a motorized fire truck, although they soon would do so. There were still only a few automobiles, chugging along city streets at 15 miles an hour. The city's first country club opened in July, and two citizens offered their gasoline launches free to transport guests along the river to the club. Otherwise, there was a bus that ran between the post office and the club, at a fare of 25 cents.

A new $10,000 garbage disposal incinerator was built on St. Patrick Street (and the operators soon were reporting that the war-conscious citizens were throwing out less garbage than usual.) Two miles of pavement, four miles of sidewalks and four and a half miles of curbs were laid, and city building figures, the first year of war, were up to $500,000, compared to $334,085 in 1913. Some new businesses moved in, and hydro, after adding 330 new customers, served a total of 1,900.

In 1915, however, the Ontario government levied a one percent war tax on municipalities, and the city shelled out $8,900 that year. Mail cost more. Gone were the one cent post cards and the two cent letters. Cards went up to two cents, letters to three. Egg prices soared to 20 cents a dozen, and butter to 35 cents a pound. Milk would soon be 10 cents a quart.

Meanwhile, Stratford and district people were digging deep into their pockets for war and victory loans. They subscribed around $175,000 in 1916, a year when $185 million was raised across the whole of Canada. The next spring, city business loaned another $382,600 through the banks, while private citizens were buying $10 war savings certificates every pay day.

By 1916, there was an acute labor shortage on the farms. A hundred high school students were released early from classes to work on the land. Private citizens also went to do farm work; so did soldiers home on leave and workers on leave from the factories.

A "vacant lot cultivation committee" was formed by the Horticultural Society, and suddenly weed patches overflowed with squash and beans. Idle city property, undeveloped subdivisions, unused private land, along with two acres of parkland along the Avon and ten lots in Avon ward taken over by the firemen, all were at the disposal of the amateur gardeners. The teachers worked an "educational plot" near the Old Grove. Schools had their own student gardens, and competed fiercely for the trophy given by Dr. E. H. Eidt for the best school garden. Hamlet School was triumphant when it won. By the end of the war, over 450 plots were being worked, and the people had become very, very fond of fresh vegetables.

And still they planted flowers, just as before.

While prohibition didn't come into effect in Ontario until September 16, 1916, the provincial government, as a war measure, began tightening the faucet earlier. Stratford remained, for a time, the only oasis in Perth County, to the disgust of the Stratford Temperance and Moral Reform Association. On the last day of the wide open bars, it was like a circus day. People thronged the streets and hundreds of farmers came in from the country, which had been dry since May 1. The city's two liquor stores were nearly mobbed, and one of them was sold out by 5:30 p.m. In the hotels, they bellied up two and three deep around the bars.

After prohibition, only drug stores could sell liquor, and then only on prescription from a doctor, dentist or veterinarian. Only six ounces could be bought, for medicinal purposes, or a pint of rubbing alcohol for bathing.

The government didn't forget a thing. Bakers could not put brandy in plum puddings. The housewives could — providing the pudding was consumed at home. Houses grew chilly with the wartime fuel shortages and, at one point, council sent a member to Algonquin Park to try to get wood. In 1918, coal cards were issued and then an alderman accompanied the driver and peeked into cellars to make sure there was no hoarding.

Sometimes consumers stormed the coal yards with sacks, sleds and wagons. Some families broke up furniture; others cut city trees. In the country, farmers with woodlots were cut off. Even at the G.T.R., there were cutbacks as the Sunday trains and the pay car were taken off to save fuel. The workers were paid through various departments.

The last summer of the war seemed a harbinger of better times. The good earth put forth a bountiful harvest and, on Erie Street, there was the North Perth Community Canning Center processing, in six weeks, more than seven tons of produce. The Ontario government supplied equipment; the Red Cross contributed vinegar, sugar, spices and containers. The Women's Institutes of the district, the Stratford chapters of the Imperial Order Daughters of the Empire and other groups all pitched in. The I.O.D.E. itself had expanded tremendously during the war. The first chapter had been formed in Stratford in 1914; now, by 1918, there were eight in the city and surrounding area.

That last war year also brought feelings of uneasiness in some quarters. In October, Stratford machinist and labor leader Arthur Skidmore was arrested for being a member of the Social Democratic Party. When the ban was lifted on party membership, new charges were laid: being in possession of seditious literature. The Trades and Labor Council backed him, but it was December before the jailer at Stratford was ordered to release Arthur Skidmore.

In the bustling downtown area,
smaller businesses were encouraged, to offset the railway monopoly.

The Armistice was signed on November 11, and the boys came home. There were soon some new, very young citizens who would have reason to remember World War I — the war babies, some of whom were forever saddled with such names as "Verdun" and "Kitchener". The nearby city of Berlin, too, became Kitchener. Germany, the homeland of many of the early, industrious settlers, had too recently been the enemy.

The war had been hard on the working man. With the country at peace, the workers again were trying to improve their conditions. Stratford bricklayers and masons won an eight hour day in 1918, and a wage increase from 50 to 60 cents an hour, the first pay raise in six years. By the end of 1918, over 1,100 workers belonged to a wide variety of organizations that were affiliated with the new Stratford District Trades and Labor Council: Plumbers and Pipefitters, Mail Carriers, Maintenance of Way, Carpenters and Joiners, Blacksmiths and Helpers, Federal Union of Wood Workers, Railroad Station Men, Railroad Employees, Amalgamated Society of Engineers, Journeymen Barbers, International Association of Machinists, Butcher Workmen's Union, Painters, Finishers, Bricklayers and Masons, Textile Workers, Railroad Conductors, and Railway Car Men.

Slowly, advances were being made in labor relations. At Imperial Rattan, the men got a nine-hour working day and a half holiday on Saturday. In some cases the labor troubles seemed frivolous, as in May, 1920, when three waterworks department men went on strike, apparently only because they wanted Saturday off.

A test case was made in Stratford in 1920. On August 31, half the girls quit at Avon Hosiery. Here, after eight years, the best workers were earning 27¢ an hour and the Textile Workers Union backed their demands for an increase. Some girls stayed loyally with management, feeling they had had fair treatment and generally liking the president of the company. The others derided them. In one family, a mother locked one of her three daughters out of the house — the one who had stayed at work.

Reportedly, the company had told the girls either to give up their union or get out, and had given them one minute to decide. They got out, keeping their affiliation with Union Local 1336 and their right to collective bargaining. The girls on the inside continued uneasily at their jobs, passing the picketers on their way to work. The mill continued operating, and the company advertised for new help. It did not help that the union organizer brought in three outside organizers from Montreal, Hamilton and Niagara Falls.

Meanwhile, going on joyously, were plans for festivities that weekend. By the 1920's, Labor Day had become a gala event in Stratford, and the energetic Trades and Labor Council was involved with arranging parades, speeches, motorcycle races and sporting events with long prize lists.

Labor Day, 1920, dawned with glorious weather and thousands crowded into the agricultural park for sports and speeches. The kiddies bought balloons and the textile girls staged a quiet demonstration, had a group photo taken, and collected $105 for their cause from Stratford citizens. They had, by then, 17 unions behind them for moral support.

The strike of the textile girls lasted for nearly two months but, when it was finally settled, the strikers were taken back on their old jobs in order of seniority, and they had won ground for the concept of collective bargaining.

There was a different feeling abroad in the land in the 1920's and 1930's, perhaps because of increased industrialization and a more complicated role of government, perhaps a reaction to the sustained sacrifice and idealism invoked by World War I. People began to accept seeing their leaders involved in scandal.

Brilliance was corruptible for Peter Smith, former treasurer for his county of Perth, and an elder of Knox Presbyterian Church in Stratford. In Premier E. C. Drury's cabinet in the United Farmers of Ontario government — a government of novices elected in 1919 — he became provincial treasurer — a job he had wanted so badly he had appeared before Drury in silk hat and frock coat to plead his cause. He was well regarded in Stratford and this helped settle the premier's choice on him. There were large sums passing through the treasurer's hands, and large sums also found their way into his Stratford bank account. He was charged with defrauding the government, in criminal court in October, 1924, and sentenced to 3 years in the penitentiary.

He was not alone in the scandal. Others were involved in the charges of conspiracy. As one writer put it, in that era there were enough officials in jail and in the penitentiary to "form a government in exile".

The frustrations of the depression years of the 1930's, the bread lines, unemployment, professional men knocking at doors seeking work — these things ate into everyone's spirits. The working men in Stratford saw their children ill fed, their own futures uncertain, and the whole country's economy apparently collapsing. The fraying of nerves in the depression was a contributing factor to violence.

In high places — Ottawa, Vancouver, Winnipeg, even in staid Toronto — the authorities kept track of where their military reserves were stationed, "in case". These low times could breed revolution, and there had already been problems. That year, 1933, there had been over 100,000 aggregate days lost in strikes throughout Canada — a whopping 100% increase from the year before.

There was, besides, a prickling, ever-present fear of "The Reds", and communist infiltration of the growing young labor organizations. The Workers' Unity League openly associated itself with the Red International of Labor Unions, and was quick to take advantage of low wages and belt-tightening for the working man of the "Dirty Thirties".

In Stratford, things continued, apparently, serene. Political activity consisted mainly of a sparring between liberals and conservatives. Trade union organization was in its infancy, and had barely spread beyond the C.N.R. shops.

As in several other western Ontario towns, furniture manufacturing had become a major industry — second only to the shops in Stratford. No panic was apparent even when there were some signs of discontent in seven of the eight factories of the city, including a branch of the Kroehler Manufacturing Company, the Preston-Noelting Company, the Stratford Casket Company, and the McLagan Furniture Company, whose president, David M. Wright, was the local M.P. The depression had reduced the already traditionally low wages of the industry, and it was natural there should be some rumblings.

Somewhat aloof from the grievances stood the eighth, the Imperial Rattan Company (later the Imperial Furniture Manufacturing Company).

Into this deceptively quiet southwestern Ontario town, came the chief organizer of the Workers' Unity League, Fred Collins from Toronto, fresh from recent union advances. He brought an incendiary message to the Stratford workers:

"The front-line trenches will be your picket line. A strong front is essential. The war is a just war and a right one — fought for the benefit and safeguarding of your homes. You are the troops!"

It was a prophetic statement, that about the troops.

The WUL found it easier than it had expected to sign up members in Stratford. The workers, deeply concerned for their families, were easily led, and Collins had strengthened his hand by bringing along several former Stratford men.

Union demands were presented to five local furniture companies on the morning of September 13, with a reply required by 6 p.m. Next morning, the furniture workers were on strike and the stoppage was ninety per cent effective. It was ironic that McLagan's was one of the ones struck. This remarkable industry had chosen to come to Stratford in the 1880's, and had expanded partly because of the city's freedom from labor troubles.

Ontario's Minister of Labor, who was also Stratford's member of the legislature, Dr. J. D. Monteith, proclaimed himself a friend of labor and then urged the strikers to consider the difficulties of their employers, but he failed to ward off trouble.

The first sign of violence occurred on the night of September 18-19 when Preston-Noelting tried to use strikebreakers to ship out some unfinished radio cabinets for completion elsewhere.

Crowds blocked the way when the trucks tried to leave. Police were called out, but no arrests were made. There were still cool heads in Stratford and H. W. Strudley, whose plant was the only one not involved, offered to act as arbiter.

Meanwhile, the aggressive and superbly organized WUL had begun to organize the women employed at Swift's meat-packing plant. It was a remarkable achievement, for the women, largely country girls employed at chicken plucking for two cents a bird, had all the traditional rural suspicions of the new trade union activity. They also knew that, in such hard times, there were many others ready to take over their jobs, even at meager wages. On September 21, the strike began at Swift's, and it quickly built up voltage.

When the workers quit, there were 11,000 live chickens trapped in the plant and public opinion was roused over the plight of the starving birds. Wisely, the strikers allowed the birds to be fed — but soon began to suspect the feeding was being used as a device for strikebreaking. Hundreds of furniture workers joined the women on the picket line at Swift's, and both local police and reinforcements from the O.P.P. moved in to protect the factory and escort the non-striking workers. Following one disturbance at the Swift plant, the provincials complained they had not had cooperation from local police. Stratford's chief of police retorted tartly that his men had been kept on downtown duty, during a mass meeting of strikers at city hall. An alert was out for possible riots which, however, did not develop.

Monday, September 25, a hose was trained on strikers trying to break into the Swift plant. Tuesday, the power and telephone lines were cut, and outside police reserves were summoned. To the average citizen, it was still somewhat in the nature of a show. The *Beacon* reported:

> Quiet reigned over the Swift Canadian plant here this morning as a strong cordon of police who had been rushed here last night from various centers in Western Ontario patrolled the area. A crowd of 2,000 people lined Erie Street last evening, the majority of them curious spectators who had gathered in the event of a flare-up.

But a doctor's car en route to the Swift plant to help an injured policeman was stoned. A Toronto photographer was attacked and beaten. Three times, the police charged into unruly crowds to push them back. At night, blinding security lights played over the Swift plant until it was impossible to distinguish friend

DEMAND TROOPS GO

THE WEATHER
Friday—Warmer.

The Stratford Beacon-Herald

INCORPORATING THE STRATFORD DAILY BEACON AND THE STRATFORD DAILY HERALD

A WANT AD. CAN EARN MONEY FOR YOU

FOUNDED—DAILY, 1887. STRATFORD THURSDAY, SEPTEMBER 28, 1933. —12 PAGES— THREE C

WITHDRAWAL OF MILITIA UP TO COL. PRICE; PLANTS STAY SHUT; NO EMPLOYEES RETUR

Removal Of Troops, Graff's Resignation Demanded By Men

Placing of Troops In City Denounced and Resolution Calling For Withdrawal Endorsed At Huge Gathering In Lakeside Park; Attempt To Intimidate Strikers Charged

Claim Action Unwarranted

Representatives of Various Railway Unions Join In Protesting Action of Province, Mayor and Police Commission; Furniture Workers Reaffirm Their Stand Not To Return To Work Until Demands Met

One of the largest gatherings of workers in the history of this city last night pledged support to strikers from six local furniture factories and the Swift Canadian Company Packing plant, and passed a resolution unanimously denouncing the actions of the "Department of Justice of Ontario, Hon. W. H. Price, attorney-general, the Police Commission of Stratford, and Mayor G. I. Graff of Stratford in the totally uncalled for and unwarranted importation of troops into the city."

Gathering in Lakeside Park, over 4,000 workers listened to a series of speeches by Labor organizers and strike leaders, and ended the meeting with a direct demand for the resignation of Mayor Graff.

The resolution adopted last night denounced "the action of importing troops into the city of Stratford for the purpose of the attempted intimidation of the striking workers, whose only desire and aim is for the immediate improvement of their conditions."

Want Troops Removed

It concluded with the demand for "the immediate and unconditional withdrawal of all troops and military forces from the City of Stratford and its environs. We further demand," it continued, "the right to organize and if necessary strike for a living wage and better conditions. We further demand the immediate resignation of Mayor Graff of the City of Stratford as we, the assembled mass, consider his action in this matter proves his alliance with the employers to further lower the standard of living of the workers of Stratford."

Nearly a dozen speakers took their place in the centre of the shell-shaped bandstand and addressed the crowd. One after the other declared there was no necessity for the importation of the troops into the city and pledged the support of their various organizations. All signed the resolution.

Protests Show of Militia

"We are gathered here to-night to present the case of the furniture workers to the public. This is a protest meeting against the action which has been taken in bringing

(CONTINUED ON PAGE SIX)

Employers Express No Surprise

Executives of local furniture companies, to which the employees failed to return to work upon reopening of the plants this morning, expressed no surprise at the result. Several of the executives had been advised by their shop committees that terms offered by the companies yesterday were not satisfactory.

"I was called upon by three of my shop committee between four and five o'clock last night," W. J. Anderson, manager of the Stratford Chair Company, said.

"I had sent the committee a copy of the Company's proposals, which appeared in last night's Beacon-Herald. The committee called to advise me that they were not acceptable to the committee. We did

(CONTINUED ON PAGE EIGHT)

Ald. Osborne Ordered To Take Complete Rest

Following his address made at the mass Labor meeting last night, Ald. W. B. Osborne suffered a nervous breakdown and temporary lapse of memory and is now in the General Hospital. His condition was not reported serious this morning. He spent a god night, and the doctor has ordered him to rest for a few days.

Chief Asks Children To Stay Off Streets

Rue to conditions arising out of the strike situation in the city Chief of Police Charles Gagen, issues an appeal, through the press, to parents:

"I would ask all parents, where possible, to keep their children, under the age of 16 years, from congregating on the streets at night," is the text of the Chief's appeal. "Keep them in the house if possible."

COMING EVENTS

5c per word per day. Minimum charge 25c. Each abbreviation, initial, figure, etc., counts as one word.

W. O. W. EUCHRE AND DANCE, Classic Gardens, Friday, 29th. Ten prizes—grand door prize. $16 card table. 25c.

DANCING, TONIGHT, STRATFORD Casino. Freddie Worker's orchestra. Admission free. Dancing 5c.

SPECIAL DANCE AT KITCHENER Park Pavilion, Thursday, September 28th, 8.30 p.m. Angelo Russo 11-piece orchestra and entertainers, from Port Stanley. Admission 50c.

DANCE, BRODHAGEN, THURSDAY. Petrie's orchestra.

TEA, SALE OF HOMEBAKING, Parkview Manse, tomorrow, 3-6. Auspices Ladies' Aid.

OLD AND NEW TIME DANCING. Friday. Tavistock Arena. Petrie's orchestra.

Preston Factory To Start Night Shift

PRESTON, Sept. 28. - The Schmidt Manufacturing Company, Preston, with start on a ten-hour night shift in adition to their regular ten-hour day shift, cmmencing Monday, it was announced Wednesday. The company has more work than it can handle, and as a result it has to increase its staff considerably to meet the orders. Company officials denied that the factory is busy owing to the inability of Stratford companies to turn out their goods due to the strike, claiming that the orders were received prior to the strike in that city.

Staging Parade This Afternoon

A big parade of striking furniture workers, their wives and families, is to be held this afternoon. Arrangements for the demonstration were announced last night at the mass meeting in Lakeside Park. The parade will form at the old Brooks Steam Motors plant on Ontario street, which is now being used by the furniture workers' union, and will proceed through the main streets of the downtown section, dispersing near the armouries, where two units of the Royal Canadian Regiment are held in readiness for action.

Children of the strikers, whether of school age or under, are to take part in the parade, and officials of the Chesterfield and Furniture Workers' Union have expressed the hope that a half holiday may be declared in the city schools.

The wives and older daughters of the strikers have been asked to assist in picket duties, so that all striking furniture employees may take part in the parade.

This will be the second parade of its kind staged within the past week. On Friday last approximately 2,000 men, representing furniture workers, railway shop men, and unemployed, paraded through the downtown area, proceeding to the bandstand in Lakeside Park, where a huge mass meeting was held.

PICKETS ON THE JOB BRIGHT AND EARLY TODAY

The photographer was on duty early this morning, but picketts had formed their lines around the east-end factories long before even he arrived. Employees gathered in groups around the factories, but not a single worker entered when the doors were swung open. Provincial, highway traffic police and local police were on duty at each of the six factories and also at the Swift Canadian Company plant on Erie street. In the top picture above, taken just before seven o'clock this morning, is shown a large group of employees gathered in front of the McLagan Furniture Company Limited. In the lower picture are shown some of the Stratford Chair Company employees grouped in front of the building.

Rooster's Loud Crowing Is Only "Disturbance"

Hundreds of roosters celebrating the advent of a new day with lusty lungs was the only "disturbance" at the Swift Canadian Company plant, scene of Tuesday's demonstrations.

A weakened squad of provincial police, with headquarters in the plant, said the night had passed quietly, although it is said a number of strikers gathered at Gore and Erie streets a block distant.

Only activity at the factory came when a transport truck drew up with a small consignment of barn salt, ordered before the strike broke out. An engineer, who is keeping fire up in the boilers, carted the shipment inside, locked the doors and went about his usual duties.

Four former employees are feeding the 10,000 chickens in the plant at the present time. They are engaged by the Humane Society at a union wage scale of 45 cents an hour which the men claim is approximately 40 per cent. higher than that the company pays.

A quartet of strike pickets were on duty at the plant all night and were joined at seven o'clock by a woman watcher.

No decision was reached yesterday afternoon at a meeting of striking employees of the Swift Company and officials of the concern. After several hours' discussion, W. K. Clark, Toronto, issued the following statement: "The walkout was a complete surprise to us as we had no indication whatever of this intent. It is our opinion the vast majority of our employees have been well satisfied and feel they have been fairly treated, and would gladly continue on the present basis if they were permitted to do so.

"We consider the present rates and hours are in line with competitive firms in the industry.

"Ontario Minimum Wage Board requirements have been fully complied with in every respect and this has been confirmed by the Deputy Minister of Labor, F. W. Crawford.

"We are very willing to discuss the situation with a committee of

(CONTINUED ON PAGE EIGHT)

Think Woman Ended Own Life

(CANADIAN PRESS)

WINDSOR, Ont., Sept. 28. After an exhaustive investigation police today were inclined to the belief that Mrs. Peter Senko, found dying in a barrel of rainwater, had committed suicide.

Questioning Peter Senko, the husband, police say they learned the woman had been acting strangely of late, frequently requesting the loan of large sums of money. Money, which Senko reported was missing from the house, was believed by the police to have been loaned by Mrs. Senko without her husband's knowledge and that she was fearful of him discovering the fact.

The woman was discovered late yesterday by her husband as he returned from work. Her legs were protruding from a rain-water barrel and the house was in a state of disorder.

Was Still Breathing.

Senko and Mrs. Annie Renakowski, a neighbor, extracted her from the barrel and she was still breathing. She died half an hour later, however, despite the artificial resuscitation methods employed. The

(CONTINUED ON PAGE EIGHT)

REMAIN OUT 100 PERCENT

"THIS is completely satisfactory," declared Ald. O. J. Kerr, prominent in Stratford Labor circles and spokesman for the Chesterfield and Furniture Workers' Industrial Union, immediately following the 'zero' hour this morning. He said that the men had remained out one hundred per cent.

"The next move is up to the employers. They can either call in the shop committees to negotiate or shut their factories," said Ald. Kerr.

Expression was given by several men on the street to what looks like a growing disposition on the part of the strikers that they will refuse to negotiate while troops remain in this area. They are backing up a resolution passed at Wednesday night's meeting demanding withdrawal of the militia.

Former Judge Stubbs Coming To Stratford

Lewis St. George Stubbs, deposed county court judge of Winnipeg, will arrive in Stratford today. The fiery Western jurist had not registered at any of the local hotels this morning, but his arrival was expected later in the day.

Stubbs cancelled speaking engagements in Toronto until Monday, when he will appear in London. His visit to Stratford, he stated, will be of a private nature, and he will not appear publicly.

OFFICERS TO STAY

Thirty-four provincial police constables will remain here indefinitely, Inspector E. T. Doyle, of Toronto, who is in charge, announced to-day. Inspector Doyle said he does not fear any more trouble, but added the officers will remain here for some time probably until both strike situations have been settled.

5-Year Term For Swindler

VANCOUVER, Sept. 28 (CP)—Five years imprisonment was the sentence imposed on William Smith, alias Leslie Barton, found guilty yesterday of obtaining $7,380 from a former Stratford, Ont., couple in a stock swindling scheme. The money was obtained from Mr. and Mrs. James Campbell.

"I can see nothing in extenuation of your offense," Judge Ellis said before pronouncing sentence. "You did a cruel thing in taking money from these innocent people; money which I have no doubt represents life-long savings."

According to the evidence, Campbell, 62-year-old retired Canadian National Railways employee, met Smith and an alleged accomplice known as Reginald Burbank July last, and with his wife, was prevailed on to give the two men money, ostensibly to make $190,000 in a stock market scheme.

Later the Campbells were advised their money and a sum supposedly put up by Burbank was lost through a mistake in the stock transaction and were given railway tickets to Montreal where Burbank promised to meet them and help recoup their losses. He failed to appear.

Smith was arrested here several days after the Campbells left when he tried to cash a $1,000 bill at a bank. Burbank has not been located.

THE WEATHER

Pressure continues unusually low over Hudson Bay, and a trough of low is passing eastward across the Gulf of St. Lawrence, while high pressure covers the greater part of the United States. Showers have occurred in Quebec and in southern and eastern districts of Ontario, but elsewhere the weather has been fair. It has been cooler in Ontario, with a tendency to higher temperature in the Western Provinces.

Forecasts: Lower Lake Region—Moderate to fresh westerly to southerly winds; fair and cool, followed by rising temperature. Georgian Bay—Fresh westerly and southerly winds; fair and cool; followed by rising temperature, and possibly more unsettled at night. Northern Ontario—Fresh southwest to west winds, partly cloudy and rather cool, probably a few ligh scattered showers.

Men Standing Firm Whistles Blow, B None Enters Doo

Workers On Strike Are Unlikely To Resume Any gotiations With Their Employers Until All Mil Units Are Withdrawn From the City

Oppose Show Of For

Pickets Were On the Job Early Today; Police tioned At Factories; Troops Held In Armouri McLagan's Night Watchman Sings For Crow Cheered As He Walks Away

"That's entirely up to Col. Price," Joseph Sedgewi presentative on the strike scene for the Attorney-Ge said this morning when asked his attitude toward the d of a mass meeting of strikers that troops be withdrawn the city. Col. Price, he said, was the one who could such a move, presumably on the advice of local author

Smiling cheerfully, Stratford's striking furniture worke morning listened to the factory whistles blow—and contin picket the factories. Despite heavy police guards at all the and predictions of trouble, the workmen started no disorder kind.

This morning at seven o'clock was regarded as the "zero for at that time the employers had declared the doors wo thrown open, that certain concessions would be made, and timated unless the workers returned to their machines, n tions would be ended.

Picketers' Lines Hold.

Promptly at seven, the whistles blew. The doors were Outside every plant, crowds of workers marched in picket They cheered when the sirens sounded. But no one moved t the open doors.

Downtown at the armories, more than 100 soldiers fr Royal Canadian Regiment, reinforced by four "baby" tanks held in readiness to proceed to the scene of any disorder. blew at dawn, and the men packed up ready to move out time. But they were never called.

Police Chief Cheered

At the McLagan plant, six policemen stood at the main entrance. Chief Charles Gagen of the Stratford force drove up to the building and got out of his car. He was greeted by cheers of the picketers and the watching crowd, strikers shouting "Good old Charlie, the squarest chief in Western Ontario." The crowd clapped and stamped its feet, and renewed the cheers when the chief greeted them.

Bob Edgar and Dan MacPherson, two of the foremen of the plant, were allowed in by the smiling workmen. "They can't do anything they haven't got any men in there," said one picket.

Squire Myers Sings

Then Squire Myers, aged night watchman, came to the door. He sang for the crowd, and they cheered him too. He went back and emerged with his dinner bucket. As he walked down the street to go home, the strikers cheered him at every step.

At 6.57, the preliminary whistle inside the factory sounded. More cheers and clapping followed. Usually the whistle indicates the machinery is being started, morning the factory was Three minutes later the whistle sounded, and ag crowd cheered.

"Well, we're late now," a number of the pickets. that's that."

They continued their circle of the sidewalk in f the plant.

Plant Stays Shut

The Moore-Bell Company remained closed. The firem three foremen under contra the company are reported quit when it was announce police would be put on the protect any of the men wis return to work. No smoke from the factory chimne morning, the employees en an iron fence, remained while half a dozen picketers ed up and down in front plant. One city policeman a provincial constables were o

At Preston Plant

It was the same story o per cent stay-out at the F Noelting Company plant, trouble had been expected of last week's disorders th James Preston, president

(CONTINUED ON PAGE EIG

11,000 Fowl At Pla Are Under Seizu

Eleven thousand live chickens and four hundred ducks, with a wholesale value of more than $5,000, were under temporary seizure here today by George Tustin, chief inspector of the London Humane Society, and Western Ontario inspector for the Ontario society. The fowl are penned in crates at the local plant of the Swift Canadian Company.

Inspector Tustin told the Beacon-Herald today that he took full charge of the fowl late yesterday afternoon. His action was partly caused by the fact that the chickens were not being properly fed by "scab" workers imported from Toronto, and also because company officials here sought his aid in the feeding of the chickens.

Cloaked with orders from the provincial society, Mr. Tustin hired four of the 80 strikers to feed the chickens and clean out the pens. They are being a union rate of 45 cen hour, with overtime, the in tor stated.

The quartet of strikers hired with the consent o central committee of the walkout workers, Inspecto tin asserted. They are, Ed Berger, 37 St. David street, man of the pickers; Frank ning, 43 Railway avenue; ence Stephenson, 37 St. street; and James Tuffna Wellington street.

Inspector Tustin has superintending the care c livestock at the plant fo past four days, acting on c from Toronto headquarte the Ontario Humane So Last night, he received a gram from J. M. Wilson, g manager of the society structing him to stay o scene as long as cond warranted from foe. The police backed up against the wall in a hail of stones and bricks. Trucks were smashed, box cars broken open and their contents tossed out. It was profitable violence for some, as residents gathered up armloads of butter and retrieved the squawking chickens that had been released by the strikers.

That night, the mayor and the police commission asked for help.

Under the national law, a hard-pressed municipality could requisition military help through the attorney general of the province. Troops could be called out under their own officers, although a civilian magistrate had to be involved in the authorization to open fire. They had not been called out in large numbers since 1925, during the strike of the Glace Bay, Nova Scotia, coal miners. It would be more than 35 years before Canadian troops would again be called out in peacetime to support civil authorities.

In response to Stratford's call for help, the men of the Royal Canadian Regiment from London arrived, detraining at Stratford in green steel helmets and full battle dress, and armed with wartime equipment. Later, a small company was brought by bus from Toronto.

Four baby tanks, each with two men and armed with machine guns, came in along Number 7 Highway until they were within eight miles of the city, then left the highway and approached Stratford by a roundabout route.

They were actually small Carden-Lloyd machine-gun carriers, forerunners of the Bren-gun carriers of World War II. An evil genius must have persuaded the commanding officer to bring those vehicles with their clanking treads as part of his regiment's equipment. It took most of the day to reach Stratford, and the crews were sick from exhaust fumes when they arrived.

The tanks rolled in along Ontario Street and turned down to the armories. There they were housed, grim reminders of military law and order — armed to the teeth. But, from the Queen's Hotel, a traveling salesman could look across and see the commanding officer keeping his men busy and venting their energies by playing handball. Citizens would drop by to chat with the young soldiers.

Members of the regimental band also were dispatched to Stratford, and concerts were arranged for the community. The soldiers themselves were not blamed for the situation, as people gathered at the armories to inspect the Carden-Lloyd carriers. Clearly, the troops were not needed in the private industrial conflict. However, the furniture companies, remembering the charge that the union was Communist-led, were nervous.

With protection at hand and some concessions held out to the strikers, the furniture factories reopened. The whistles blew, but the strikers smiled and continued to picket. The unfinished cabinets were finally shipped out, but the pickets remained, and so did the tanks.

Over 1,500 citizens staged a protest parade with mock "soldiers" and a miniature "Big Bertha", demanding the troops go home. The baby tanks were never used, but, with their entrance, there had been introduced a new element of bitterness. The intervention had also attracted unwelcome publicity. In Toronto, people raised funds for the downtrodden Stratford workers. Even newspapers lukewarm to organized labor castigated Stratford for calling in the military.

The wily Mitchell Hepburn, the Ontario Liberal Leader, took advantage of the Stratford ruckus to place his loyalties with the workers who were "victims of circumstances beyond their control", and not like "the manufacturers who are increasing prices and cutting wages at the same time".

The military wanted their equipment and soldiers back and, finally, the tanks went on October 27. To pacify an edgy furniture business, with winter coming, some troops stayed.

It was early November before agreements were signed in all plants. The furniture workers got a 44-50 hour week and a ten per cent increase. The poultry dressers shortly got similar treatment. The Perth Regiment was left to assess how much damage had been inflicted on the officers' mess furniture by its bored guests.

The strike was a shocker to Stratford — that there could be tanks on Ontario Street, and machine guns to keep the peace. The show of force had proven no answer in labor disputes — and Canada's leaders took note of the lesson learned at Stratford.

In Stratford itself, the whistles blew again.

There were some political consequences in the city. Mayor G. I. Graff resigned at the end of his term and Alderman O. J. Kerr won the next mayoralty contest at the head of a predominantly labor-endorsed slate of councilors.

Stratford continued to be a strong union town, with the outlook of the workingman often reflected in the city's government.

By the 1970's, unions everywhere were strong, and collective bargaining fully established. Ottawa set up the Anti-Inflation Board to put a brake on rising prices and wages and, by 1975, Stratford was appealing an arbitration award of 26% to the firemen. The A.I.B. did, finally, order some rollback of the wages.

As elsewhere, the main, umbrella organizations of the unions, headquartered in United States or Canada, were reflected in the locals. The old Trades and Labor Congress, founded in 1886, merged, in 1956, with the Canadian Congress of Labor to form the new "C.L.C." — the Canadian Labor Congress. Stratford and District Labor Council was chartered by this.

Since 1956, there have been about 26 recorded strikes of various durations in the city; over 260 contracts have been signed without trouble. At a 10:1 ratio it is a bit better than the national average.

By 1978, the Labor Council in Stratford had 32 affiliated locals, with about 3,500 members. Plants were about two-thirds organized, with a few exceptions, and the largest industrial employer, Canadian Fabricated Products (United Auto Workers Union), had about 750 employees.

Stratford has come a long way from chicken plucking at two cents a bird. Management and labor have mixed fairly well since, with few class barriers. The city, through the years, has maintained a good track record in labor relations.

The armed camp that Stratford became during the black days was at least understandable, placed in context, and against the backdrop of fears fomented by the escalating problems of the depression decade — the infamous "Dirty Thirties".

12

"The Dirty Thirties"

NEW YEAR'S DAY.
January 1, 1930.
The beginning of a new decade, the end of an era. At the end of ten years, there would be changes in lifestyle for the whole city.

The stock market crash in October, 1929, had scarcely ruffled the surface of life in Stratford. Except for a relative few — bankers and some citizens rich enough to dabble in stocks and bonds — the market crash had been only scare headlines in newspapers. The Canadian people had been assured Canadian banking was in no danger of failing and Stratford believed this. There were no millionaires committing suicide by jumping from apartment or office windows, or throwing themselves off the stone bridge into the Avon River.

The city's economy was solidly based on railways and the manufacture of furniture, with textiles a close third in importance. It also had smaller, well-established industries and services, along with the stores and shops that carried on a steady, if not spectacular, business.

Except for the pay cheques of railway employees, wages were on the low side of the national average. Teachers in elementary schools were starting out at $400 to $500 a year. But the cost of living also was low. There was little real poverty in the city, where many residents could not only live on what they earned, but also put a bit of money aside to buy homes. This was a comforting fact of life, but home-ownership soon would haunt many, and affect the city's economy.

In Stratford, one did not live on the right or wrong side of the tracks. Here, the fairly sharply defined social line was drawn by the river. The majority of the workers lived south of the Avon; presidents and managers and professional people built their homes on the north side.

There was some mingling, noticeably in places like Hamlet Public School, which drew its pupils from both sides of the river. Although the social distinctions were there, each group was content to let others live their own lives in the comfortable existence which was Stratford at the beginning of the 1930's.

These were the halcyon days of boating on the river . . . of shopping leisurely along Ontario, Downie and Wellington Streets . . . of cheering for the home team in sports. The first indication of the severity of the depression came with the arrival of the first of the depression transients, who were a different breed from the rootless, happy-go-lucky hobos of pre-depression years.

These new drifters were not unemployed by choice, but of necessity. Many were skilled tradesmen, professional men or young university graduates who, unable to find work at home, set out in search of jobs anywhere, doing anything, and sometimes just for a square meal.

Eventually, there were four hobo jungles in the city. The largest, and most popular, was along Romeo creek, behind the Griffith saddlery at West Gore and Erie streets. Children of the neighborhood would sneak out after they were supposedly in bed and visit the jungle, huddling around small camp fires and listening, enthralled, to stories of the men who "rode the rails". And they were worth hearing, the tales of these extraordinary "hobos".

The depression hobos didn't stay long in any one place, and created few problems. Periodically, the police raided the jungles, and gave the men a few hours to leave town. The children waited impatiently for the next ones to come. They always did.

The earlier hobos still made their rounds, as usual. East of the city, the King of the Hobos would often be seen resting beside the spring and watertrough at the Little Lakes, before continuing on his way through Stratford. For him and his people, this nomadic existence was a normal and pleasant way of life, as it also was for the bands of gypsies who for years had traveled the county roads and stopped from time to time near Stratford.

That first year of the depression, there was one civic gain, in the upgraded sludge sewage disposal plant and its activation. It was fortunate the project had been set rolling before the 1930's, because, for the next 10 years, there would be little public money available for new projects, or even for maintaining established works and services. In Ottawa, the federal government had been able to find a little money to remodel the Ontario Street post office, and, at city hall, municipal officials had approved the start of work on a municipal golf course. But the public purse was already getting thin.

As the depression began to eat into Stratford, the city had to find funds both for unemployment relief and for direct relief. The population then officially stood at 17,742. Employees were being laid off in some businesses and industries; those still with jobs had their wages cut. In some firms, the employees themselves agreed to take less pay so that their fellow workers would not be out of work. City employees were all docked a set sum each week for relief.

Only the railway employees continued to enjoy a preferred position. With their wages on a higher scale to start with, they were living comfortably, and were not faced with the spectre of layoffs, in an essential Canadian service. They had little difficulty keeping up mortgage payments on their homes, and they could obtain credit.

Ed Doadt ran a grocery at the corner of Downie and Brydges streets, and served customers employed mainly by the railway. They settled their accounts on pay day and they were always good for the money, but Mr. Doadt didn't refuse credit to others in less lucrative employment. Some accounts he carried for three or four months, and estimated he lost only $300 to $400 in bad accounts during the whole depression period.

Understandably, the storekeepers were reluctant to run up bills for families in which the breadwinner might, at any time, receive a substantial wage cut or be laid off altogether. Yet, the mainstay of the average citizen was the small corner grocery store. The modest little establishments were to be found in every section of the city, including downtown Stratford, and the proprietors were usually sympathetic.

They were difficult days for all the small businesses. Griffith Saddlery, a family firm that sold primarily to the western provinces, was badly hit by the depression. Larger companies also suffered. Many a worker at Kroehler Manufacturing was paid only 25¢ an hour, and one young couple, married in 1933 with a nest egg of $35 (which they borrowed) furnished their first home with only a chesterfield suite.

A newspaper item, of March, 1932, underscored the depression's progress: "160 persons added to the relief roll and given money for fuel, groceries and children's shoes and rubbers." Some said families on relief were better off than those attempting to eke out an existence on miniscule salaries.

Many a boy went to school with patches on his pants or in clothes made over from adult garments. Families made do, bought only necessities, and somctimes did not even have the money for those.

Local organizations helped as far as their exhausted funds would allow. The home and school clubs aided the needy, and the Perth Regiment donated $25 from funds already nearly exhausted. There were campaigns and special events organized to raise money. The Salvation Army issued meal tickets to hungry people, many of them transients.

Into this deteriorating situation, came the strike by the furniture workers and meat packers in 1933, a crushing blow to both spirit and business in Stratford. It was, itself, to some extent a product of the city's unhappiness. The soup kitchen that opened next door to the strike-bound Kroehler plant was the only one to be set up in Stratford during the '30's.

Fortunately, there were some safety valves, the spiritual support of the churches and the synagogue, the home-made entertainment that drew families and friends closer for mutual comfort, the ball games by the river. During those low years, there were some high points in sports with the winning of championships.

In 1932, the city's senior soccer team repeated its 1929 achievement and won the Western Ontario championship. In baseball, the Stratford Nationals, in 1934, brought the first Senior A Ontario baseball championship to the city. In 1939, the Kroehler men's softball team took the Ontario Intermediate A title — the only occasion on which the championship came to Stratford. Hockey also was bringing home championships with morale-building regularity.

*Whyte Packing Company, organized in 1899,
was still doing business in the 1930s, despite depression cutbacks.
Later, failure of overseas markets after 1960 would close the historic
meat-packing firm.*

They wanted to build a softball field but there was no money to hire
contractors and so, as was the custom in those days, everyone — players, fans,
even the children — pitched in to help. Great was the individual satisfaction
when the field was ready. They showed movies under the moon after the games,
and, in winter, the ball field doubled as a skating rink.

They began building a stadium in the depth of the depression in the early 30's.
Laid-off C.N.R. employees found work erecting fences, doing tiling and sodding,
laying the cinder track and building grandstand and bleachers with reclaimed
lumber from scrapped boxcars. It took nearly three years of hard work before
the project was completed in 1934 and named National Stadium.

The sports action moved indoors in winter. The arena, on the south bank of the
Avon River, had the only indoor ice surface for hockey and for public skating. As
for the curlers, they played on the "natural ice" in the old casino, until, finally,
there was no more money to repair leaks in the roof, and it became impossible to
maintain the ice at all. Every year, Stratford hoped for a winter without too much
snow so there would be skating on the river and on the neighborhood rinks
which appeared by magic in schoolyards and backyards.

The Lions Club Pool was undertaken as a relief project early in the depression, and officially opened in 1932. The club scrimped to make the final payment of $2,000 on its debt to the city six years later. A staff of four, two lifeguards, an office worker and an engineer-maintenance man, received a total of $14 a week in salaries from the city and often worked up to 70 hours a week. Many days, the pool stayed open until 10 p.m. All swimmers, including male lifeguards, were required to wear bathing suits with tops. A swimmer who showed up only with trunks, went into the pool with his undershirt on.

In spite of cut-down inventories and reduced consumer spending, it was business as usual in downtown Stratford, and most of the stores managed to survive. In the heart of the city were most of them, including the four large ones, Canadian Department Stores, J. A. Duggan's, Northway's and Crosier's.

There were offerings of everything from shoes to hats, from hardware to drugs and men's and ladies' wear. Bradshaw's China Hall specialized and so did Moore's Leather Goods. Others sold mainly furniture, or even candy. The Whyte Packing Company, a retail outlet at Downie and Wellington, was famous for its meats, while, down the street, early each morning, shoppers were met by the tantalizing aroma of freshly baked bread.

Financial business could be transacted at any one of the city's five banks: the Royal, Bank of Nova Scotia, Bank of Montreal, Bank of Toronto or Canadian Bank of Commerce; or at the British Mortgage and Trust Company, which celebrated its diamond jubilee in 1937.

Coal and wood were the fuels of the 30's, and trucks made the deliveries except, occasionally, during the winter, when horses drew the sleds door to door, through heavy snow. Anthracite, a hard coal from Pennsylvania, was popular. Canadian bituminous lump coal was sold for hand-fired boilers and stokers and, for the apartment dwellers short of storage space, there was coal in 100-pound bags. There was wood by the cord for furnaces and fireplaces. There was also the local fuel, coke, a by-product of the gas works. Many electric stoves in town had an attached section for burning either wood or coal — a handy annex, also, for disposing of garbage. And no one kept the fires stoked up after bedtime.

Neither hydro nor water was to be wasted, even by the railway, the biggest user of both. Citizens used hard earned dollars to pay their bills at the Public Utility Commission retail store at the corner of Ontario and Church Streets. In 1934, an average depression year, the total amount of water pumped in Stratford was 575,545,000 gallons, a large percentage of which went to the steam locomotives and the motive power shops. Forty years later, in 1974, with the steamers gone and the shops closed, the total was 1,042,470 gallons. In 1934, the average kilowatt hours of power supplied to customers was 4,853.5; in 1974, in the age of electric appliances and heating, the average demand was 37,968.2.

Leisure time was precious, and entertainment not too costly. Stratford had a choice of two movie houses, the Majestic on Downie Street, which once had been Theatre Albert, and the Classic on the south side of Ontario Street. Both did capacity business at 40-50 cents a show and 5-cent Saturday matinees. Many a youngster slipped in free when kindly managers pretended not to see.

The Majestic was often rented for local productions that could not be accommodated in the city hall auditorium. Sometimes the shows were directed by professionals who traveled from town to town staging musicals or extravaganzas.

By the 1930's, radio had lost its first bloom of novelty, but those fortunate enough to own radios spent hours listening. In 1935, it was to the silver anniversary festivities of King George V and Queen Mary; at other times, talented residents of the city put on live programs.

The station, which had been known as 10 A.K. in the mid-thirties, adopted the call letters CJCS. At one point, manager Jack Kent Cooke drew a tremendous salary of $35 a week. Cooke's marvelous pay was even more impressive when Charles Trethewey joined the staff at $5 a week, and, along with his other duties, would sally forth each Saturday morning to collect money from the advertisers in order to pay the employees their week's wages.

As money became tighter, numerous little groups sprang up almost overnight, and city residents offered time and talents to create amateur productions. Each church had its own entertainers who raised funds for church and community projects, and Stratford gained a certain amount of fame for its performances of Gilbert and Sullivan operettas by the all-male Masonic Chorus. Its ranks were swelled by ''the girls'', as needed to fill the feminine roles and to work backstage on costumes and makeup.

Once, the stage at city hall was found to be too small for the ambitious set built for it. There was a frantic, last-minute switch. Nothing if not resourceful, all night the members of the company were carrying chairs, borrowed from churches, up two long flights of stairs to the drill hall. There, next day, the show — rather breathlessly — went on.

They scrounged wood to heat the hall, and anything else they could. Sometimes the costumes had to be rented, but, more often, they were made or borrowed. Some properties were created by clever-fingered people and some were on loan. It was an exercise in creativity for all the depression performers, whether the Adanac Dramatic Society, the Masonic Chorus or the Tamarue Players. They were providing the city's citizens with an opportunity to forget, for an hour or two, the less pleasant aspects of living during that era.

Nerves were badly on edge. Yet, in spite of the times, there was little serious crime in the 1930's. City lawyers were engaged mainly in litigation — the legal work involved in the sad business of foreclosing mortgages on homes and business properties in the city, and arranging the extension of mortgages on farm properties.

Those who did steal during the depression years were not criminals in the usual sense. They stole food to keep alive, and clothing for their families. Some stole deliberately and openly, so they could be sentenced to jail with a roof over their heads, a place to sleep and three meals a day.

''Every night the cell block in the old police department in the basement of city hall would be loaded with transients,'' Police Chief A. T. Day later recalled. ''We became famous for our soup. Every night we boiled up a big pot of soup and, before releasing our 'tenants' in the morning, they got a big bowl of the night's boil. We canvassed city restaurants for bones and leftovers and tossed them all into the pot. It was mighty good soup!''

In the daytime, the unemployed read endlessly in the public library, just to have some place to go, and to keep warm. There was no vandalism, although there was raiding of gardens for vegetables. People on welfare, or "relief", were given plots of ground behind Avondale cemetery, and these remote gardens often were the ones from which produce was stolen. Some made a few extra dollars with bootlegged homebrew. Cheating and stealing from the coal companies aroused no feelings of guilt because there was not enough money to buy fuel for cooking or heating.

For city council, the depression years were exceedingly trying, and heavy was the responsibility of establishing priorities. The demands on the city's coffers were more than the city could handle, with taxes not being paid on many homes and some businesses.

As depression year followed depression year, relief rolls lengthened, and city revenue did not keep pace with the increased demands.

As tax money became only a trickle, there was little available at any level for new buildings, for educational advances, or even for maintenance of public buildings, roads or sidewalks. Some suffered from causes not even of depression origin. In 1938, when compulsory pasteurization was introduced under provincial legislation, it forced out of business some local dairymen who had been delivering fresh milk to homes in Stratford.

On January 1, 1939, as church bells ushered in a new year in Stratford, war clouds were gathering in Europe, but few took notice, as they pursued their deadening day-to-day existence. Then, in June, came anticipation of a break in the greyness of their lives. King George VI with his Scottish wife, Queen Elizabeth, would be paying the first visit to Canada of a reigning British monarch, and Stratford was included in the royal itinerary. The city was jubilant.

The ceremonies were planned for June 6th at the C.N.R. station, with arrangements for thousands of students to have vantage points all along the route. The little girl chosen to present a bouquet to Queen Elizabeth was nine-year-old Goldie Rosenberger, granddaughter of Stratford pioneer Thomas Brittiff McCarthy. Children came to Stratford from all over Southwestern Ontario.

But the visit was yet another depression-time blow. The stop at the Stratford station was heartbreakingly short. The train whizzed through town and few of the children who had come early and lined the route even glimpsed the monarchs. The royal couple did not even know about all the children until later, and then sent a note of apology.

With a shrug, Stratford turned back to the depression and its problems, and to assuring each other that war had been averted by British Prime Minister Chamberlain's trip to Munich. They were wrong. Germany invaded Poland, followed by a declaration of war by Britain two days later. Canada declared war on Germany September 10, 1939, a week after Britain.

A pastime club
could raise the spirits of its members in gloomiest times.

Along with other Canadian regiments, the Stratford-based Perth Regiment had been mobilized September 1, when Hitler marched into Poland. Sealed orders addressed to the commanding officer of the Perths had been waiting in safe-keeping in the vault of a Stratford bank. The recruiting of men from Perth, Waterloo and Bruce instantly began.

In World War I, the Perth regiment had served mainly as a recruiting unit. This time it would be different.

Officially, "The 28th (Perth) Regiment" originally was organized in 1866, the year of the Fenian Raids scare, along with a number of other county regiments. In the early years, besides sending volunteer companies to the Niagara and Detroit frontiers, it had supplied troops for the Northwest Rebellion and for the Boer War. It existed until 1914. Reorganized in 1920, it was given its colors and shortly became simply "The Perth Regiment". In 1930, it was affiliated with the Cameronians.

Now, with World War II beginning, the old McLagan furniture factory was converted into barracks that would at times house not only the Perth Regiment, but before long also the Highland Light Infantry of Canada and the Royal

Netherlands Army. Leftover uniforms from World War I were hastily assembled for the early recruits. The Perths shivered through one November inspection by the Lieutenant Governor because greatcoats had still not been issued. Both the county and the city chipped in with money to help outfit the local regiment before it moved out in May, 1940. The Canadian forces were woefully ill-prepared for World War II.

In Stratford, suddenly the depression and its troubles were over. The hobo jungles melted away. Jobs opened up. Money was more plentiful in the crescendo of preparations for war. Women were starting to fill jobs vacated by men called up, and the click of knitting needles was heard in the land. Soon, gift packages were on their way to men in the armed forces spending their first Christmas away from home.

On December 31, 1939, the eve of a new decade, Stratford citizens sang Auld Lang Syne and looked back over the depression years and marvelled. They had coped with ten years of hard living which, for most of them, had produced radical changes.

Many social distinctions had disappeared forever. The "hads" had worked side by side with the "had nots", to provide for everybody not only essentials of food, clothing and shelter, but also the brighter moments of sport and entertainment.

There were some Stratford residents who celebrated New Year's Eve in a festive mood, and, throughout town, to herald the new year, all factory whistles blew for five minutes. Many filled Stratford churches to watch out the old year with prayers for a brighter and happier decade. No one knew how long the war would last.

Throughout the years of war, in Red Cross workrooms, in church basements, or behind the curtains of the homes, Stratford kept exceedingly busy. Comforts sped to the city's adopted ship, the minesweeper, H.M.C.S. *Stratford*, on duty on the high seas. There were drives for funds and for reading matter; in one year alone, the city collected and sorted eight *tons* of magazines for overseas.

Once again, the locomotive power shops of Stratford geared up to make shells and other instruments of war. In the old factory building on King Street, Imperial Rattan turned out wing spars for Mosquito bombers. From Stratford were shipped plywood parts for Mosquito and Lancaster bombers, furniture for cargo vessels, molded rubber parts for tanks and armored cars, brass parts for war equipment and machine tools with which to make war equipment. Knit wear, battle dress serge, over a million pairs of army, navy and air force gloves — even felt shoes for men on the Alaska Highway — all were made in the humming plants in Stratford. At home, experienced knitters were turning out socks, balaclavas and mittens, while less experienced women were knitting scarves by the yard.

Airmen on 48-hour passes from Clinton or Port Albert came to Stratford. The foreign servicemen posted to the city also were welcomed into private homes, a spontaneous gift of kindness that the people of the Netherlands in particular would never forget.

ADELAIDE LEITCH

*In the tiny Dutch Memorial Garden, an injured bird symbolizes
the Netherlands, supported by the strong hands of Canada.*

Netherlands troops were stationed in Stratford from January 7, 1941, to October 31, 1942. The furniture factory in which they were quartered became *Juliana Kazerne,* and here they were visited by their future Queen, then Princess Juliana, and her husband, Prince Bernhard. The royal family had sought safety in Canada.

After the war, through the efforts of Capt. Sidney J. van den Bergh, one of the Dutch officers stationed at Juliana Barracks, a lovely little statue came to the Classic City. On the base was the inscription, in Dutch and in English: "To the people of Stratford in grateful memory of their kindness and hospitality to the soldiers of the oppressed Netherlands." Later, the Netherlands ambassador to Canada arranged for the Dutch Bulb Growers Association to ship 1,300 bulbs of tulips, daffodils and hyacinths, to the city for planting around the monument. A tiny park became the Dutch Memorial Garden, just north of the river, and part of the city's parks system.

Stratford's own Dutch-Canadians contributed a plaque of their own to the Perth Regiment memorial, a thank-you to the men "who contributed to the 1944-45 campaign that led to the liberation of the Netherlands".

The Perth Regiment saw action in Italy and northwest Europe and, when the war was over, came home to the welcome of conquering heroes — and also to a handsome gift. Six sets of bagpipes and five drums had been ordered from Scotland in 1944, as the Perths received permission from Ottawa to become a Scottish unit. The pipe band committee had placed the order after an exchange of letters with the commanding officer during the campaign in Italy.

The Perth Regiment was one of the last of the county battalions to be disbanded after World War II, and was one of the 58 military units eventually abolished by the Canadian government in the name of economy at the end of 1964. A month later, the colors were deposited in St. James' Church.

There were new directions in Stratford in the decades following V-Day. Through the '40's, Stratford was a strongly labor-minded city. The working men and their families, with the belt-tightening and the fuel shortages of the depression fresh in their minds, were still saving bits of string, stretching the Sunday meat loaf with bread crumbs, patching worn work clothes. Their generation would never again be wasteful.

City politics were, in general, dominated by men interested in keeping taxes down and the workingman happy. Many politicians had been associated, in one way or another, with the C.N.R. shops that had seen them safely through the depression. They believed the shops would forever provide employment for Stratford's workers.

"My grandfather worked for the railway, I worked for the railway, and my grandson will, too!" That was the comfortable belief, but it was an attitude that limited thinking in the area of industrial expansion. Council was more interested in improving existing labor conditions than in expanding Stratford's industrial base. Executives of companies considering locating in Stratford were often met with a barrage of questions: "What are your working conditions?" "What wage levels?" ".... overtime?" ".... holidays with pay?" City council, in turn, would not spend money on the municipal services that would attract new companies.

It added up to one thing: stagnation.

Consumer shopping within the city also was suffering, partly because those who worked for the railway had travel passes and could shop in larger centers such as Kitchener and London. People were not spending their money in Stratford and the city was on its way to becoming a dormitory community, a city with little investment in its future. Ironically, back in 1931, the city's resigning industrial commissioner had left a list of 130 companies considered possible prospects for Stratford, with 22 actively considering coming. He had, by that time, contacted some 10,000 firms.

There was, however, a small group of politicians and concerned citizens interested in changing the direction (in their opinion, *lack* of direction) which the city was taking. The primary objective of this new breed of municipal leader was beautifully simple: to build a diversified industrial base to replace the city's dependence on the C.N.R. shops. It was not as easy as it sounded, for the shops, at their height, employed almost half of the city's workers, and had been geared up to capacity during the war.

By the middle of the 1940's, however, changing technology was heading the shops toward obsolescence, as diesel engines began to replace the steam engines for which the Stratford operation had been designed.

In 1950, a new, forward-looking council took office, and this city administration, and the ones which followed it, were ready and willing to spend money, not just to attract industry, but even to promote culture.

When the railway shops closed and the whistle was silenced for good, a big new tenant, Cooper-Bessemer, was found, and it was a godsend. So, too, was another employer that providentially came to town in 1953 — the Stratford Shakespearean Festival.

The city was committed to industrial expansion for the next two decades. Stratford became a recognized leader in industrial promotion; it spent more, per capita, than any other city in the province. This program sometimes drew fire as being extravagant, but it brought results. Between 1951 and 1966, Stratford added almost 5,000 in population. It earlier had had an industrial commission. Now, between 1950 and 1959, 20 new industries and 1,000 new jobs were introduced. Stratford got back on its feet and, by the end of 1959, it had turned the corner industrially.

Through two wars and a depression, the city of Stratford grew, if sometimes slowly. This picture, taken around 1969, looks east along Ontario street, where the highway still generally follows the route of the old Huron Road.

LLOYD DARK, BEACON HERALD

The magnificent 21-globe chandelier adds a touch of drama to City Hall. Below, on stage at City Hall, with the cast for Shakespeare's Comedy of Errors, *which was performed by the Normal School students on Tuesday, May 23, 1922.*

PERTH COUNTY ARCHIVES

13

Stage Setting for a Hundred Years

I F ECONOMIC GROWTH sometimes rode a roller coaster, Stratford itself was a community that always seemed to know where it was going, and its progress through the century that followed Little Thames seemed, at times, eerily inevitable.

The settlers lugged in over the Huron Road not only practical pioneer necessities, but equipment also for the mind: worn volumes of the classics tucked into their bulging bags, books on architecture and horticulture, small heirlooms and miniatures they could carry. They were young, most of them, and they coped purposefully with the pioneer conditions and blistered their hands at the pioneer chores, not because they liked them, but because they fully understood where they could lead.

This was the society that, in the 19th century, produced a judge of the Supreme Court of Canada, as well as a brilliant and corruptible Provincial Treasurer who ended up in the penitentiary. It nurtured the creative Lizars sisters . . . built an enormous concert hall in a market building . . . floated blissfully in flotillas of small boats upon the Avon River, while listening to the music from the bandstand, and later tuned in to broadcasts of the Metropolitan Opera from New York City on Saturday afternoons.

It yearned for the printed word, and produced, in the 19th century, a rash of newspapers, including two weeklies that published in German. It early had a country club, and the people held elegant garden parties. Culture came easily and early to Stratford, like Scottish porridge or German schnitzel on their tables.

Add to this basic cultural fabric the influx of Grand Trunk families for the railway shops — active, eager young families with money to spend. Add a rising and vigorous furniture industry, attracting skilled, old-country craftsmen.

By 1911, there were over 2,000 craftsmen in Stratford, and these people had built beautiful homes and planted gardens in which they took almost snobbish pride. By 1914, there were 500 members in the Stratford Horticultural Society that had been going since 1878. They were holding regular flower shows and

179

tending 60,000 tulips planted in 50 flower beds throughout the city. When W. H. Strudley went to Europe that year, he brought back $10 worth of seeds of a new variety of sweet pea to divide among his fellow members, a generous sharing that averaged out at four seeds per person.

By the mid-1870's, influential townspeople and 28th Regiment officers were including fox hunting in their social life, and membership in the "Tally Ho" was a mark of prestige. Another hunt club was established at the turn of the century, primarily to encourage the breeding of saddle horses, which were in demand by the British army. It, too, attracted the Stratford elite, among them Albert Brandenberger, Stratford's first theatrical "angel", and Judge J. A. Barron, who would follow the steeplechase races by road, with his pony and gig.

But, of all the accomplishments of early Stratford, the most remarkable was surely the first concert hall in the market building.

If the German settlers brought one outstanding thing into the life of the village, it was an early appreciation of theatre and music. In the German homeland, it was commonplace for every little village to have an impressive hall and stage. Many little communities of Upper Canada had their central halls and auditoriums too, but none produced them on so grand a scale as did Stratford. Nor did they use them so constantly and enthusiastically.

In 1857, when only a few more than 2,000 people lived in the village, they built a market building with a concert hall that could seat 500 of them. That was a quarter of the population — proportionately more than for the 1,500-seat Festival Theatre that would be built a century later in a city of 19,000, and draw its audience from a continent.

In that tremendous hall, they produced plays and performed concerts to packed houses. In a slack season, small groups would use the hall, and sometimes just a handful of students would be rattling around in it for a music teacher's recital. There was a fine upright piano, and an excellent stage across the whole width, sometimes draped with a four-foot-wide Union Jack.

In April of 1864, Stratford celebrated the 300th anniversary of Shakespeare's birth and put on a Commemorative Festival, with a ball, a military review, a band concert, a regatta, and a program of "Shakespearean orations, readings, recitations, and songs". Heavy rains and muddy roads kept many people away from the ceremonial planting of a "Shakespearean oak", and the regatta was cancelled because the water had been let out of the lake; but the evening program in the town hall was a sellout.

In the concert hall around 1889, Stratford watched a British motion picture, *Scotch Gray*, on the cinema circuit that was probably the first in Canada. On a Saturday night in January, 1889, they got a spectacular *Uncle Tom's Cabin* that had run 100 nights in New York City. (Admission: 10 or 20 cents.) There were also "comedy-dramas", each with a long pause for the changing of a reel.

Interspersed with the marvels of the movies, were the live, local productions. Late in the 1800's, a Mrs. Junck gave enormously popular recitals on piano, harp and musical glasses. "She could and did also handle spade and pitchfork," added a newspaper account admiringly.

One night, late in the 1890's, there was even a prize fight on stage, with a sellout audience at 25¢ a head, and every church in town denouncing it as scandalous. The out-of-town contestants got into an argument of their own, after the first blow. The referee took a long time sorting out the rules and, while he did so, both fighters vanished — and so did the cash receipts.

When the old market building burned, toward the end of the century, many, including the press, were suddenly awed that Stratford "had had the nerve" in the 1850's to erect that far-more-than-adequate municipal building! From the wreckage, they raised a new city hall, and the mayor promised it too would have a concert hall with seating capacity for 500. But cost-paring reduced it to less than half the size, and this new hall now was to serve a population of over 10,000. It was planned and conceived as a concert hall, but a sign-painter ill-advisedly put "auditorium" on it.

They fitted it up in style, however, with its painted ceiling, painted figures in the alcoves, wall coverings to deaden sound and a fine stairway leading to the balcony at the back. When balls were held, they strung strings of colored lights, and the balcony was festooned with flower wreaths. Up there sat the chaperons, watching as ladies came in rustling silks and long white kid gloves, and men arrived in their "monkey tails" — full dress suits. There was a "sitting out space" under the balcony with comfortable chairs and romantically shadowed corners.

In the early 20th century, with six choirs in town, there were at least three events — drama, music or recitation — taking place in the auditorium of city hall every week.

Like other small Ontario cities, there were theatricals, perhaps more of them than in most places. There were plays put on by the ladies' aid societies of the churches. There were the Tamarue Players on stage in the 1920's, and the Temple Choir of the Masonic Lodge with an annual Gilbert and Sullivan operetta. There was the music festival, to which the audience could come prepared to stay, with lunches and knitting. It was used by the first Stratford Little Theatre, which, at its peak, had 1,700 subscribers, produced three plays a year, and became one of the most active in Southern Ontario. There was also the Shakespearean Society of the Normal School presenting *The Merchant of Venice,* or *As You Like It.* Eventually, the Shakespearean Festival itself would use the city hall, with an exhibition spilling out of the auditorium into both rotundas, upstairs and downstairs.

Meanwhile, following the fire, Albert Brandenberger, who had backed many of the shows in the old hall, had determined that Stratford should still have its "opera house". He opened his 1,250-seat Theatre Albert January 1, 1901, with *The Female Drummer,* the first stage show in the city's first legitimate theatre.

Stratford saw the pick of the shows on the circuit. It was a regular point of call for the touring companies, and to Theatre Albert came the great of their day: Maude Adams, in *Peter Pan,* the Marks Brothers (a Canadian troupe, not the later Marx Brothers), Elsie Janis, Forbes Robertson, John Griffith, and Sir John Martin Harvey.

*The first Town Hall and Market Building
had a remarkable concert hall for a handful of people.*

A large and appreciative audience was "contained" in Theatre Albert, so the *Beacon Herald* said, for John Griffith's presentation of *Macbeth*. The theatre-goers were hardly purists, for the text of the play had been altered and some scenes omitted; yet "a fair representation of the spirit and action of the drama was witnessed." The paper went on: "Shakespearean tragedy is not strongly in favor with the average theatre-goer . . . In a place of Stratford's size, it is very seldom that a company of necessary ability and numbers can be brought together to give it adequate presentation." The *Beacon Herald* was not clairvoyant.

The famous "Dumbells" of World War I came annually to Stratford for some years after the war, although the movies had already marked the end of the era of touring live theatre. Theatre Albert survived the changes. It became the Griffin, then the Majestic, finally the Avon, and, as such, was taken over by the Festival and converted once again for the presentation of live theatre.

There were other smaller concert and theatrical stages in Stratford, in schools, church basements, and sometimes just out of doors. Post Office Park was used to hold money-raising events — which did not greatly please the downtown merchants. In 1910, when the ladies' aid of Knox Presbyterian Church was given permission to stage a summer festival in the little park on Ontario Street, the

Merchants' Association complained to the Parks Board that such things interfered with their business. The Board replied that, on the contrary, such things would stimulate business, and bring people downtown; it continued to encourage the gatherings.

The conservative, temperate and concerned Local Council of Women in Stratford, soon after its organization in 1922, was concerned with the elimination of vaudeville, with providing more movies suitable for children — and with the ringing of the curfew bell. However, the city, by then, was sold on theatre, and Stratford's appetite for the stage was further whetted during the depression of the 1930's, as people turned gratefully to the home-grown concerts and plays. Meanwhile, many little movie houses blossomed, sometimes just in old stores that had been fitted with hard seats and given gaudy new fronts. Ontario Street, some claimed, "was becoming a little 42nd Street".

In summer, there was nothing to top the band concerts, and Stratford attended virtually en masse.

There were a number of bands, playing in bandstands in various parts of the city, including Queen's Park. The first railway band formed up in 1871, with the Grand Trunk bandsmen resplendent in scarlet and blue. The first city band, which organized about the same time, decked its members out in grey with heavy black braiding and put red and white plumes in their hats. The first regimental band started around 1891, 20-strong, assembling for practice in the old drill shed.

By 1905, programs for summer band concerts by the 28th Regimental Band were regularly published on the front page of the *Beacon,* and music lovers could buy the program and the whole paper for two cents.

Like many small cities, Stratford built a handsome downtown bandstand in the 19th century, a fine, open, octagonal stand that aged gracefully with concerts, the skirling of bagpipes and the martial music of the bands. Like the village pump before it, it became a meeting place for the whole community, and there was an outcry when the aging bandstand was slated to be moved and probably replaced.

Three sites were possible for a new stand: in the willows by the river, facing the river on York Street, or abutting on Cobourg Street. There were two choices of style: another open stand or the new shell, which was just becoming popular.

In 1929, the matter came, innocently enough, before the parks board, and it quickly fanned the biggest row Stratford had seen since the C.P.R. had tried to usurp the tranquil parklands by the river.

There was much ado about a bandstand as they battled over location and over style. Opposing sides seemed about evenly matched. All of them circulated petitions, demanded that council intervene, and wrote long, windy letters to the newspaper. The city engineer added the information that the proposed bandstand contravened the city's fire bylaw, since it was to be constructed chiefly of wood.

Even within the parks board, there was disagreement, and, in their stormiest session in over two decades, the commissioners finally voted, four to one, for a shell and a location among the willows of Lakeside Park.

The historic "Battle of the Bandstands"
ended with the official opening of the shell stand.

The boaters were irate. The shell would face away from the river, they protested, and they would be unable to hear, as they floated upon the water. Also opposed, were the people in the trades and labor council and the ratepayers association. The Musicians' Protective Association was worried about mosquitoes. Besides, the association slyly pointed out, big cities like Toronto, Chicago and San Francisco didn't have shell stands, did they?

As for the musicians, who would be most affected, the Perth Regiment Band didn't want a shell stand, but the C.N.R. Employees' Band did, although not in the mosquito-laden willows. The Local Council of Women objected. Alderman Wigglesworth argued plaintively that, as council was paying half the bill, it should have something to say about design. And it did, finally. It approved an open stand, to the disgust of Dr. E. H. Eidt, "Father of the Parks Board", who then came out in favor of a shell.

After the smoke cleared, the parks board had the final say and clinched it. On June 4, by majority vote, the commissioners accepted a tender, over howls of anguish and shouts of glee, for a band shell, and set about erecting it in the willows.

It opened, on schedule, on September 21, 1929.

The Royal Canadian Regiment band came over from London and played lustily afternoon and evening, its leader claiming he had never played on a better stand. There was a display of living statuary. There were Scottish dances and Scottish pipers, and several numbers by the Brunswick Male Quartet.

It was proclaimed "Tom Orr Day", in honor of the man who had introduced the idea of a shell stand, after seeing them in southern United States. Later, he was vindicated in his choice. When the Canadian National Exhibition was considering a bandstand, they came up from Toronto and looked over what the Classic City had chosen. Toronto, in 1938, also built a shell. As for Stratford's old stand, it was given to the Agricultural Society and moved to the fair grounds.

As always, Stratfordites had abhorred the unimaginative, the static, the trite and the mass-produced! Domestic architecture, too, produced some striking buildings, almost from the beginning.

On the way into the Huron Tract, many settlers had seen what could be done with backwoods resources for, in 1827, John Galt had built his headquarters, the "Priory", in Guelph, using logs but building in the style of a masonry house. It was the show place of the Canadas, and its impact was not likely lost on the settlers for Little Thames.

J. C. W. Daly established himself on a fine location that looked straight down Ontario Street. At the other end of Ontario Street was W. F. McCulloch, who built "The Grange" in 1840, with impressive ornamental gates guarding the two entrances. An oval driveway led to the house, surrounded by neat paths, formal gardens and a fine stand of pine and spruce — the show place of the day owned by the village's largest taxpayer.

The property came into the hands of James Trow around 1860, then was bought in 1907 by George McLagan, who tore down the home and built afresh, apparently on the original site and foundations. What he built was magnificent. Today it is Stratford's one surviving "mansion".

In many new homes, there began to be lovely gothic arches, windows with twelve lights, attractive dormers to break harsh lines, sometimes richly imaginative "gingerbread" for trim. The cold Canadian winters soon dictated a lowering of lofty ceilings for the elegant rooms, and more attention began to be given to the realities of snow.

As late as the 1870's, there were still small and classic houses being built, and Belden, compiling the *Atlas of Perth County* in 1879, took note of both private streets and public places . . . In Stratford, he found much to please the eye . . . "streets lined on either side with shade trees" . . . "a pleasing air of comfort" . . . "On Ontario Street . . . some of the finest business blocks in any town of equal size in the Province . . ." "The Albion, Dufferin, Easson, Odd Fellows, Phoenix, Rankin and Waverley blocks are such as would do credit to any city. . . ." He counted twelve churches, "some exceptionally fine in architectural design, mechanical execution and interior decoration — Knox Church (Presbyterian) is one of the finest specimens of architectural models we have ever seen. . . ." He admired the High School: "of modern style of architecture . . . this beautiful building. . . ."

A Piccolo Band tootled enthusiastically around 1912,
in a city devoted to bands.

Only the Market Building, "a fine building for its time", he found possessing "no very great pretensions to architectural excellence." The local people still thought it outstanding.

Except for a few outbursts like the 1845 riots, Stratford usually was one of the most tolerant communities of Southern Ontario. In pioneer days, there was Mrs. Thomas Sargint, free to attend mass while her husband, the brother of the pioneer innkeeper at the Shakespeare, remained an Anglican until he died, and was buried beneath a flat white stone in St. James' churchyard. There was a Boys' Home established at 51 Avon Street to bring poor boys out from London and give them a fresh start.

Annie McPherson, daughter of a Scottish educationalist, bought this huge old house, one of the finest in Stratford, in 1883, and to it she personally escorted dozens of the waifs of England, until the time she died in 1904.

The predominantly Irish population had a healthy leaven of Europeans, mainly German. There were also some Americans moving north as well, and from the south came American slaves, able to settle happily in the city on the Avon, establish their own church and prosper. Some of them became the town's best businessmen.

"Ben" Sleet, was born in slavery in Kentucky, and, with his wife Betsy, had arrived about 1850. In the early sixties, this ambitious man acquired the ice cutting privileges on the river, ran a stable and also contracted with the town to water the streets. In 1864, Ben Sleet built his Victoria Rink, the first real skating rink in Stratford. To do it, he hollowed out low land, let in the river, then built an embankment. It wasn't covered, but it was better than the river, and immensely popular.

He offered memberships: men, $3; ladies, $1.50; families, $5. Single skaters and spectators were charged a York shilling, or 20 cents each. At one time, he was operating the Royal Exchange, later the Royal Hotel, on Wellington Street, said to have had the finest saloon in town. Ben Sleet, when he died in 1891, was a satisfied and respected man.

When assembling riverfront land, the parks board bought the old Sleet property from Ben's son, James, who, with a partner, William Keane, was still operating the old ice house. The two men used the ice house until it was razed, then moved the business. Betsy Sleet was given life occupancy of the cottage at 20 Waterloo Street, for the rent of $15 a month, until she died in 1925. Her cottage was finally removed, and the old Sleet property became sloping green lawns, such as old Ben Sleet might have remembered in Kentucky.

Stratford had a climate of success for those willing to work at their ambitions. James Trow, when he arrived in the mid-1840's, was a 15-year-old lad from Wales, penniless and friendless, but with a will to succeed. He went on foot to Goderich for his certificate to teach. Later, he became warden of Perth County, whip of the Liberal party in the House of Commons, and owner of one of the city's finest homes.

From the days of J. J. E. Linton, Stratford was good to individualists, whether great men or scamps. Even among the clergy, there had been some renegades in the 19th century. Kathleen and Robina Lizars, as everyone knew, modelled the reverent rascal in their novel on a local minister.

The city may have kept a low-profile, genteel appearance, but it must have acquired a widespread reputation for broadmindedness for, in the fall of 1905, datelined Chicago, there appeared in the local press the story of two Chicago wives fleeing their homes to come to Stratford, where they registered as sisters, the Misses Allen, and then struck up questionable friendships with local businessmen.

Their husbands, a Mr. Anderson and a Mr. Horn, set out in pursuit of their errant ladies, found them, and hurried back to Chicago to file divorce proceedings. The *Beacon* reported in detail, but tactfully refrained from naming the Stratford co-respondents either then or later.

Then there were the genuine Stratford characters.

Once, during a local holiday, a man raced a horse — and won. Another, Jimmy Patterson, raced a freight train from Shakespeare to Stratford with horse and buggy. He, too, won. Everyone knew Jimmy, going about town in his "coat of many colors" made from badger, coon, dog and squirrel skins.

There was Harry Crouts, the bill poster, with his pail and coconut game, gleefully urging on the contestants: "In the hole — 'pon my soul!" There was taxi driver "Dusty" Rhodes, who doubled as volunteer fireman. And the Devon and Yorkshire men who would gather at Getschell's Hotel on Erie Street for a game of kicking shins.

In this interesting Stratford pastime, the contestants would roll up their trousers, leaving their shins bare, and then, grasping each other's shoulders, they would just kick each other's bare shins until one gave in.

There were Sunday school picnics in the Old Grove, and there was "Tinker Tom" getting tarred and feathered because he was suspected of murdering three women. (Actually, his wife and two other women had been on a drinking spree, and had become indifferent to what they poured. They drank a bottle of muriatic acid he used in his tin work, and, all three of them, died on the floor.)

There was Mayor William Roberts being nabbed among the found-ins during a raid on a house of ill repute. When he entered the council chamber next time, the councilors rose in a body and left. The mayor wouldn't resign. "It deals with my private conduct and character, and with those council has nothing to do!" said he indignantly, and stayed right on to the end of his term in December, 1883.

There were colorful characters-about-town, tagged with nicknames descriptive of their specialties: "Four-Eyed" Stewart, a lawyer who wore glasses; "Oh My" Mosely (who, no matter what you said to him, would reply, "Oh *my!*"), and "Fixey" Wilson, Chief of Police. "Fixey", who was chief in the 1870's, would take after the unruly and the unclad at the swimming holes, hollering at the top of his lungs, "I'll fix ye!"

There was Dr. W. N. Robertson, called "Long Robertson the Bicycle Man", because he owned the first bicycle in town and took it on his professional rounds as well as to meets and conventions all over the country. He distinguished himself, when he was 70 years old and living in Toronto, by returning for a Stratford Old Boys' Reunion — and cycling both ways.

There was "Old Man Pencil", selling his wares, and locally famous "Cowkitty" Bryden, who ran the first commercial dairy in town.

"Cowkitty" was Miss Katherine Bryden, Scottish-born. She lived with her cows, sharing the long building where they were housed, and going about her chores, winter and summer, wearing an old black hood that came down on her shoulders and turned greener and greener with age. She loved her "beasties". Also, she was a good woman. She went faithfully to services in Knox Presbyterian Church, leaving her pails behind the door as she entered, and she gave all she could afford to mission work. They said once she had planned to marry a missionary, and the unhappy love affair had kept her single.

In the days when councils had trouble collecting the city's share of the poundage fees, there was James, "Spring Heeled Jimmy", Brown, an exception, and a model of honesty. As the *Beacon* in 1859 reported, he had "since last week actually paid to the town treasury about $20 of poundage fees".

Stratford's early professional community was both outstanding and colorful. One of Stratford's finest and most popular doctors was "Old Iron Teakettle", whose father had come north with the legendary Mohawk chief, Joseph Brant. He himself married the chief's granddaughter, Irene Hill.

His name was Oronhyatekha and he had been born on August 10, 1841, on the Grand River Six Nations Indian Reserve. He picked up his nickname at the University of Toronto, because his classmates couldn't pronounce his Indian name. If this bothered Oronhyatekha, he never let on. When Edward, Prince of Wales, visited Canada, Oronhyatekha was selected to make a presentation, and the young prince was so impressed he invited the Indian to attend Oxford University. Oronhyatekha completed his medical training in England, later returning to Ontario to establish a practice in Frankford.

He was in Stratford for three or four years in the 1870's. He set up practice with Dr. J. A. Robertson, and earned a reputation, particularly, for his treatment of nervous diseases and throat and lung problems. He was active in local politics and his eloquence may have influenced the Conservative victory in the election of 1872.

He left in the mid-1870's, to work with the Mohawk Indians on Quinte Bay; later he moved on to London, Ontario, and Toronto. He instituted No. 53 lodge of the Independent Order of Foresters in 1880 and, in the latter part of his life, he was the chief ranger and its medical officer of health. Oronhyatekha was a high ranking officer in the Orange Lodge and the Masons as well. The brilliant Mohawk doctor died in Savannah, Georgia, on March 3, 1907.

Another even more colorful doctor who found the tolerant Stratford community much to his taste, was the controversial Norman Bethune. He treated his first private patients here in the spring of 1917 when he was 27 years old, a holiday replacement for Dr. J. A. Robertson and his son, Dr. Lorne Robertson. He filled in for them again in 1919, and the office nurse found young Dr. Bethune "broke as usual", but, in his two months in Stratford, certainly much devoted to his profession.

He was, besides, eligible and attractive. He charmed completely the young ladies of the city, in spite of his eccentricities. He escorted one of them to a dance, splendidly outfitted in a light blue suit, a red tie and yellow shoes — to her utter humiliation.

Stratford warmed to him. A group of citizens offered to back Dr. Bethune financially if he would stay and set up practice. The unconventional doctor by then had other stars to follow, which would lead him eventually to Mao Tse-tung's China, where he died in 1939, the Chinese people's great and beloved surgeon, but still little honored at home.

Through Stratford came, at various times, a number of high-voltage notables. Among them was Dr. Gordon Murray, the "blue baby" doctor, internationally famous for his cardiac work and for completing the first kidney transplant in Canada. There was the brilliant physicist, Sir John Cunningham McLennan, Ph.D., O.B.E.,F.R.S., who succeeded in liquifying helium. Margaret Addison, who taught in Stratford, later became Dean of Women at Victoria College. Agnes MacPhail was the first woman to sit in the House of Commons. Charles A. Hanson, a future Lord Mayor of London, preached his first sermon in the little red brick Methodist church, when he was 20 years old and had recently arrived in Stratford to live with an uncle.

New Queen Zephra *had a record run of three straight years at*
Theatre Albert. This Stratford playhouse later became the Avon
Theatre for Festival productions.

Rev. David Williams of St. James' Church became archbishop of the Church of
England in Canada. James Reaney graduated from the Stratford high school to
become an outstanding poet and playwright. T. M. Daly, grandson of J. C. W.
Daly, became a Stratford lawyer, and went on to be the first mayor of Brandon,
Manitoba, and the Minister of the Interior. There was Peter Dierlamm, whose
paintings were sent to a world's exposition in Paris, representing Canada; and
John Idington, Judge of the Supreme Court of Canada, and oldest sitting judge in
the British Empire when he retired, aged 87; and R. S. Robertson, Chief Justice of
Ontario. There were two private secretaries of high rank — William Buckingham
to Prime Minister Alexander MacKenzie; Kathleen Lizars to Premier John
Robson of British Columbia. John Luke Poett, veterinary from Glasgow, arrived
soon after the railway repair shops did, anticipating there would be endless need
for his services with the increase in the carriage-driving population. He worked
out of his office in the business block William and Caroline Brandenberger had
built on Wellington Street and, after Stratford, went on to become the first
veterinary surgeon of the North West Mounted Police.

Swedish Frederick Hansen became a citizen of Stratford in 1902. He applied for patents for a "flying machine" in 1909 and, in September, 1913, he came before city council seeking support to build and market his airship.

It was not, however, an airplane that Fred Hansen was making — it was a dirigible balloon. He had sent his first design to the German War Office in 1902, and, he claimed, many of his ideas had been stolen and used in the Zeppelin dirigibles. (Actually, Count von Zeppelin had built his first dirigible in 1900, a craft to serve as the prototype for many subsequent models, but it was not used for commercial air passenger service until 1910.)

Although Hansen improved his model and secured patents, lack of funds and inability to sell the patents ended the venture. He died in Stratford in 1936, at the age of 87.

About the time Hansen was seeking public support for his airship, an expatriate Londoner, Albert Sugden, secured a United States patent for a "flying machine". Sugden and Hansen had worked together in the "brass corner" of the G.T.R. shops, and shared their aviation projects. The Sugden plane had eight propellers, driven through gears and shaftings, with provision in the two wings for gasoline. He never really tried to get financing for his invention.

Probably the first airplane flight in Stratford took place June 10, 1913, from the agricultural grounds. It was an exhibition flight, but, for the Toronto company that promoted it, the flight was not a howling success. Gate receipts were $79.64, with about 500 people inside the grounds and 1,000 more outside.

Next seriously air-minded man was Albert Holmes who, with partner Albert Mantelow, put together the "Heath Parasol Monoplane". It taxied grandly down Stratford's first airstrip on May 26, 1931, took off and stayed up ten minutes, then made a perfect landing to the open-mouthed delight of 50 spectators.

It had been more than a year in the making, first in the Holmes basement, then in the garage and backyard. The spruce wings were from a local lumber mill, and fashioned according to blueprints from a Chicago company. The engine was fundamentally a Henderson 4 motorcycle engine, with refinements. To cover the wings, Mrs. Holmes sewed cotton fabric over the framework, and the whole thing was doped with a solution to tighten and strengthen it, and give it a silvery appearance.

Completed, it had a fuselage 16 feet, eight inches long and a wing spread of 25 feet, could carry 300 pounds of freight, and, best of all, it could fly — at up to 85 miles an hour. After Mr. Holmes died, the plane, still airworthy, was sold.

Stratford took a flyer into auto manufacturing in the 1920's, with probably the only Canadian car using steam as a power source in an age of gasoline. The Brooks Steamer (price tag $3,800) actually made the trip from Stratford to Vancouver, mountain and plain, averaging 300 miles a day.

Earlier, Henry Ford sold stock in Stratford, as wherever else he could, and found sales excellent here, where the people prided themselves in being adventurous in new ventures. In 1902, Moses Schlotzhauer drove Stratford's first car down the main street. George Wettlaufer owned the first steam car.

With improving communication in the 20th century, there had been frequent and friendly contact with the other Stratford in England — visits, greetings, and unofficial letters. In 1927, Hon. Archibald Flower, former mayor of Stratford-upon-Avon, came on a fund-raising tour for the establishment of the Shakespeare Memorial Theatre in England, and urged Canadian Stratford also to embark "on something that would contribute to more frequent productions of Shakespeare's plays". Nothing came of it — then.

In August, 1952, when there was talk at last of the actual possibility of a festival, J. M. Dunsmore was commenting in his column on the availability of Kathleen and Robina Lizars' local novel. "There's not a copy of it in our library . . . We have forgotten it, yet we're bustin' our braces trying to start up a Shakespeare theatre here!"

The next year, into a nicely prepared setting, came the Stratford Shakespearean Festival.

14

The Stratford Festival

CORONATION YEAR IN BRITAIN saw all London decked with bunting, and preparing for the pageantry that would accompany the crowning of Queen Elizabeth II. It was a hard act to follow, if you were an actor or an actress.

Harold Hobson, theatre critic of London's *Sunday Times*, took a cheap shot. British actors, he said, were taking the easy way out in 1953, either by appearing in safe plays or by leaving town.

To which Alec Guinness retorted tartly: "I do not consider that going to Canada to play in a theatre-in-the-round not yet built, in a town of 18,000, in a program quite impossible to present commercially in the west end, is entirely unadventurous. The possibilities of disaster are *quite* formidable!"

Guinness was soon to sail for Canada, and the word from the colonies was not cheering. Possibilities of disaster were not only quite formidable but practically inevitable.

Opening night was just two months away and, in Stratford, there were financial problems. The committee of citizens, beset with critics and buying a dream with money they didn't have, were wavering between cancelling and postponing. There was a chance that the Shakespearean Festival so enthusiastically envisioned would not take place at all. Guinness was supposed to sail the first Tuesday in May, just a few days hence. He wondered if he was going to do so.

This respected British actor was not worrying alone. Deeply alarmed also was Tyrone Guthrie, most outstanding director in Britain, along with Tanya Moiseiwitsch, stage designer with the vision of genius, and actress Irene Worth. Over the weekend, the committee in Stratford phoned across the Atlantic to Guthrie, who asked for an immediate decision. The citizens, practically committed, terribly afraid, but still trusting to Guthrie's genius, gulped and telephoned back.

"We'll go ahead."

Two months later, on a July night in 1953, Alec Guinness walked out on the balcony of the revolutionary thrust stage, the hunch-backed king of *Richard III*, in the largest circus tent in North America, with the sounds of picnics and pigeons and swans and trains outside, and delivered the play's opening lines:

"Now is the winter of our discontent
Made glorious summer by this sun of York."

Next day, the critics raved. The editors of *Life*, who had planned a special, grass-roots feature on the Stratford Festival and then had dumped it to feature a tornado in Kansas, were kicking themselves. It was the scoop of the year. And how, in the name of all the swans of Avon had such a "Miracle of Stratford" been pulled off? Because that was what they began calling it.

Oh, not the people of Stratford! Not the members of the original committee, nor the local contractor, nor the secretaries and businessmen in the Gordon Block! It was the audience that came flocking from outside Stratford that dubbed it "The Miracle", and also "The Stratford Experience". It was theatre people and critics in Toronto, in London's west end, and in New York. Mainly, in Stratford, the mood was pleasure, and relief!

A few citizens still viewed with alarm, but, for the most part, the city took its sudden fame calmly. The times were right. Stratford had both the social climate and the setting in the 1950's, and neither could have been better. There were the long traditions of cultural life. There was a backdrop of parklands, and that elegant river with its swans. There were the Shakespearean names long established on streets, wards and schools. There was nothing recently contrived about the Stratford in which the Shakespearean Festival swiftly took root.

The one thing needed to bring about that heart-stopping moment in *Richard III* had been a catalyst. And that, perhaps, was already in the making years before in a school room at the Stratford Collegiate, where Rose McQueen taught English.

During the fall classes, and through the grey Stratford winter, and on through the dragging spring to exam time, Rose McQueen talked with enthusiasm of the plays of Shakespeare. In her classes, young Tom Patterson was enthralled.

Tom Patterson's father was a Stratford manufacturer, Harry Patterson, proprietor of the Stratford Brass Company. As a boy, Tom had prowled about Stratford's parks and along the Avon River, and had grown up amid the Shakespearean names. With the Canadian army in the Second World War, Tom had his first contact with professional theatre, and came home fired with the idea of producing Shakespeare in the Canadian Stratford.

At the same time, he had an education to complete and a living to earn. In Toronto, he became associate editor of *Civic Administration*, a Maclean-Hunter magazine. But still he kept turning his grand idea around in his head, and dinning it into any sympathetic ears turned his way. Tom's dream was truly visionary. The Canadian Manufacturers' magazine *Industry* later called it "a conception so colossal that it almost reaches the realms of impudence". Oddly, on a smaller scale, the same thing was also developing locally.

The newly organized Chamber of Commerce was looking for ways to enliven its town and attract visitors, and it hit on the obvious idea of capitalizing on the parks and the Shakespearean theme. Independently, the Chamber was considering a Shakespearean play which might be performed for a week or ten days, perhaps using the local Little Theatre group as the nucleus of the company. Performances could be in the open air, in the bandshell, elsewhere along the river, or maybe on the Collegiate flats.

It was the first action towards a Shakespearean program taken by any official body in Stratford, and it occurred without the group even being aware that Tom Patterson was, at the same time, promoting the idea on a much grander scale — a professional, high-quality, summer-long Festival, as good as that held in the city's English namesake. When they were approached, members of the Chamber of Commerce and an increasing number of citizens were attracted to the Patterson idea. Tom came before city council and asked for $100 for a trip to New York to talk to Laurence Olivier. One alderman said, "Oh let's make it $120!" They gave him $125 and waved him off at the station.

However, that year an overworked Olivier was not only acting on Broadway, but also directing a play in Philadelphia, and commuting daily. He simply had no time to see his young Canadian visitor.

Meanwhile, back home, a citizens' committee was formed, with, as chairman, Dr. Harrison A. Showalter, a prominent industrial chemist much involved in the city's activities. They set about investigating ways and means and costs. Out of this came the Stratford Shakespearean Festival Foundation of Canada. With the help of Dora Mavor Moore, founder and director of the New Play Society, and a strong influence in Toronto theatre, Tom Patterson finally was put in touch with the man many considered the finest director in the English-speaking world — Tyrone Guthrie.

Guthrie, between plays, was home in Ireland, when Tom telephoned to outline his plans. The overseas connections were not good. There was difficulty also because the colleen who was village postmistress would not believe that someone was calling from Canada. But Tom Patterson got from Guthrie an answer he would never forget.

"When do you want me?"

During a second phone call, there was a technical interruption just as Tom named the fee which the committee was prepared to pay out of their own pockets. This did not prevent Guthrie from coming to Stratford to talk about the "proposed" festival. He arrived on July 9, 1952.

Guthrie deeply mistrusted all committees. He came, expecting, as he said later, "little old ladies of both sexes". In Canada, he got, instead, a serious, somewhat nervous, but altogether very sensible and open-minded group, with men outnumbering women five to one. They were, to his astonishment, not just eager for advice but — *humble!* He had never met their like before. Guthrie was charmed.

The Irish director was, by nature, an adventurer in the theatre. He had already directed plays in the United States, Israel and Finland, and had worked in Australia. He had been in Canada 20 odd years before, to direct a series of radio plays for the Canadian National Railway, and had been thrilled then with the vast, developing land he saw.

ONTARIO MINISTRY OF INDUSTRY AND TOURISM

The Festival Theatre after dark.

At the time Tom called him, he had, for some years, been turning over in his mind the idea of producing Shakespeare with closer actor-audience relationship. The possibility of returning to something like the thrust stage of the Elizabethan theatre of Shakespeare's own time was irresistible, and he also liked the idea of being again in Canada.

Sitting in the parlor of a local home, looking like a great, benevolent eagle, he told the citizens' committee franky that if they wanted to bring in tourists and make money, their best plan would be to get some bright lights and hire some dancing girls. For this they didn't need him. But if they wanted to do something worth while, he would be glad to advise them.

They told him they wanted to do something worth while.

"At three o'clock we came out into the marvelous starlit clearness of a Canadian midsummer night," Guthrie wrote in a letter. "It had been a Midsummer Night's Dream, and there were 15 or 20 of us that night, in other respects sensible, respectable, ordinary citizens, who vowed to ourselves that we would make that dream a solid, literally a concrete, reality."

On Guthrie's advice, the committee, without demur, raised its sights from a $30,000 budget to $150,000. Tom Patterson was sent shopping for talent in London. He talked to Alec Guinness (sitting in his long underwear in his dressing room, putting on his make-up for *Under the Sycamore Tree*). Afterwards, Guthrie wrote Guinness a long persuasive letter.

Guthrie also recruited Tanya Moiseiwitsch, who would create the thrust stage with its seven acting levels, nine major entrances, trapdoors and balcony. The audience would flank three sides of the stage, and the theatre, to start with, would be an enormous tent.

That fall, at the end of October, the citizens' committee incorporated, and the Stratford Shakespearean Festival of Canada Foundation (later the Stratford Shakespearean Festival Foundation of Canada) came into existence. Dr. Showalter became first president, and Tom Patterson quit his job in Toronto to become the first manager. In December, Guthrie returned to Canada on a whirlwind talent hunt, holding auditions in Toronto, Montreal and Ottawa. Publicity offices opened in Stratford and Toronto. A teacher's wife organized what she expected to be a small class to study Shakespeare in depth and was swamped with 160 applicants. A huge tent was ordered from Chicago to house the first production, while the more cautious urged delays, more thought, more time — especially after council contributed a modest amount of their money to the Festival. The cautious voices were drowned in the enthusiasm of a city caught up in an irresistible idea whose time had come.

Theatre people, too, were busy. Cecil Clarke, former production manager of the Old Vic, and now assistant director of the Festival, arrived to continue auditions and organize production facilities. A financial campaign was launched in Stratford, and Guthrie set about negotiating with high calibre talent.

To quiet the rumors of financial difficulties for the festival, president Showalter, with a nice blend of idealism and determination, had bulldozers standing by with engines running during the ceremony of the turning of the first sod in April, 1953.

However, the festival board *was* in difficulty. As work began on the theatre site, only $60,000 of the needed $150,000 had been raised. Some businessmen saw their own careers at stake if the grandiose project failed. And for what? For a few plays in a circus tent! The crisis of May, 1953, was terrifying.

There was no money to pay either the tent maker or local workmen. Although the tent makers stopped work in Chicago, Stratford contractor Oliver Gaffney kept his crews doggedly at the job, not knowing whether he would be paid or not, but determined that, if the Festival failed, it would not be the fault of a citizen of Stratford. And Guinness did sail for Canada on the Tuesday, perhaps for a non-existent festival.

On Mother's Day weekend, the Atkinson Foundation told Dr. Showalter it had found it necessary to cancel its $50,000 donation to the enterprise. Monday afternoon, the Festival board met glumly to decide whether to cancel or proceed, and miraculously came help — $35,000 in last-minute donations, $25,000 of it from the Perth Mutual Fire Insurance Company, which had already contributed,

The tent watchers gathered, among them R. Thomas Orr, right.

and another $10,000 from "an anonymous donor" who later turned out to be the Massey Foundation.

That first year, Stratford's financial contribution to the Festival would amount to about $73,000 — prompting Guthrie to write to a friend, "I don't see that happening in many of our country market towns, do you?" The big donations, and the little ones, were put up with little belief in any financial reward, and, with the surprise $35,000, the Festival again got under way.

Guinness arrived, looked around the city, was delighted, and then went fishing. The cast assembled for rehearsals, using a makeshift stage with terrible acoustics in the Agricultural Hall at the fair grounds. In Chicago, the tentmakers went back to work. The Festival tent was the second largest in North America, after that of the Ringling Brothers' circus. Each tent pole weighed a ton and a half and was sixty feet high. There were ten miles of guy-rope and cable.

All week, after it arrived, tent-watching was Stratford's favorite outdoor sport. People sat in their cars around "the site", as they had called it for months, or they brought lawn chairs and sandwiches. On Saturday and Sunday, the crowd

BEACON HERALD

Alec Guinness came to town.

was swelled with arrivals for Old Home Week, a gala and a highly successful celebration which enhanced the pre-Festival excitement. ("Do you do this *every* year?" Guthrie asked in bewilderment.)

In the midst of it was the tent master, Roy "Skip" Manley, a man of great friendliness, a droll sense of humor, and enormous industry as he sorted his complicated tent hardware and directed his crews. Hopes of meeting the deadline showed a faint glimmer when the great 60-foot poles and 250 stakes arrived on June 22, a Monday. The canvas, terra cotta red and aqua blue, came on Thursday. By late Wednesday, tractors and teams of men hauling on guy-ropes had raised the four main poles, each with its spaghetti-like cluster of ropes, all numbered. The nine canvas sections of the roof, weighing half a ton each, were laced together on Saturday; and on Sunday, to the cheers of a large crowd, the big top went up. Rehearsals in the tent could begin. "Skip" Manley had worked non-stop for almost 60 hours.

Now everything was rushing to completion at breakneck speed. Ticket sales had gone quite well, although it was not a sellout. Journalists were taking notice.

THE TELEGRAM

Tely Want Ads—Em. 3-7531
8 a.m.—6 p.m.
Monday Through Friday

Want Ads Placed By 10.45 a.m.
Appear Same Day
Closed On Saturday

SECOND SECTION

TORONTO, TUESDAY, JULY 14, 1953

SECOND SECTION

'KING RICHARD III' COLORFULLY LAUNCHES SHAKESPEARIAN FESTIVAL

And Guinness Is King
Garbed in Royal purple and bearing Orb and Sceptre, British actor Alec Guinness enacts the role of King Richard III in last night's premiere presentation at the Stratford Shakespearean festival.

Under The Canvas
From high in the "gods," Alec Guinness and fellow cast members can be seen taking bows following their dramatic performance last night. Under canvas and without scenery, as in Elizabethan times, the presentation stimulated the audience's imagination.

Between Acts
Ornately costumed, George Alexander forgets his role as the bearded Earl of Derby for a minute as he stands at the stage door between acts to catch a quick smoke.

'Downtown In A Hurry'
DISAGREES WITH MAYOR ON EXPRESSWAY

By WILLIAM BRAGG
Telegram Staff Reporter

'This Sun Of York' Converts Winter Into Avon Summer

By ROSE MACDONALD

Planes, Trains, Crickets Liven Bard At Stratford

By DOROTHY HOWARTH
Telegram Staff Reporter

Outdoors with PETE McGILLEN

PRINT BY MICROFILM
RECORDING CO. LTD.

The National Film Board, which had come to do a ten-minute production, ended up with a 38-minute feature, *The Stratford Adventure,* which was an Academy Award nominee the next year. Just about everyone in town took part in the film, playing waiters, garage men, or pedestrians in the street.

The afternoon before the opening performance, E. B. Radcliffe of the *Cincinnati Enquirer* came driving through western Ontario, muttering to himself: "This is a bit of a put-on . . . When I get to the end of all these wheat fields, I'm not going to see Alec Guinness . . . It will have to be some other Guinness — Joe Guinness or somebody."

At the last minute, coco matting was rushed in and laid over the cement floor to improve acoustics. All the church bells in the city began to ring at eight o'clock that night, opening night, July 13, 1953. Then all the factory whistles joined in. At 8:15, the Shakespearean flag, a gift from the Memorial Theatre in Stratford-upon-Avon in England, was raised under the Union Jack at the court house. Trumpets lifted in a fanfare to summon the audience, a cannon was fired to announce the start of the play, the orchestra played the National Anthem, the great theatre bell boomed, and Alec Guinness appeared on the stage balcony to thunderous applause.

Richard III came to life under flapping canvas. The tent theatre was packed. To the young players who had worked and believed, it was the night of a dream come true.

Long before that swirling, tumultuous, colorful, thrilling evening of theatre was over, it was evident that Patterson, Guthrie, and what Guthrie called "that gallant committee" had succeeded, perhaps beyond their highest hopes. Between 15,000 and 20,000 words were filed that night at the telegraph office. The second production of the show season, *All's Well That Ends Well,* received raves the following night. The "glorious summer" had begun.

The *New York Herald-Tribune* called it the theatrical coup of the season, achieved by "this inaccessible town and this impertinent theatre". Brooks Atkinson of the *New York Times* wrote of "a little gem of imaginative theatre". Some unlikely publications gave it space. A British medical journal, *The Lancet,* in its July edition, lauded the festival right next to an article on "Comfortable Childbirth". Even Canadian history books, before long, began to mention it.

For that first season of 42 performances, the house averaged a remarkable 98 percent of capacity. Guthrie later itemized the three reasons for the enormous success: first, the Festival was right for its time; second, the citizens' committee was right for the Festival; and, thirdly, "the productions were not bad!"

The tent theatre was used for four seasons for a succession of plays . . . *Oedipus Rex . . . Measure For Measure . . . Julius Caesar* — nine of Shakespeare's plays in all were performed beneath the blue canvas ceiling. There was no stage setting as such, just the breath-taking costumes. When the big top finally came down in 1956, after playing to 443,000 people, the permanent theatre that replaced it was built with a tent-like design. This time, with the Festival a success, the money was there.

Funds came from large foundations, from provincial and federal governments, from private patrons. Stratford itself, through the Corporation, local businesses and private citizens, contributed $140,000. By 1979, Stratford's total contribution would be nearly three quarters of a million dollars — a figure to boggle the imagination of the first, frightened committee, turning out their own pockets more than two decades before, to try to pay the men digging "the big hole in the ground". The new Festival Theatre opened in 1957 with the rising young Canadian actor, Christopher Plummer, as Hamlet.

Plummer moved into the Queen's Hotel, temporarily, and couldn't be budged from the historic hostelry. The proprietors finally vacated their own suite so he could stay on, while *they* went to the furnished house that the Festival had thoughtfully provided for Plummer.

The new theatre was designed by the same architect that had designed the tent theatre, Robert Fairfield, who later won the Royal Architectural Institute of Canada gold medal for the most outstanding work of the year.

The composer of the trumpet fanfare would hear his summons to the plays sounded for the next quarter century — and never collect a cent of royalties. Lou Applebaum, the first music director, passed up a tidy fortune when he "just decided he didn't want" the royalties. He went on to become the executive director of the Ontario Arts Council which, in 1977, gave the Festival a grant of over a quarter million dollars.

The Festival launched into almost continuous expansion, with more performances, longer seasons, added musical programs and increasing professionalism in the backstage arts and crafts and costuming. There were tours abroad, and also other theatrical stages. The board rented the old Casino on the river in 1955, and the downtown Avon Theatre in 1956; it used both for expansions, for experimental works and for the training of upcoming talent. Later, it bought the Avon.

An outstanding Festival Archives developed, the oldest formally constituted theatrical archives in North America and one of the most complete in the world, with its thousands of pictures and sketches, shelves laden with all the prompt books back to 1953, even a chair believed to have been Shakespeare's own, and a prized Fourth Folio of 1865. The crowded collection finally moved down the street to share space with the Perth Mutual Insurance Company in the great, pillared mansion once built by the furniture king, George McLagan, on the old pioneer Grange property.

Some alterations eventually were made to the original Festival stage, including replacing the nine slender "feminine" pillars supporting the balcony with five larger ones. The Casino was converted into the concert hall, then became The Third Stage for workshop productions and original Canadian plays. In 1958, began the highly successful school performances, in spring and fall, with matinees at reduced prices and with a member of the cast coming back for questioning afterwards. The millionth student, arriving October 9, 1977, to see *The Tempest,* was given a lifetime pass.

Other playwrights joined Shakespeare, among them Stratford area writer, poet and playwright, James Reaney, who saw his *Colours in the Dark* performed on

Tom Patterson:
he saw his imaginative dream
come true.

BEACON HERALD

the Avon stage in 1967. Earlier that year, the Festival Company of players and musicians made its first coast-to-coast tour as part of Canada's Centennial celebrations. It coped with not only winter storms in Newfoundland but also a cello. The huge and valuable instrument was an official headache, for it occupied a passenger seat that had to be accounted for. And so an airline ticket was made out to "Miss Cello", the cellist put a hat on the instrument, fastened its seat belt, insisted on an airline dinner for "Miss Cello", and then ate it as well as his own. The musician — and the tour — got national press.

The year 1975 brought to Stratford the brilliant, sometimes controversial young Britisher, Robin Phillips, as artistic director of the Festival. In a Canada still riding the wash of nationalism, Phillips was considerably nonplussed later, when he tried to evoke that great Canadian patriotism for a revival of *Richard III*. To stir up patriotic fervor for the play's red rose and white rose theme, he suggested the cast join in singing *'O Canada'*. They thought he was out of his mind.

The playgoers came from all walks of life . . . Lieutenant Governor Pauline McGibbon in full evening dress, glittering with jewels . . . two teachers from Ohio in cotton frocks . . . a man in sport shirt, his wife with Mexican stole . . . teenagers in faded jeans, in the balcony. In a community where Saturday night at the movies had been a lively weekend for many young people, now Tom Patterson could turn up at the Edinburgh Lounge of the Queen's Hotel with Ethel Merman. And once Edward Everett Horton had to stand up at the bar because he didn't have a reservation for a table.

*School performances brought bus loads of students to fill the
Festival Theatre and to question the players after the performances. This was 1973,
after* The Taming of the Shrew.

Princess Margaret came in 1958; Queen Elizabeth and Prince Philip in 1959.
Governor General Vincent Massey, who saw the plays the second week in the
tent, returned to lay the cornerstone for the permanent theatre. Prime Minister
Louis St. Laurent came on his election campaign; Jose Ferrer and Rosemary
Clooney on their honeymoon; and author Nicholas Monsarrat, to write a book,
To Stratford With Love.

When the U.S. President's daughter, Lynda Bird Johnson, showed up with her
escort of five gleaming Cadillacs, the U.S. secret service men insisted she have
police protection since the entourage ''would attract so much attention''.

''Five Cadillacs?'' shrugged Stratford's chief of police. ''Cadillacs are like
bottoms in this town! Everyone's got one.'' She got her escort all the same.

The Festival had five artistic directors in a quarter century: Tyrone Guthrie,
1953 and 1955; Cecil Clarke, 1954; Michael Langham, 1956 to 1967, Jean
Gascon, first Canadian director, from 1968 to 1974, and Robin Phillips, who
came in 1975.

Meanwhile, with a success on its hands, the city did not turn its festival wholly over to the outsiders. Nine of the thirteen Foundation presidents between 1953 and 1979 were from Stratford. The city itself began awarding a $1,000 prize to enable a local, upcoming actor or actress to further a theatrical career. Tom Patterson, who bowed out of active management of the festival and moved to Toronto, was given an enduring reward — an island named after him in the Avon River, where kids could dangle their toes, and, through the lace of willows, look up to the Festival Theatre that his dream had built on the hill.

In a large downstairs workroom at the theatre, a computer began purring away in 1978, able to produce over half a million tickets for the festival season. It was a theatrical first in Canada.

The same year, the Festival completed the entire range of Shakespeare's plays with a stunning performance of the early, violent *Titus Andronicus*, not one of The Bard's best, and considered, by some, to be "unplayable". Presented with total realism, the stage would have been awash with ketchup-blood by the final act. At the evening performance of *Titus Andronicus*, September 7, 1978, the eighth millionth theatre-goer arrived at the Festival theatre. Yet still a few were unconvinced.

It was frequently and reliably reported in Stratford that there were two little old ladies (or was it two little old men?) strolling past the huge theatre parking lot by the river just as the revival of *Richard III* was starting. There were a dozen empty parking spaces and one turned to the other triumphantly.

"You *see!* I *told* you this thing would never last!"

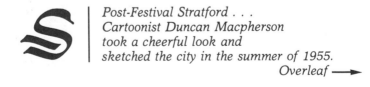

Post-Festival Stratford . . .
Cartoonist Duncan Macpherson
took a cheerful look and
sketched the city in the summer of 1955.
Overleaf ⟶

SPREAD here, for the Delection of the Beholder, lies a Vista of *Stratford*, in *Ontario*, the scene of the North American *Shakespearean* Festival where from June 27 to August 27 will be presented the *Merchant of Venice* and *Julius Caesar*, also the Tragedy of *Oedipus Rex*, (by another author).

MINISTRY OF INDUSTRY AND TOURISM

Fort Henry guards in 19th century uniforms took part in the summer festivities in 1972. A few years later, demolition of the Royal Bank building in the background outraged many citizens and drew the wrath of Heritage Canada, as Stratford set about modernizing its historic downtown core.

15

The Festival City

AFTER THE ARRIVAL of the Festival, there was much assessment and reassessment of a city suddenly caught up in international fame and fortune. There had to be a credibility gap between the theatre lifestyle and the nine-to-five, predictable and pedestrian rhythms of Stratford.

They used to say that some townspeople went to church to pray for the actors, and others went to the priest to confess uncharitable thoughts. City youngsters were mesmerized by the colorful world of show people. The theatre people, for their part, at first mistook the conservative surface of the city for the face of dullness.

Unaware of the past, the Shakespearean Festival of Canada Foundation published an otherwise excellent booklet, *The Stratford Story*, and posed a question that many were asking: "Why, with no particular previous claim to cultural importance, should Stratford suddenly become the hub of such a project as a festival of Shakespeare? Until the first stirrings of the infant idea began to be felt in the press, Stratford had been notable only as a railroad divisional point and the home of the Stratford Indians Hockey Club. . . ." The answer, as they saw it, was the hundreds of acres of parks and gardens.

What the Festival actually brought was the impact of a new culture superimposed on a strong, already existing one, night people coming into a day people society.

There were a few incidents in the '60's with the "gazoonies", the youths with duck-tail haircuts, calling out to actors and wardrobe men, "Hey *Gearbox!*" — their name for men they thought effeminate. One gang jumped a long-haired actor and discovered, too late, that he was a former boxer. Three gazoonies promptly landed in hospital and all of them kept sheepishly quiet about the cause of the "accident".

Once in a while, Stratfordites could make a useful scapegoat of the Festival. Half a dozen years after the theatre came, the local wets mustered up a 60%

majority and voted in cocktail lounges, for which many townspeople blamed the theatre — among them Rev. Stuart MacLeod of St. John's United Church. He thundered forth from the pulpit on the eve of the liquor referendum: "I'm sorry that some of the promotion for a 'yes' vote comes from citizens clearly associated with the Festival. By implication it means that they regard cocktails as essential to cultural development!"

The Duke of Edinburgh, on the other hand, was not at all amused at the restrictive liquor laws in Ontario and, because of his complaints in Stratford, the "Edinburgh Lounge" at the Queen's Hotel got its name.

For the most part, the Festival and the city were gamely trying to understand each other and the effort produced, occasionally, rare and sweet flashes of friendship. Actors and actresses were charmed when, in the lounge of a downtown hotel, a local stranger would come over and order them drinks "because you've brought us so much enjoyment. . . ."

Celebrities, both theatre people and visitors, shopped and window-shopped in a city with the heart of a good small town, and it minded its business and let them alone — this was only good manners. The city, meanwhile, managed to keep a low key profile on its tourism, and, following the unwritten policy of council, rarely lapsed into what one writer called "creeping ye-olde-ism" in naming new, festival-oriented enterprises. Stratford had usually been careful about naming things.

Social changes for the city were subtle . . . a broadening of horizons, increased tolerance, wider interests. People traveled more than before, although they had always "taken trips", for pleasure or for business. Early merchants like J. A. Duggan regularly sent buyers to Europe — Duggan cannily sending his brother to save expenses. Duncan Ferguson, after buying the Idington Block, would himself take frequent buying trips to enhance his line of "silks, fine dress goods, millinery, mantles and domestic staples".

In festival season, the people opened their homes to the visitors that overflowed local accommodation, and, the first year, there were local church suppers to increase the city's strained dining facilities. First to benefit in the business community were the house painters. The city was proud of itself, and wanted to present a clean and shining face to its visitors. Senior citizens and old age pensioners had extra cash from paying overnight guests and, with the money, they painted and planted. It added to the air of well-being along the city's shaded streets.

Members of Stratford's Little Theatre group had speaking parts or walk-on bits; all the ushers, including the captain, and some of the dressers behind the scenes were local people. Stratford musicians played in the orchestra, and a Stratford boys' choir, drawn mainly from the Alpha Juvenile Choristers, sang in *Richard III*. The city invested heavily in the financial campaigns launched by the theatre; both the parks board and normal school donated land to permit the Festival to promote a bond sale. The Festival company, in turn, involved itself in civic affairs, even to participating in "A Rescue Review", a benefit show to aid the Perth branch of the Humane Society. Some members of the company found

Stratford a congenial place to live, and they stayed, sending their children to the schools with the Shakespearean names. Among them was Maggie Smith, who made her home in the city for several years.

There had been some momentum building up in acquiring new industries even before the railway shops had actually pulled out, and the Festival arrived, with perfect timing, to take up the slack. In that first astounding festival year, bank clearings in Stratford in June, July, and August of 1953 were $4,000,000 higher than in the same period in 1952. The C.N.R. reported a 55 percent increase in its sale of tickets from Toronto to Stratford, and set about sprucing up its station, putting up welcome signs and hanging baskets of geraniums.

Twenty-five years later, theatre ticket sales were still booming and an estimated 20 million dollars was being spent in the city every summer. Besides the full-time staff of 120, over 660 more had jobs at the height of the season.

To obtain new industrial space, the city nearly doubled in size in 1965, annexing land from all four surrounding townships to expand to an area of 4,663 acres. The 1953 population of 19,000 had topped 27,000 by 1980, although, even with the festival, it still fell short of the 35,000 figure planned for it by the Canada Company in the 1830's.

The out-of-town press took note. The improvement in Stratford's economy was due solely to the theatre, they said. *Weekend* referred to it as a "meat and potatoes town" before the coming of the Festival, and "no more than a genteel but shabby railroad switching center".

The Festival people, understandably, saw the summer flocking — the theatre-goers, the new money that had not been there before. Just as understandably, Stratford business wasn't exactly willing to admit that there had been *that* much of an impact at all! The Stratford Industrial Commission, in a 1968 summary of business conditions, pointed to the acquisition of new industries and economic progress generally and allowed that the Festival Theatre had been "*one* of the reasons".

Somewhere in between lay the truth.

The Festival was the biggest business in town, but not the only one. Some 40 new diversified industries had arrived, along with some younger industrialists. The small, long-established businesses in Stratford were sound, and probably the first major entry due to the presence of the Festival was that of Samsonite, which frankly felt it would benefit by the excellent ready-made publicity. The first heliport opened July 6, 1967, on the roof of its plant on Ontario Street. The first helicopter arrived, and out climbed the pilot, holding the millionth piece of Samsonite luggage made in Stratford. The inaugural flight also carried 1,500 helicopter first day covers to be cancelled at the city's post office.

"Even our industries are pretty industries!" the manager of the Chamber of Commerce earnestly told a T.V. radio interviewer, pointing out the absence of pollution. One of the post-Festival businesses of Stratford was the largest book publishing company in Canada, Harlequin Enterprises, which established a distributing branch. Another was FAG Bearings Ltd., celebrating its 25th anniversary in town in 1979 by opening a new $3 million addition to the plant, entertaining the top officials from the parent plant in Schweinfurt, West Germany — as well as the mayor of that town — and throwing a six-hour birthday party for 1,400 guests, complete with steins of German beer, an oom-pah-pah band, and a lunch of roasted pig tails and sauerkraut.

Automobile plants were at times discussed but, mindful of the monopoly of the old C.N.R. shops, Stratford backed away from becoming once again too greatly dependent on one industry.

After some earlier, unsuccessful attempts, there also was a city airport by 1973, located in North Easthope, about two miles north of town. The site had begun as a 2,800-foot grass landing strip, with no facilities and a gas supply that had to be pumped by hand from 45-gallon barrels and filtered through a felt hat. By the 1960's, council's attention was attracted to the man who owned the strip, a young R.C.A.F. veteran, Bruce Dale. Dale and the corporation worked out agreements to improve the 220-acre site originally called the Festival City Air Park. Aware of the value of air facilities in a growing economy, the City renewed the contract in 1978, subsidizing improvements and including an option to buy, good until 1985.

Stratford council actually had begun discussing a municipal airport when commercial flying was still very young. The failure of several early efforts had not daunted it. Now it was talking of air commuter services with other cities. Meanwhile, over 500 people received pilot's licenses after a flying school opened in 1963 at the airport — among them some Eskimos from Quebec, Manitoba and the Northwest Territories, sent to Stratford for training under a government program. And an increasing number of Festival visitors were flying to Stratford in their own planes.

Stratford women did the traditional behind-the-scenes jobs of all conservative and well-bred ladies in the early days, particularly in the service of the growing churches. Around the turn of the century, they had begun sitting on community boards, or volunteering for the Victorian Order of Nurses and other organizations. For the Women's Hospital Aid, they were responsible for erecting a driving shed and stable as well as for furnishing an operating room. They worked in the Home and School Council, the Catholic Women's League, and the Red Cross Society. They were solidly dedicated to the welfare of their city.

But they also valued themselves as persons, and they traveled outside Stratford for many of the things they needed. After the coming of the Festival, the women of Douglas Street and Delamere Avenue could shop downtown in Stratford boutiques for expensive lingerie, instead of having to go to Toronto. At home, they continued their community projects and support of local endeavor.

One project that swiftly caught the interest of the people of Stratford was the art gallery set up in the old pumping station at Confederation Park. Originally, it was funded by Rothmans. When the Company finally withdrew its support in 1975, it was taken over by the city — and by an eager corps of 75 unpaid volunteers who ran it year-round and with outstanding success. Part of the pattern of Stratford life had always been financial support for various causes, with often more than 100 fund-raising events in a year.

The rich variety on shaded streets

Number 19 Grange Street, simple and attractive in style.
Thomas Edison reputedly boarded here.

An iron dog,
once on guard at "The Elms",
Dr. J. A. Robertson's home,
now guards a Queen's Park
entrance.

*A lovely home north of the river
once was owned by Judge John A. Barron.*

*A Grecian touch on Mornington Street.
Pillars were added to this Italianate
house in 1939.*

An outdoor cafe behind city hall never materialized, but new restaurants catered to after-theatre crowds one of them in the old, deconsecrated, Congregational Church. The turn-of-the-century neighborhood grocery store established by Eli Heimrich became a high-class gourmet and crystal shop, selling imported coffees and snails, and shipping gourmet gift baskets to England, Europe and Australia. A lovely old house became a book store. And there were those who thought it time to remodel the city core.

Doubtless, the redevelopment plans were hurried along by the presence of the Festival and the influx of summer people, but change and renovation in the whole downtown area were long overdue. Concurrently, in the early '60's, in a country not yet a hundred years old, there was a growing nationalism, and an appreciation of Canada's architectural heritage. In Stratford, economics and culture clashed head on, and the fury of the impact was awesome.

The people of Stratford could be mulishly obstinate once they attached themselves to a cause — a trait they had already amply demonstrated in bringing about the Shakespearean Festival. Now, in the 1960's, council began planning to remove their city hall, bulldoze it right to the ground.

Since the turn of the century, the proud "Queen of the Square" had gone quietly along fulfilling her role as focal point of civic life. Here, people had come to transact business in her offices, to entertain, or be entertained, in her auditorium. She welcomed royalty and visiting dignitaries, received conventions, presented exhibitions and rallies, offered comedy and drama, held political meetings and tea parties. She had installed a succession of mayors in the chair with its steaming locomotive on the back. She heard many wise and far-reaching decisions made by her councilors. She had heard idiotic and retrograde decisions, as well. Through it all, she had lorded it grandly over market square.

By 1964, City Hall was aging. Compared with that shining theatre by the river, she appeared downright dumpy to some. As civic departments expanded, the original interior design had become increasingly inadequate. Finally, the police department and court officials moved out and city council, urged by Mayor "Dutch" Meier, determined to do some overhauling.

The decision to tamper with the old city hall blew up into headlines all over Ontario, but the idea was not new. Council had, off and on, been trying to get rid of the huge building for years, and, in 1964, the time seemed right.

The building, basically, was still sound, but the innards required an estimated $660,000 worth of surgery. This was too rich for the civic purse, and an architectural report, which had cost the city a tidy $36,000, was shelved. For three years there was silence from city hall, although a committee went quietly to work, investigating alternate sites, looking at fresh new designs.

Meanwhile, the Festival clearly flourishing, the Ontario Government became much interested in the growing tourist possibilities, and sent out a team to investigate. The 1966-7 survey found that visitors would attend two or three performances and often repeat the visit another year. About 26% of their money went for Festival tickets: 54% for food and shelter, and 20% for purchases within Stratford. In 1966, it amounted to over 39 million dollars altogether, $8 million of it within the city proper, and it was a very interesting figure to city hall, already aware that tourist dollars were being siphoned away from the downtown area and spent in the outskirts.

With this very real economic pressure, with a clear need for more tourist facilities (as everyone, including Guthrie, had been urging since 1953), it was no wonder the small and special city of Stratford took a flyer into big-city planning that could have wrecked it.

In October, 1967, Mayor Meier produced a sketch of what the city could have in its historic triangular square — a round, 10-storey hotel with a revolving restaurant on top. With stores and offices at ground level, it was a complex modeled on the C.N.R.'s Chateau Lacombe, in the city of Edmonton, Alberta. The Victoria and Grey Trust Company might be persuaded to sell its building, and Stratford City Hall could then move to Number 1, Ontario Street.

The plan gained wide publicity, and there were nibbles from several interested developers, one of whom proposed a $3 million development, "Bard Square", with an international hotel chain as the prime tenant, and the city renting offices. However, the scheme strangled on costs, for the city already had a debenture debt of $9 million, third highest per capita debt of any city in Ontario, and by far the highest for any city of its size.

Next spring, a new council, under a new mayor, John Killer, recommended that the city hall site be made available for redevelopment, and the Chamber of Commerce approved, but council itself was divided in opinion. In September, the special committee was expanded to include businessmen, and, almost nine months later, in early June, the enlarged committee presented its verdict: get rid of city hall. "The costs of necessary renovations, either for city offices or other uses, cannot be justified. The building is a fire hazard. The auditorium is not needed and seldom used, the plumbing and heating systems are completely inadequate and the building has serious cracks in the outside walls and inside walls and ceilings."

Few citizens attended the special council meeting. However, as soon as redevelopment rather than restoration seemed imminent, the lethargic city bestirred itself. Six angry women, all citizens of Stratford, met privately. They involved others and, before the end of June, 1969, the militant "Save the City Hall League" was in full cry. They lobbied. They hired a lawyer. They sold Christmas cards of a city hall nostalgically festooned with Christmas decorations. They got 1,939 signatures on a petition asking council to go to the ratepayers with a plebiscite. Council was horrified.

Considering the work that had been done with full public knowledge, and until now with lukewarm interest shown by the citizens, the last thing the mayor wanted now was a plebiscite!

"I suggest to you that this is not a question that can be referred to the public and get a responsible answer!" snapped Mayor John Killer.

The *Beacon Herald* called the mayor arrogant, and accused council of ignoring the people. The weekly *Times* didn't want a plebiscite, and demanded the resignations of two aldermen who did.

John Idington, Q.C., was appointed to the Supreme Court of Canada in 1905. Earlier, in 1885, he had built the Idington Block, which became part of Festival Square.

A new mayor and a new council took office in 1970. Council was still divided, but it went doggedly on with the redevelopment schemes, and there were some wild new opinions put forward: that the previous committee had been biased because all members had been men; that a plebiscite ballot couldn't be worded satisfactorily; that — even sillier — another committee should be formed. The City Hall League was asked to prepare a brief, the public was asked for suggestions, and (as it usually did when pressed) council called a public meeting.

There were 81 briefs submitted, 65 of them wanting to save the building. "Fight City Hall!" might be a normal pastime in most Canadian cities, but here *city hall itself,* like Caesar's wife, was beyond reproach. Many citizens wanted to restore their queer, historic, beautiful old lump of a building sitting there in market square like some old dowager queen from a more opulent age. Others wanted it out.

Another new mayor and still another new council in 1971 inherited the ongoing problem, and they voted, by a narrow margin, to accept the proposals of a Montreal developer and proceed with the demolition. Immediately, some aldermen began receiving threatening telephone calls. One man's wife was told, "I'd like to see him blown up!" The mayor got a toy bulldozer, with a note, "It's time to do something!"

Meanwhile, the plight of City Hall was attracting unwanted attention elsewhere. Eric McLean, instrumental in preserving Old Montreal, said it would be "sheer insanity" to tear down the Stratford City Hall. A professor of urban and regional planning at the University of Waterloo said it was "absurd" that the city hall had no historic value. "They don't want to pay for the upkeep of the municipal building!" he snapped.

Mayor D. S. Davis replied drily, "He didn't tell us anything we didn't know."

Council proceeded with plans that would cost $1 million, and the citizens took sides, as they normally did.

While the actual proposal for redevelopment did not come before council at its August meeting, more than 200 Save-City-Hallers did, with their solicitor. James Beatty was a former Stratford lawyer. He pointed to the city as the home of a national theatre, and suggested trying for a government grant to restore the building. The city's own official plan, he said, contained a clause calling for "the retention and improvement of the present city hall area as the focus of the central business district".

A group from the Architectural Conservancy of Ontario, including its vice-president and an architectural historian, came to the city on a walking tour of market square and admired what they called "that proud structure — city hall". This was marvelous encouragement to the citizens, a horrifying turn of events to the developers.

No developer in his right mind would consider becoming part of any such political issue. Retaining or razing city hall was the city's own business and the firm wanted no part of it, as it beat a hasty retreat.

In May, 1972, believing the city hall had been saved from the bulldozers only for the time being, the Save the City Hall League regrouped as the "Citizens For Stratford", to deal with "other areas of civic importance that are also being neglected."

August 1, 1972, council finally scrapped redevelopment of the city hall site, and began to study renovation plans instead.

The arguments, of course, were not over, and, at the storm center, was often the question of the auditorium — whether to foot a sizeable bill for its restoration to its former glory, or whether to convert it into office space that was sorely needed. The capacity of the hall by the 1970's was only 153 for a banquet and dance, 235 for a meeting; and the balcony could not be used at all because of fire regulations. Mention of the plight of the auditorium could be counted on to set off fireworks anytime, both in and out of council, and the issue dragged on.

However, some needed renovations were made to the city hall, including buying a clock for the building from an English clock maker. The tower had been waiting for its clock ever since 1898.

On Sunday, June 2, 1974, Stratford gathered to pay homage to the "Queen of the Square" resplendent in new raiment. It was rededication day, but a strained one, after a decade of conflict. None of the Save-City-Hallers were included in the program, but their name tags were prominently displayed in the audience.

The mayor and the president of the Perth County Historical Board unveiled the plaque of the "Ass Architect" inside the main entrance, where it was intended to be placed when the building was first opened in 1900. They took note of the cost of the project, as recorded in the city treasurer's records: exterior, $89,700.14; interior, $746,767; furnishings, $40,022.49; total, $876,485.63.

And they went home.

Meanwhile, up the street from city hall, sat a huddle of wall-eyed buildings, city-owned and empty — a new battlefield in the making.

The coming of the Festival, with its staffs and companies of players, its thousands of theatre-goers in a holiday mood, all had given the downtown merchants urgent incentive to revitalize the downtown core. They saw business heading out to the perimeter; the visitors commuting to the theatres from motels on "the strip". Some visitors never saw the downtown city at all, as the merchants well knew.

Urgently, they wanted to bring business back to the center core, and council was sympathetic to their requests. Anticipating the multi-million-dollar development of hotel, offices and stores, and encouraged, for a time, by the expressed interests of large concerns, including the C.N.R., the city had methodically assembled two acres of vacant properties. Having purchased them, the city failed to find a developer, and this collection some people soon were calling "that monstrosity", and some others were calling "historic".

The whole area echoed Stratford's past. The red brick Gordon Block at the Ontario Street apex of the gaunt triangle had been built by Stratford's first city mayor, William Gordon, in the 1890's, and was the last significant structure of the 30-year era of brick construction. John Idington, later Judge Idington of the Supreme Court of Canada, had built the block alongside, and later sold it to Duncan Ferguson. Nearby on Wellington Street, clearly etched in the roofs of old buildings, were the profiles of four early hotels. Two active banks, the Commerce and the Toronto Dominion, sat within their Victorian quarters near the wide-angle junction of Wellington and Downie. Another, the Royal, was across the street, and all three wanted to modernize.

A cluster of shabby frame buildings had stood at the Downie-Ontario-Erie triangle in the middle of the 19th century, when wags had called the group "the fire-proof block", in sarcastic reference to the fact that, while fires burned useful buildings, this eyesore always escaped unscathed. But the brick replacements, like city hall itself, were prime samples of heritage architecture, and their fate attracted outside interest, as plans were laid to replace them.

An Ontario Municipal Board hearing in the fall of 1976 pointed out that the local business community could suffer, too. The proposed development with large hotel, enclosed mall, apartment building and six-storey parking garage was a "big city" solution, and it could overwhelm the very downtown merchants the scheme was trying to help. The Corporation, however, won its case, and the right to proceed as it saw fit for the ultimate good of the citizens.

Heritage Canada, the Ottawa-based foundation dedicated to the preservation of the man-made past, considered the Stratford center core well worth saving. Author Pierre Berton, did too, and, in midsummer, 1977, got off a stinging letter to Stratford's mayor, blasting as "perfectly scandalous" the plan to raze the 65-year-old Royal Bank, and replace the heritage architecture of Stratford with new and shiny buildings. The local architectural advisory committee agreed. But the city saw its two-acre block of empty buildings occupying prime space. The vacant, staring windows and the lost tax dollars haunted city council at every meeting, and the buildings were deteriorating badly.

While the outcries rose several decibels, the Royal Bank was bulldozed, and a new bank building took shape. For the building across the street, what the city arrived at, in due course, was a compromise, a three-way agreement between the corporation, downtown banks and a London developer with a flair for history. To rescue the historic brick block at the apex of Erie, Downie and Ontario Streets, government help was available through the Ontario Heritage Foundation. Work began in 1978, on a $2 million budget, to turn the three old buildings into boutique-oriented "Festival Square". The Bank of Commerce and the Toronto Dominion were soon to follow the Royal and be replaced, but the old skyline down Wellington Street was still at least partially intact.

And so ended a small and special city's flyer into big city planning.

Stratford through the years had responded predictably to an international festival, which it saw as an extension of its own cultural tradition. Two and a half decades later, the fine early fervor had, naturally, cooled. The crusaders who had said "Go ahead" to Guthrie when they had no money to back their dreams, were older now, more settled. Tom Patterson had left. The fine fire of challenge was banked, and the people who had plunged into establishing a festival, even at risk of their own jobs and homes, now took the same festival for granted.

There were now some who could add "O.C." after their names for the Order of Canada, mainly for service to the Stratford Festival; and "Sparky", the tour train, loaded with summer visitors, trundled about the quiet streets of the city three times a day. But the swans still nested up Idington Creek, and business went on pretty much as usual on Ontario Street.

The 25th festival season brought another spate of reviews and assessments from abroad, by writers who honestly still seemed surprised — some even a trifle irked — that Stratford had not been more transformed. But an associate editor of a national magazine, whose grandfather had been born in a little wooden house beside the Mansion House Hotel, still found it unhurried and friendly — "a nice place to go home to".

In market square, City Hall stood, a little smugly. Would someone, sometime, again raise the cry — "*Fight City Hall!*"?

PART

2

THE SUPPORTS

Every good city has its supports. They do not change its destiny, or alter its history but, without them, no city could long survive . . . . the schools to train its young . . . . the churches to feed its spirit . . . . sports to stir its blood . . . . even the housekeeping jobs of police, fire and sanitation to keep the city operating. They are a continuing fabric of its existence. And, threading it all together, are the communications, the communicators, and the press . . .

ADELAIDE LEITCH

Typical of Stratford is the St. James'
Church spire rising in the background
on this post card made around 1914.
Tall iris bloom, left, in memorial
flower beds planted for a beloved
priest, Father Corcoran, through
whose efforts the iris became the civic
flower of Stratford in 1925.

Avon Bridge, Stratford, Ont.

PERTH COUNTY ARCHIVES

16

The Continuing Church

IT BEGAN LIKE any normal church-raising in Stratford in the 1860's.

The Baptists were replacing their first little frame church with a larger one. But, after the construction had been under way for some time, it became increasingly apparent that the churchmen were not going to supply the customary whisky. The workmen were first incredulous, then indignant. No whisky — no church! They quit and went home.

The Baptists rolled up their sleeves and put their shoulders to the beams, Deacon Thomas Birch among them. As he later told it:

"We lifted until we saw stars, but the frame did not go up. We felt something slipping and knew if it fell someone would be hurt. Suddenly there was a roar by an unfamiliar voice and the frame went up as if by magic." A group of Perth County farmers had come to the rescue.

It was typical of the ecclesiastical order of things in early Stratford, where everyone pitched in.

Tiny houses and log cabins first served for family prayers. Then the large room of an inn or tavern became a first "Church home", with liquor flowing during the week in sociability and, on Sunday, for sacramental wine. The first proper church was inevitably of logs, the next one usually frame, and both were built with the help of hand labor.

Early congregations, in appallingly stiff and uncomfortable Sunday best, came not only from the hamlet of Stratford, but from the surrounding townships, Downie, Ellice, North and South Easthope; later from as far away as Shakespeare, to hear the preacher when he came. So hungry were they for divine service that many would walk barefoot over bush trails to save their shoes, putting on their shoes and stockings only when they got in sight of the little church.

The first ministers were, of necessity, itinerants, traveling on horseback to the scattered settlements, staying a few days, then moving on along the Huron Road. To Little Thames came the famous "saddlebag preachers" of the Methodist

223

circuits, working out of York in the early 1830's, later attached to the Brampton circuit after it was ''set off'' in 1838.

Presbyterian and Anglican ministers never were so dedicated to an itinerant ministry as the Methodists, nor were they so easy in the saddle or so much at home in the woods. But all faiths came, and all held services wherever heaven could provide a spot.

On the hillside that sloped down to the river and the mills, before 1837 Rev. William Rintoul would gather together the Presbyterians, baptize children born since his last trip, and celebrate communion in the open air. Sometimes, it would be Rev. Donald Mackenzie of Zorra preaching on the slopes. For the Anglicans, the first Stratford service was in the Shakespeare Hotel. The Roman Catholics worshipped in a still-unfinished church before the settlement was a decade old. In 1843, the Wesleyan Methodists had a more-or-less-regular place of worship in James Rust's log cabin and, later, his wagon shop at the corner of Ontario and Nile Streets. Two years after that, for five shillings, they bought lots 116 and 117 on Erie Street. Here, they built their first modest frame building — Wesleyan Methodist Mission, forerunner, by 80 years, of Central United Church.

In June, 1847, appointed to the newly-designated Methodist circuit of Stratford and Peel Township, came Rev. William Dignam, a man of boundless optimism and good humor. For him, the parishioners rolled up shirt sleeves and, faces dripping with sweat, hewed out timbers not only for the church he wanted, but for a religious center as well. Meanwhile, as a conference report said, the minister ''stood from time to time on the stumps and offered words of encouragement, or prayed for blessing on their efforts''.

After three years, he was followed by Rev. John Wakefield, who traveled a longer circuit that now included Stratford, New Hamburg, Bell's Corners (Shakespeare), New Dundee, Ayr and Drumbo. His camp meetings were famous, often lasting from ten to twelve days. He was truly a ''saddlebag preacher,'' as the *Beacon* described him.

> He rode horseback, and his saddle was specially constructed, with loops in front and behind for the valises which held his little all, his library, clothes and everything else. This wonderful saddle had been made in the village of Ayr.
> He arrived at Stratford on a Thursday and was directed to Robert Monteith's. Sunday morning he preached, and a desperately hard time he had. The church was unplastered and not properly heated. But to the unaccustomed preacher it seemed as large as Westminster Abbey, and the audience filled him with awe. So ill did he succeed that he went back to Monteith's, strapped up his valises and departed, determined that Stratford should see his face no more.

Stratford, of course, did. After bearing the confusion of several such early sermons, he accepted his calling and, as he said, was ''secured for better or worse to the ministry''.

The Canada Company, mindful of its charter to develop the Huron Tract, gave land to fledgling churches when they were ready to build: an acre and a quarter for the hamlet's first church, St. Andrew's, in 1837; other grants to the Anglicans, the Roman Catholics, the Methodists, the First Congregational Church, Zion Lutheran and others.

The actual building of a house of worship, the never-ending scrounging to pay the salary of the minister or raise the money for furnishings, melodeons, pipe organs and carved pulpits — these things were the responsibility of the congregations. Wealthy families in Stratford made gifts, dedicated windows, or supplied communion silver. Others gave work and time.

Behind the unending work stood the organizations of the women — the early Ladies' Aid, holding bazaars, buying the carpet or setting up a new church kitchen; then the "W.A." — the Women's Association that became eventually the "United Church Women"; and the Catholic Women of St. Joseph's.

Stratford's first established church was the "Auld Kirk" — St. Andrew's Presbyterian, organized for Stratford and North Easthope Township in 1838. A log building complete with steeple was up by 1840, and here worshipped the first congregation of the Established Church of Scotland in the whole Huron District. The church would be rebuilt twice, in 1868 and in 1911, always on the same site, above the slope where Rev. William Rintoul first preached in the open air.

Before any church building went up, however, there arrived Scottish-born Rev. Daniel Allan, dispatched to Canada as a missionary by the Colonial Society of Scotland under the auspices of the Kirk of Scotland. He was inducted as first minister of the joint charge of Stratford and Woodstock at Stratford on November 21, 1838, and he had orders to preach equally in English and in Gaelic.

Names of those who subscribed to the minister's first yearly stipend of 63 pounds, 27 shillings and six pence (as listed in a church record book) read like a roll call of clans in Scotland: McPherson, McNaughton, McDonald, McTavish, Anderson, Crerar, Stewart, Monteith, Scott, Fraser. . . . There were also the names of the early Makers of Stratford: J. C. W. Daly, the Canada Company agent, (and everything else in the 1830's) . . . William Sargint of the Shakespeare Hotel . . . J. J. E. Linton, teacher and crusader . . . John Sebring who built the mill . . . John Sharman, the blacksmith . . . Alexander B. Orr. It was the Auld Kirk and the only kirk, and everyone attended.

The estimated cost for a simple church building, 50' x 40', without counting in the cost of belfry or steeple, but including two stoves with pipes, was $600. During the winter, when the sleighing was good, provisions of lime, putty, nails and shingles were assembled for a framework slated to go up in the spring.

The laying of the cornerstone took place July 16, 1840, in the fourth year of the reign of Queen Victoria, and a jar was placed beneath, containing a number of documents and copies of the *Canadian Christian Examiner,* the *British Colonist,* the *Upper Canada Almanac,* the *Home and Foreign Mission Record* and the *Woodstock Herald,* the nearest local paper. There was also a copy of the deed for the Canada Company property, and some coins. Before long, Rev. Mr. Allan resigned the Woodstock charge and became, in 1840, minister for Stratford alone.

Stratford churches were elegant,
as W. H. Smith noted in Picturesque Canada *in 1882. The poetic engraving*
looks south across the river, toward "the beautiful Presbyterian Church [with]
Gothic Spire towering to the height of 215 feet".

Three years later, like a thunderclap from across the ocean came church war — the disruption of the established Church of Scotland, as a seceding group formed the Free Church of Scotland. In Stratford, St. Andrew's congregation also split. The next year, the minister left, taking much of the congregation with him, to form a Free Church. The departing Rev. Daniel Allan also took all the church records with him, including the original deed to the property.

St. Andrew's struggled along without a minister for three years, until it got a probationer, and, at the same time, it had to carry on a battle for the possession of the church building. The Established Church, the St. Andrew's group, derided the very recent beginnings of the seceders:

> "The Wee Church, The Free Church,
> The Church without a steeple!"

The seceders replied:

> "The Auld Kirk, The Cauld Kirk,
> The Kirk without the people!"

For several years, the dissenters petitioned and wrote and generally badgered Thomas Mercer Jones, commissioner of the Canada Company at Goderich, for a deed in their name to the lots originally granted to St. Andrew's, and upon which the church of St. Andrew's stood. Cannily, they refused to give up the papers they had proving the Auld Kirk's claim that the grant was made to the Established Church of St. Andrew's *in common with the Church of Scotland.*

Finally, in late 1848, the Auld Kirk's members pulled out the foundation stone and unearthed the jar containing the papers. They presented them to Commissioner Jones, who upheld their claim and assured their title to their ministry, "for the consideration of Five Shillings of lawful money". The Canada Company grant was in connection with the Established Church of Scotland "and for no other purpose".

The church minutes noted: "The jar with all the coins, together with the papers which it contained and the additional paper, was again deposited in the same spot under the northeast cornerstone of the Stratford church, and we hope it will rest in peace."

The next year, 1849, Knox Church was founded, and held its first services in the school house until a church could be built the year after.

The second church of St. Andrew's, in 1869, was a bit bigger. The city directory of 1870-1871 described it as a white building, 75' x 44', of Gothic style, with a lecture room and Sabbath School in the basement, and windows of richly stained enamelled glass. It seated 400, and cost $7,000.

The first little church was moved across the street, to become a dwelling. By 1911, with attendance up, the congregation again decided to build a new church, and the cornerstone of this third and final St. Andrew's was laid Oct. 30, 1911. The dedicatory opening service was Sept. 15, 1912.

While St. Andrew's was establishing its rights of possession, other churches were taking root in Stratford, attracting congregations and raising their first church buildings. They all had mortgages and eventually burned them triumphantly and with great celebration.

In the 19th century, Scrimgeour Brothers were increasingly busy with church carpentry, either building or renovating. Many a Sabbath service moved temporarily into the town hall, the county court house, a school basement or even a livery stable. The congregation of St. James' moved so frequently that the press, in time, took note: "The Stratford Anglican has been a very Noah's Dove in the matter of visitation. This time it was to allow the first brick church, an ugly, red-barn-doric affair, to be built; so the melodeon migrated across the road into one of the jury boxes."

By the time Stratford had become a town, it had active congregations of most of the major churches of Canada, as well as many of the smaller ones; also at least one that came to it for asylum.

Fleeing slavery in the United States, there came a handful of colored people seeking a new life. One of the first recruits in an early Baptist membership drive was a black lady, a Mrs. Young, once a slave in Louisville, Kentucky. In time, Stratford's colored people built a church more suitably their own. A little frame Primitive Methodist Church stood on Waterloo Street in 1857. Locally, they called it "The Colored Church" because almost the entire congregation was made up of escaped slaves who had been given homes by nearby farmers.

Eagerly, these people seized the opportunity to attend services in a village that allowed them to worship in peace. Few outsiders attended, but, when they did, they were gathered in and welcomed. It was an unfamiliar, strange service to people brought up with Presbyterian, Anglican and Roman Catholic forms of worship. Yet it was so unforgettable that young Christine McNaughton still remembered it vividly even when she was an old lady.

She had come unexpectedly upon the Primitive Methodist Church when out for a walk one evening, and had gone in. Many years later, she could still tell a newspaper interviewer about it, in detail:

"The church was a low, narrow building with no paint either on the exterior or the walls inside, but the white pine floor was scrubbed to a highly polished state. In the front, there was a desk for the preacher and a small melodeon, which was played by the minister's wife. . . . The first part of the service was a 'Love Feast', and, after the sermon, the colored people participated in a testimony meeting, rising to give praise and thanks for being free from bondage."

The United States abolished slavery in 1863. The little Stratford slave church still existed and, in time, merging with other churches, wound up by 1926 as part of St. John's United Church.

There apparently was another "Colored Church", perhaps an offshoot of the first, for among the entries in Vernon's *Stratford Directory* of 1909 was: "Colored Church, 327 Birmingham". Its formal name was "British Methodist Episcopal Church", and its pulpit was supplied, usually, by preachers from Toronto; although, sometimes, they came from local city churches and the Salvation Army.

By 1934, the assessment department estimated there were only 13 members of the British Methodist Episcopal Church. As families moved away or moved to Memorial Baptist Church, it dwindled, being discontinued altogether in 1935.

Growing in strength and size, however, was the Church of England parish of St. James', founded by Canon William Bettridge, who came riding up from Woodstock to preach in the Shakespeare Hotel. In 1843, a resident minister arrived for the little congregation — Reverend William Hickey, who held his first services in the small, newly-built log school, before the frame church went up in 1849 north of the river. The second church, of rather forbidding red brick, was built in 1855. Meanwhile the Anglicans sought temporary quarters nearby in the court house.

When it came time to build the third and final church, founding families of the parish helped with church construction by hauling stones and lumber at a dollar a load. The new St. James' Church on McCulloch's Hill opened March 20, 1870, and it was a lovely one, of early decorated Gothic design. It was one of the churches that reflected the elegance of the era, and St. James' superbly showed the fine Anglican layout of deep chancel and altar placed in a sanctuary, which called for a divided choir. In time, this invited improved forms of organs. After the coronation of Queen Elizabeth II in Westminster Abbey, it was one of the Commonwealth churches fortunate to obtain a piece of the special blue carpet, enough for the chancel and pulpit.

The Home Memorial Church was an extension of the Anglican faith, in 1875, into the south end of town. It began as a Sunday school in the waiting room of the Grand Trunk Railway station, encouraged by the mother church, St. James', and it had, as one of the early teachers, the mayor of Stratford, Thomas Mayne Daly, as well as the mayor's wife and sister.

To house the Sunday school, St. James' put up a small frame building on land donated by Judge Lizars, and the church that later developed was named for his young son, "Homie" Lizars, who died when fifteen years old. It became, later, St. Paul's Anglican.

The Roman Catholic priests also came early to Little Thames, on horseback or on foot. First mass was celebrated in late autumn, 1832, by Rev. Father Dempsey from St. Thomas. The next June, he conferred the first sacraments in what would be Perth County — a marriage and a baptism. If there was no better means of transportation, the priests walked. Father J. B. Werreat, a dedicated German priest, came walking all the way from Waterloo in a bleak November, carrying his vestments on his back as he trudged toward Stratford and Goderich.

News of his coming spread like wildfire, and the settlers came hurrying from outlying homesteads to be there to see him next morning. When he finally set out for his next stop at Irishtown, half way to Goderich, a young lad of Little Thames volunteered to carry his vestments that far for him. By the time the good priest returned to Stratford, he was nearly worn out, his feet half frozen in their low shoes. Still he walked to other settlements, although it was by then December.

The first frame church — still unfinished, still without plaster — opened some time in the late 1830's or early '40's, and here the sacrament of confirmation was administered for the first time in 1843 by the Bishop of Toronto. The area that would become Perth County at that time was still in the Diocese of Toronto, and remained so until 1856, when the Diocese of London was formed. That same year brought Father P. J. Canney to Stratford as first resident priest.

The new and final church of St. Joseph's, with seating for 900, was opened November 8, 1868, by the Bishop of Sandwich. In 1878, the Loretto sisters from Toronto came as teachers, to the delight of the Catholic families. The party of lay sisters and choir nuns was met at the railway station in Berlin by the carriages of prominent Stratford families, and thus, in style, they came to establish a convent and separate school.

The parish divided after the turn of the century; a cornerstone was laid for the new Immaculate Conception Church, in 1905. One of its most beloved priests, Rt. Rev. William Tillman Corcoran, D.P., V.F., affectionately was known just as Father Corcoran, and he was the man largely responsible for the iris becoming the civic flower of Stratford.

Father Corcoran loved flowers and his garden was open to everybody, regardless of faith. He took joy in growing and hybridizing iris, giving them to people, donating some to horticultural societies. His "City of Stratford Iris" found its way into the Royal Botanical Gardens of London, England, the Spring Garden of the Royal Botanical Gardens in Hamilton, and many other places. Beside the river in Stratford, after he died, the Horticultural Society planted memorial iris gardens for the gentle Father Corcoran.

At year's end, 1846, a small group gathered at Rev. A. C. Geike's house and formed the "Congregation-church of Stratford-on-Avon". This little Congregational Church was new for Stratford, but old historically, with roots in 17th century England. Its emphasis was on close-knit fellowship and an immediate, direct line between believer and God. It reached America with the Pilgrim Fathers, but there continued little association with United States when the Congregational Church was established in Canada.

The Dalys and the Sharmans were among the early members and, in the early 1850's, the first Sunday School in Stratford was held here. The new church opened in January, 1874, a fine white brick building with stained glass windows in memory of the pioneers and an exquisite rose window, later bricked over. The belfry had four unusual open arches to enclose its bell.

By far the most colorful preacher the church ever had was Rev. George A. Mackenzie who, in two separate terms of office between 1898 and 1937, served his people for 25 years. For him, the church later was named "Mackenzie Memorial Gospel Church".

As a boy, Mackenzie had joined the Salvation Army in England. Noted for fiery oratory, as well as for generosity as a salvationist, he once spent seven days in jail for defying police orders. At 16, he was private secretary to William Bramwell Booth, son of William Booth, the Salvation Army's founder. Later, with another one of Booth's sons, he came to Canada as chief secretary of the Army. Eventually, he broke away and returned to England. His first stint as pastor in Stratford began in 1898.

The Stratford church was one of the very few Congregational churches that stayed out of church union in 1925, as most others throughout the country were swallowed up in the United Church of Canada.

A lovely statue of St. Joseph and the Child
stands before the Roman Catholic Church that bears the saint's name.

After the United Church was established, however, there was vigorous pirating of church members of all denominations, and groups began to leave. The Congregational membership was badly eroded, although it continued as an independent church until the 70's. Then, on February 1, 1975, an item appeared in the *Beacon Herald:*

> It was announced to the congregation of Mackenzie Memorial Gospel Church last Sunday that their church had been sold to Joseph L. Mandel of Stratford who plans to convert the century-old building into a restaurant.

Members found new homes in other congregations; but some could no longer bear even to walk past their own lost church, when it became the Church Restaurant.

Because of many German settlers in the area, the cadences of German prayer rolled through the market building every other Sunday after 1859, as the Lutheran Church established itself in Stratford. In that year, Zion Evangelical Church was formed with 18 charter members, and it was 1910 before — with some dissent — the church became bilingual and the first services were held in English.

Four years after it was established, the congregation finally had a first little wooden chapel, but it was 1908 before the church moved into its permanent home.

While the founding minister, Rev. J. A. Hengerer from Seebach's Hill, and those who followed him, were anxious to end Lutheran dependence on the States, from the time of the first organizational meeting in 1859 in Christian Ubelacker's home, the group cherished its German background. The first resident minister came from Pomerania, Germany, in 1876. From Germany, in 1910, came the black paraments (altar and pulpit hangings) to be used on Good Friday; also an altar bible bound in leather and sterling silver which was given to Zion by former Empress Augusta Victoria of Germany and the Grand Duchess Marie of Mecklenburg-Schiverin.

The bible was used whenever the service was in German, but, gradually, the old language fell into disuse until around 1956. Then, with more German-speaking people arriving, occasional services once again were held in the original tongue.

Two more Lutheran churches followed, as the German population increased. In 1911, St. Peter's Lutheran began with a small gathering in Heinbuck's Hall, and a first pastor commuted weekly by horse and buggy. By 1964, there was need for another congregation, and first services for the new St. Matthew Lutheran Church were in the auditorium of Avon Public School. It had its first church up two years later.

For the Baptists, a small house at the corner of Cobourg and Nile Streets served as the first gathering place. In 1857, shortly after young Thomas J. Birch arrived from Brantford, a dozen Baptists were also holding prayer meetings in their homes. Meetings next moved to the town hall, with students from the Baptist Literary Institute of Woodstock conducting services.

With Rev. R. McClelland as the first minister, on April 3, 1859, the "Regular Baptist Church of Stratford" was organized. They drew up a declaration of 18 articles of faith and a church covenant, including their affirmation of belief in baptism by immersion, a central feature of Baptist faith. They built a first frame church at the corner of Front and Brunswick Streets, and opened it on the first Sunday in May, 1861. The members then set aside 13 cents a week each to pay off the church debt.

In 1866, they took down the church, and rebuilt it on Ontario Street. This was the church raised without the tot of whisky! Later, when the building was outgrown, it served as a livery stable, then housed Stillman's Creamery, Silverwood's Dairy, and finally the Union Gas Company.

The Baptists expanded, with missions and with new congregations. The mother church finally became Ontario Street Baptist, and it marked its centennial in 1959 in style, with a three-day celebration and a large, mock birthday cake in the sanctuary, lit with 100 electric candles. This was a church much in tune with the times. After reviewing the constitution in 1963, it had it rewritten to suit modern needs. In 1966, it appointed the first two women to the Board of Deacons, six years before St. Andrew's had its first women elders.

April, 1970, a drug clinic was held in the church and letters went off to the Perth County Board of Education, Ontario's premier and other officials, recommending factual information on drugs be included in the public school curriculum. The church also held English classes for new Canadians whose first language was Chinese. A minister of Ontario Street Baptist, Rev. John B. McLaurin, became, in 1874, the first missionary in India supported by the Baptists. To preserve its past, the church filed historic old documents with the Archives and History files of McMaster University, Hamilton — among them the first mortgage and the land conveyance agreement.

The Methodists, who had received their saddlebag preachers and held their camp meetings under the trees, soon moved indoors. By 1855, Wesleyan Methodist Mission had outgrown its early frame church, and the new, red brick building was ready for services in November, 1856.

There had been neither organ nor choir in the first little frame church, but the year 1857 brought music to its successor — a humble tuning fork in the hands of Samuel Vivian, directing a first choir and demanding perfection. Musical discord from the singers brought a sudden *"Stop that!"* A few years later, the church had a melodeon and an organist, although that didn't prevent it from expelling at least one member for dancing!

More genteel outings were allowed, as announced in the paper in 1863:

> "PIC-NIC" — The Sabbath School Pic-Nic in connection with the Wesleyan Methodist Church in this town will be held today in Mr. McCulloch's Grove.

In 1858, the senior minister's budgeted salary and expenses were: salary, $240; table expenses, $200; horse keep, $60; horse shoeing, $8; wood, $50; conference expenses, $17; moving expenses, $11. Total: $586. But the mission's income was less than the budget forecast, and the minister was paid $419.87.

Later, when a janitor could not be afforded, two church members took turns lighting the fires and preparing the church for service each Sunday morning. If they were careful, one gallon of coal oil, costing 50¢, fed all the lamps for one week. The little church was eventually swallowed up in a new building, although the old red bricks were, it was said, used in building its successor.

Around 1865, the church debt, for which the congregation had once paid "the exceedingly Christian" sum of 20 percent interest, was nearly wiped out, but it was followed by a larger one, with the building and furnishing of the third church in the 1870's. With a two-manual pipe organ replacing the old melodeon, the sexton soon had a new duty: "blowing the organ" as well as cutting the year's cordwood.

Southside Methodist Church was established as a mission in 1876, and the mother church became "Central Methodist"; later, with church union, it became "Central United".

Methodist churches vanished in Stratford, as elsewhere in Canada, with church union in 1925. Methodists, most Congregationalists, and some — but not all — Presbyterians joined to become the United Church of Canada.

Both St. Andrew's and Knox Presbyterian Churches elected to stay out of union, although both ministers favored it, and both left. At St. Andrew's, after a vote of 532 to 232, the continuing Presbyterians not only asked — but insisted — that the minister resign immediately.

Meanwhile, the strong, new but homeless United Church, seeking a physical home, took a long look at the two exceedingly fine Presbyterian buildings and came to a natural conclusion. Surely, with so many people gone from the congregations, the Presbyterians would not need *both* church buildings? They took this request to the Ontario Church Property Commission.

The Auld Kirk, St. Andrew's, which previously had staved off a proposed takeover by Knox and the dissenters, now rose up in righteous wrath — and so did Knox, which had had to rebuild after a fire in 1913. They successfully protested the application at the hearing in the court house, Stratford, and "First United Church, Stratford" had to look elsewhere.

In the end, it joined Trinity and chose a new name, St. John's United. The amalgamation took place solemnly in the Majestic Theatre, and the new St. John's went home to the former Trinity Church building on Waterloo Street. In St. John's eventually, were the remnants of a number of early Methodist churches.

The year before union, an interdenominational Union Sunday School had been organized to meet needs in the eastern section of Stratford. Supported by Methodists, Presbyterians, and, later, by United churchmen, it began in Juliet School on Sunday, April 6, 1924, with five classes and 75 young people. Church services were added and, shortly after church union, it became a congregation of the United Church.

The superintendent of Central Sunday School, D. M. Wright, donated a large lot at the corner of Ontario Street and Parkview, for a new church building. From its location, close to an increasingly lovely Queen's Park, came its name after church union: Parkview United Church. The ousted minister of St. Andrew's was invited to conduct services.

After a disastrous fire on September 20, 1959, the Central United Church congregation moved temporarily to a unique house of worship: the Stratford Shakespearean Festival's theatre. People flocked to see a church in action, with the church choir on stage, flanked by a rented Hammond organ, and the minister using a spotlighted lectern, not yet discarded from the props for the summer production of *Othello*. The Sunday School held classes in the upper hallways and dressing rooms, and Cora Thistle's kindergarten squeezed into the powder room. There were after-church gatherings in the huge foyer — a fact that later influenced the building committee's preference in styles, when it came time to rebuild.

In two "off season" years, rarely were there fewer than 500 worshippers on Sunday, some of them city visitors seeing the Festival Theatre for the first time. During the summer Festival seasons, services moved around: to a movie theatre, to share joint services with St. John's, and to the city hall.

After much soul-searching, there came a reluctant decision that Central United Church, (previously Central Methodist, previously Wesleyan Methodist) could not be rebuilt on the old Erie Street site its continuing congregation had occupied for 112 years.

On a chilly June day in 1961, the retiring chairman of Perth Presbytery turned the first sod on a new site on Avondale Avenue, battling a whipping breeze that ruffled hair and threatened to carry away mortarboards. The new church they built did not, perhaps, tug at the heartstrings as the old one had done, but the inscription on its cornerstone recorded a long and honorable history:

CENTRAL UNITED CHURCH
FOUNDED 1845
ERECTED 1845 1855 1870
ENLARGED 1917
DAMAGED BY FIRE 1959
THIS BUILDING ERECTED 1962

Usually, the Protestant churches got along among themselves reasonably well, although it caused quite a stir in the early 1900's when the Presbyterian minister, Rev. Dr. Thompson, preached the sermon in St. James' Anglican Church when King Edward died!

There was room in Stratford for many religious beliefs. First gatherings of the Gospel Hall (Plymouth Brethren) began about 1865. The Reorganized Church of Jesus Christ of Latter Day Saints reached Stratford in 1889, and, for a first church, they bought a little house on Douro Street, and turned it around on its foundation because the back had a more church-like appearance. When it, in turn, was replaced by a larger building, the little Douro Street church was sold and once again became a private dwelling.

*Central Methodist Choir around 1900. It and others
contributed to the rich heritage of church music that was developing in Stratford.*

Just two years after the Salvation Army was established in Canada, in London, Ontario, the Stratford Corps was formed, August 1, 1884, with "Irish Annie" in charge. Three other women followed Captain Annie Maxwell as commanding officer in the 1880's, in one of the most beloved organizations in the world.

The "Sally Anns", with their bands, their Christmas kettles and their outdoor meetings, were highly visible — and a little strange, at first, in Stratford.

"I can never forget the opening in the city of Stratford by the Salvation Army," wrote Mrs. Jane Crocker, one of the first group of soldiers to be accepted. "I was there to hear what these peculiar people had to say as each of them gave their testimony. . . ."

Music and worship both were important, and, in the early 1960's, a Salvation Army diarist noted, with obvious approval, "New carpet on mercy seat kneeler." One musician of the Stratford Corps band, Martin Boundy, became the leader of the London (Ontario) Civic Symphony Orchestra.

A new century brought new religious communities. In the early 1900's, a small Jewish congregation met for prayers at the home of Benjamin Gerofsky, the start of Beth Israel Synagogue. For the high holidays, the Synagogue would rent one of the Stratford halls until, in the 50's, a building was obtained.

The Stratford congregation of Jehovah's Witnesses was established in 1901, with ten members. Bethel Pentecostal Tabernacle began with home worship services, or "cottage meetings", before its official establishment in April, 1907. In the 1920's, four students meeting informally began the First Church of Christ Scientist in Stratford; in 1927, it was granted group recognition and privileges by the Christian Science mother church in Boston. In 1922, came the Spiritualist Church, with 100 members. In 1947, Faith Bible Church was organized and, next year, was affiliated with the Associated Gospel Churches.

Stratford also was on the circuit of many outstanding evangelists, among them Rev. H. T. Crossley, who had a profound effect on the grandson of the first blacksmith — Henry Burton Sharman, a recent graduate in animal husbandry at the Ontario Agricultural College, Guelph. Harry moved west with his family in 1885. Later, he became a pioneering religious leader in his own right, and the man largely responsible for formation of the Student Christian Movement in Canada. One of his many books, "Jesus in the Records", became almost the standard handbook for religious teaching in both United States and Canada.

The musical heritage of a Stratford deep in the woods of the Huron Tract had, of necessity, small beginnings.

The Anglicans arrived, bringing traditions of church music with them. The Presbyterians came, thinking music was the work of the devil. As late as 1876, Rev. Mr. Wilkins resigned his charge at the Auld Kirk of St. Andrew's, because of what he called "lack of harmony" — mainly the reluctance of some in the congregation to accept the organ as a fit instrument for holy services. His successor found the same attitude not only regarding the organ but also in the matter of singing during the taking of collection. Later, it was in this same St. Andrew's that a future Sir Ernest MacMillan, conductor of the Toronto Symphony Orchestra, gave an organ recital — as a boy of 12.

Perth County's first choir was that of St. James' Anglican Church, and one of its voices was that of Robert McFarlane, law partner of Judge Lizars. The church also had a trio of flute, horn and clarinet which would rise to crescendo pitch and (said William Johnston in his *History of Perth County*) "so terrible was their melody that the wild fowl on Lake Victoria took flight in dismay, never resting their weary wings till a secluded spot was reached in the Ellice swamp."

The Wesleyan Methodists were ecstatic when they got a tuning fork in 1857, and could begin their first choir. They had a little melodeon, and, in the 1870's, they bought a pipe organ. They invited an outstanding Montreal organist to come for the opening services and, next evening, he gave a recital which drew a rave review from the *Beacon:*

> The music, of a very beautiful character, and probably above the comprehension of an average audience, afforded to lovers of classical music a treat such as never before has been listened to in Stratford!

Central Methodist also developed a fine choir and began 40 years of Good Friday sacred oratorios that became a musical event in Stratford.

Meanwhile, across town, the Congregationalists were forming a choir of their own in the 1870's, and a private citizen loaned them a small red melodeon as an aid to the voices.

When young Margaret Schoedel, aged 12, became organist for St. Peter's Lutheran Church when the church still used a pedal organ, she was the youngest organist in Ontario. When Zion built their new red brick church in 1908, the dedication service included a special children's service with choirs from New Hamburg and Berlin.

The city's lovely old churches nurtured music, encouraged fine young choristers, acquired several Casavant organs from the hand-crafted workshop of Casavant Frères in St. Hyacinthe, Quebec. St. Paul's Anglican bought their early-model Casavant organ for $7,000, and it operated at first with a water-powered pump which occasionally left the organ without wind in the midst of a hymn. In 1916, it got an electric motor. The church also became well known for its fine choir of boy choristers.

The Baptists bought their Casavant pipe organ in 1922, and dedicated it to a well-loved organist who died before he ever had a chance to play it.

St. John's United developed a Sunday School orchestra, which was a feature of the sessions, and the St. John's pupils, whistling the hymns, acquired a reputation of their own as "The Whistlers." St. John's became almost synonymous with music. In Music Festival competitions between 1944 and 1975, its choirs won 115 first awards.

Music was important — and all the choir leaders were resourceful. While waiting for its building to be raised, Parkview United — while still a Union Sunday School — moved its first Christmas concert into the assembly hall of the Normal School.

The Stratford churches had come a long, long way from tuning forks to Casavant organs!

17

The Absolute Realm of the School Trustees

I T WAS MID-SUMMER, 1882, when young "Cam" Mayberry arrived from Ingersoll in pursuit of a fast-disappearing job. He trudged the streets of Stratford, seeking out the school trustees one by one and presenting to them his case for being hired as the new classical master at the Stratford High School.

These were important men. They could make or break a new master. In early days, they laid down not only what a teacher could teach but where the teacher should live and how his or her private life should be conducted. In Stratford, these gentlemen presented almost a cross section of the town: among them, the harness maker who now was a letter carrier, the county magistrate, a former mayor, the minister of lofty St. James' Anglican Church, the builder who was erecting the new post office on Ontario Street.

Cam Mayberry's pursuit of the school trustees follows, in his own words . . .

☆   ☆   ☆   ☆

In Aug. 1882 I came from Ingersoll and made application for the position of classical master of the Stratford H.S.

This was my first experience in the (to me) humiliating ordeal of begging the favor of a school board. I came to Stratford shortly after graduation at the University of Toronto, to answer an advertisement in the *Globe* for a teacher of Latin, Greek, French and German. The ad asked for a personal application; hence my journey to this northern town. The first man for me to interview, of course, was the Secretary of the Board. This office was held by Mr. John Buchan, a fine old gentleman who lived in the cottage on Caledonia Street nearly opposite the north end of St. Vincent. My interview with Mr. Buchan was completely discouraging; he told me in as kindly a way as possible that the headmaster, Mr. Macgregor, had already made the selection.

"Mr. Robert Barron will be appointed tomorrow evening," he said.

However, I asked the names and addresses of the trustees, and, after partly recovering, I sallied forth like a soldier who has been badly wounded but not utterly undone.

Fortune took me next to Mr. Thomas Stoney. He kept a little harness shop in the rear of a store at the foot of Ontario Street. I told him how I had come leagues to please the Board who had asked for a personal application, only to find that the decision had already been made; and that the effort and expense on my part was of no account.

The old man looked me straight in the eye and said, "Young man, you go on and put in your application."

Is there any greater benefactor of the human race than the man who puts hope into the hopeless? Thomas Stoney had seen better days himself: he had been a man of importance in the town of Stratford and had been its mayor. He was born probably in the 20's and his knowledge of the pioneer days was prodigious. If Thomas Stoney were living, I could, with his help, write countless volumes of history — such volumes as would rejoice the hearts of even Dr. Silcox or Tom Orr! Now, Mr. Stoney was in somewhat straightened circumstances, but he had been a good stalwart Tory all his days and a grateful and generous party had given him his reward. He was made collector of letters in the city and for years he tramped the dusty streets of Stratford picking newspapers, postcards and dunning letters from the boxes that are nailed up against telegraph poles, and drawing the splendid remuneration of $200 a year.

As I journeyed between filling stations, I mentally computed my chances. At the first call on a trustee I figured I had made one possible vote out of the six very doubtful ones. But the urge was pressing and on I went.

At that time, the Police-magistracy of Stratford was in the hands of Mr. James O'Loane. He was one of the six who held my fate in their iron grasp. He was a big, powerful man with a wonderfully kind face and a beard that reminded me of the High Priests of Israel. How I admired his mighty physique and his easy manner! His courteous treatment of my recital roused fresh hope in me till he frankly told me he had promised his support to another applicant, Mr. Isaac Levan, a young teacher in St. Marys. He assured me with all the good-will of a true-born son of Erin that he would rush to my assistance in case he could not get his own man.

The score after the second skirmish: about one-and-a-half possible votes.

Mr. James Steet was next to be sought. I was unable to see this trustee but I learned, in my much traveling, that he would support, as was perfectly logical, the Headmaster's choice.

Prospects were not improving. I was next to interview the Rev. Mr. Patterson[1] on whom I expected it would be necessary to use my most deadly ammunition. Mr. Patterson was already an expert in the business of education: he had been at one time Superintendent of Town Schools.

I regret to record that the only ripple of distraction that disturbed my usually serene nerves occurred during my interview with that mild, cultured, scholarly, episcopalian divine. I was ushered into the parlor, I suppose, of the rectory and

[1]Rev. Canon Ephraim Patterson, rector of St. James' Church.

informed that Mr. Patterson would see me shortly. I had not long to wait. He was a tall, slender man, with striking and reverend aspect. At once, I told him that I was an applicant for the vacant position on the staff of the High School. I had scarcely finished this much of my story when, with undue abruptness, (as I thought) and a somewhat aloof attitude, he said, "I never give any promises!" I had just enough spirit left to feel hurt.

I reasoned thus:

(1) This gentleman is a member of the H. S. Board.

(2) The Board has asked for applications, with personal interviews.

(3) I have gone to considerable trouble and expense to meet the Board's wishes.

THEREFORE, I should not receive too curt a reception.

This is exactly how I felt and I told Mr. Patterson so flatly, and rose to leave. He insisted I continue. I apologized, and we conversed with the utmost harmony during the rest of the interview. He came to the door with me when I left and shook me warmly by the hand, wishing my every success in the great calling of a teacher.

He omitted to add that he hoped to see me again soon. I knew the worst. The Rector's vote was not for me.

The air had turned decidedly chilly when I left the rectory. It was hard for me to realize that we had been sweltering in the heat of the Dog Days. However, the chill was welcome, as I trudged around Stratford.

Mr. Robert Smith, chairman of the Board,[1] was unable to see me on account of illness and I moved on to the last member.

He lived away to the east of the G.T.R. Station. William Roberts was the father of Mr. Roberts who kept the secondhand store on Erie St., and brother of John Roberts, a popular alderman. William Roberts was the exact opposite of his mild brother John. He was big and bluff, with a voice of authority: he used strong language. He never called a spade a hoe or a club. He was a builder by profession and, at the time of my visit, was erecting the Post Office on Ontario St. My interview was exactly what such a meeting should be. He was friendly and business-like, asked many shrewd questions, but did not commit himself. He appeared to me as a trustee who was selecting his candidates on merit alone.

Nothing now remained but to await. I did not stay in Stratford the night of the meeting. But, early next morning, I sent this telegram to Mr. O'Loane as being the most convenient one to reach — "Who was appointed last night?" In a few minutes the answer came, "You were, come to see me when you come up."

In the final vote, Mr. O'Loane had transferred his support to myself, and, by this simple act, fixed my fate as a school master forever.

☆   ☆   ☆   ☆

The fate of the young schoolmaster from Ingersoll was, indeed, fixed, even though, almost immediately, a very tempting offer came to him from the Brantford High School.

[1] Also legal adviser to the City of Stratford; later Honorable Mr. Justice Robert Smith.

C. A. "Cam" Mayberry became Stratford's most durable master, with 36 years at Stratford's first high school.

Loyal to the Stratford trustees who had picked him over 11 others, he felt he must tell them first, and the man he went to see was William Roberts. The builder, hard at work at the post office site, heard him out, and minced no words.

"Young man, I stood strong for you when you were appointed and, to make a long story short, I won't agree to release you!"

Mayberry gulped, then grinned broadly. "You win — I stick!"

Stick he did, for 45 years, becoming principal of the Stratford Collegiate eight years later, and quickly winning the respect of the whole community.

The school trustees of 1882 were followed by others, just as awe-inspiring to new, incoming teachers, as the Stratford school system progressed from one log pioneer school to a city-wide network of schools appropriate for a 20th century city.

There had been no secondary education at all when Stratford was founded. Indeed, the settlers were lucky to have even the innkeeper's wife to teach rudimentary lessons, and these were supplemented in the homes by the small libraries many people had brought with them.

By 1834, J. J. E. Linton had opened a private school in his home, the first school in what would be Perth County; his wife, also, was teaching, out in the country. The first little schoolhouse was built in 1843, and the school bore the lengthy label, "No. 1, Union Section of Downie, Ellice, North Easthope and South Easthope" — not without reason! By taking in the neighboring rural lands of the four townships that came to a point in Stratford, the school area had sufficient population to support a public school; more to the point, as the trustees well knew, the common school grants were more easily obtained for schools designated as rural. John Linton may have taught briefly in the log school, before a first master was officially named for Stratford, and he was on the first school board that was set up in the little hamlet in 1843.

Stratford's first school, of logs, was built near the Presbyterians' first church. It was a little building, 20 feet by 30 feet, raised by the manual labor of almost the entire population of Stratford — about 50 souls. There were 33 pupils listed in the first report sent to the Department of Education. By 1845, there were 31, among them John Linton's own children.

A big box stove warmed the single room in winter. The flies droned in summer against the panes of the small windows, and the master sat enthroned throughout every season, with desk and chair on a platform that gave him a fine, unobstructed view of the students squirming on the long, hard benches below him. Outside, were beech nuts for the gathering on the river flats; hide and seek to be played in the sawmill property that was marvelously tangled with brush and strewn with logs.

Inside the schoolroom, there was the screech of pencils on slates, as the young scholars devised short cuts to solve the multiplication problems set by headmaster McGregor. Each had a good slate, strengthened at the corners with tin caps to "stand the racket" — which was considerable when an arithmetic competition was in progress. In the center of the room, the master placed a small table, and the first pupil to finish a problem would slap down his slate, face down. Others would follow, with a great din from the reinforced slates.

In this school, presided Stratford's first teacher, Alexander McGregor, appointed for the 1843-44 school year.

Alexander McGregor was a learned man who had come out from Scotland with his teaching certificate crisp and fresh in his pocket. His records were kept in a fine, slanting hand, and in his first classes labored the young of all the hamlet's leading men, the children of Linton, Daly, McCulloch and Orr.

The spirited young Woods lad, son of one of the first trustees, was often a sore trial to the master, as he also was to Andrew Monteith, the county treasurer, for the steps of the Monteith store were an irresistible launching pad for a boy's sleigh. Young J. P. Woods turned out all right, however, and became a County Judge.

The classroom quickly proved as confining to the schoolmaster as to his pupils. Briefly, Alexander McGregor left, to pit his wits against the business world. He found it unsuitable to his academic nature and was back within a year — to the unconcealed delight of the school trustees who had had the devil of a time replacing him.

The first teacher they hired, a Mr. McKee from the West Indies, died soon after he was engaged. The next, William Boorhead, was probably hired as a temporary replacement, until George Purday signed an agreement with the trustees "for three months of one year, if both parties are pleased with each other". He was a bit of a rascal; the trustees were *not* pleased, and thankfully reinstated McGregor on November 10, 1847, and raised his salary to 85 pounds — about $340 a year.

For this, he taught, with considerable dedication, all subjects on the curriculum: the three R's plus grammar, history, geography, and some basic Latin. Once, he bought a large Canadian school map out of his own money, when the school board would not.

First teacher hired for the common school was Alex McGregor from Scotland.

The headmaster was not, however a man to cross. It was his habit to return to his home over a footbridge across the Avon. At one end was a piece of square timber laid angle-wise over a ditch, and the right of passage went, as a matter of course, to the strongest. One day, a particularly loutish young man caught Mr. McGregor just there and did not offer to retreat. Scarcely missing a stride, the master dumped the fellow into the mud and continued on his way.

The boys at school knew him as a fair and understanding man. In winter, he ignored their sport of coasting from the schoolhouse down to the river. However, when the master chose not to stop the sport, a trustee and one-time chairman of the board, the respected Dr. John Hyde, tried to end it. The boys dubbed the worthy doctor "Old Mercury", a name that stuck, rather unfairly, for years afterwards.

Like all Canada's teachers in mid-century, schoolmaster McGregor did more than teach for his meagre salary. The brunt of *all* school business fell upon the teacher's shoulders, since he was also secretary of the board of trustees. He made up the accounts for school repairs, prepared the collection roll whereby each person was assessed for the education of his own children. One widow, unable to pay, applied for, and got, free tuition for her child — an early foreshadowing of the free schools.

In 1848, McGregor became involved in straightening out some irregularities in the deed for the school property, apparently a lengthy process still in the works after he retired. Eventually, the school trustees of the village of Stratford, for the sum of five shillings, finally acquired a satisfactory deed from the Canada Company for Lot 59, "containing by admeasurement, thirty-two perches of land". It was one of the documents that survived the city hall fire.

Stratford's first schoolmaster, for some reason, when he was well on in years left the city where he had spent his entire professional life. He died in Texas.

Until the late 1840's, education in the southern townships, as elsewhere in the area, remained oriented to the Canada Company stronghold on Lake Huron. From Goderich was supposed to come, at least once a year, the superintendent of education, John Bignall — a man big in name and big in belly. He stood six foot three and grandly headed his correspondence "Education Office, Goderich". Those who journeyed there to see him on school business rarely found Bignall — nor, for that matter, any "education office" either.

He did appear in Stratford from time to time, and observed a class or two at work. In 1848, this portly gentleman, faced with an upcoming public examination of his books, stuffed his pockets with $1,560 in $10 notes which he had removed from his department funds and fled, never to return.

In 1851, the school trustees reached a major milestone and hired Stratford's first female teacher, Miss Annie Watkins Coleman. Very shortly thereafter, she marched all the girl pupils down the street to a room that had been secured for them on Erie Street, leaving the little log school to the boys.

With talk of the new county of Perth on everyone's mind, and Stratford slated to be the county town, it seemed appropriate also to have a new schoolhouse, to accommodate the expanding classes. At the annual meeting of the school board in January 1852, high on the agenda was the matter of "the erection of a new schoolhouse to be built of brick". A public meeting followed, in the "long room" of the Union Hotel, presided over by the two champions of the new county, J. C. W. Daly, chairman, and J. J. E. Linton, recording secretary. Before long, an advertisement appeared in the newspaper:

FOR SALE,
cheap . . . the building
now used
as the male schoolhouse.

The historic old log "male school" was carted away and, in its place, in 1855, rose the new Central Common School, sporting a new fence and a fine old pump with a tin cup chained to it.

Meanwhile, there was crying need for more advanced education, beyond what the little log schoolhouse could give. It was a widespread need for, in all Canada West at the time, there were only 64 grammar schools (the forerunners of the high schools) to give this continuing education, and few of them were adequate, with 30% of the students unable to read and 24% unable to write. There was no set course of study, although there was one man who was setting about changing the entire school system: Dr. Egerton Ryerson, provincial Superintendent of Schools 1844-1876, and the architect of Ontario's school system.

For a while, in 1853, grammar school classes were held by Rev. Thomas Russell in the grand jury room of the court house. The arrangement was a stopgap only, and the quarters were small and dingy, as the county judges also were finding.

Council borrowed 6,000 pounds from the Municipal Loan Fund to build, among other things, its grammar school. The trustees met January 8, 1855, to appoint the new teacher for this first "High School". As it happened, there were two clergymen on the board — one an Anglican and one a Presbyterian — and, for their consideration, there were two well qualified applicants — one an Anglican, one a Presbyterian. The ministers were not much for turning the other cheek, and there was a bit of an ecclesiastical dust-up. However, when the dust settled, it was decided that the master for the new grammar school on Norman Street would be the Presbyterian, Charles Macgregor, B.A., graduate of the University of Toronto, at a salary of 150 pounds a year.

In the first written report of the school inspector to Egerton Ryerson, dated March, 1855, was an assessment of Macgregor's prospects: "The master is mild but firm, seldom using the rod. He is young and inexperienced but, as he is willing and winning in manner, he is likely to succeed." He succeeded well enough to still be there when young Cam Mayberry came to Stratford, also young, inexperienced and willing!

From the time of Perth's becoming a full county, the visit of the school inspector had been a matter of some consequence in the classrooms. More than once, the county inspector, journeying to Stratford in the 1850's, found a curious lack of animation in the junior classes — and three quarters of the children between the ages of five and 16 not in school. It was the beginning of the railway age, the time of the Gravel Road scandal — and one inspector noted that the parents were "not too concerned about absenteeism".

Other comments by the early inspectors in that era were often enlightening.

On Stratford society: "All classes (of society) are so busy getting rich that they have no time for visiting the schools or troubling much about them."

On discipline: "There is . . . want of proper discipline. This evil, I think, arises from a fashionable doctrine — an importation from the United States — that teachers should never on any occasion use the rod."

On the new grammar school: ". . . a large, lofty, brick building, 45' x 45', with a cupola over it, small hat rooms not completely furnished; one acre of ground, not fenced."

The *Beacon*, meanwhile, was urging the school contractor to "put on a little more steam" in laying the sidewalks on Mill and Norman Streets, in the vicinity of the fine new school.

The first Separate School was built in 1860, a little frame building facing the street in front of the early St. Joseph's church. Even after the new St. Joseph's was built in 1867-68, some classes were still held in the frame building. By 1879, the Belden Atlas noted the presence of two separate schools with a combined attendance of 200; one of them a large and handsome brick edifice, the other the Convent of the Ladies of Loretto, organized a year before.

The first grammar school was not far away, and it was not long before the husky grammar school boys and the separate school boys were joining forces in snowball fights, pelting the common school youngsters with snowballs that had been well and sadistically water-soaked and frozen the night before. In summer,

The class of 1899 at Central Public School

however, the younger students escaped, with the public school excursions to Port Dover, return fare 25¢ for children.

After the school act in 1871, the Protestant schools became "high schools" and "public schools". "Grammar school" and "common school" vanished from the vocabulary. But, even in the 1870's, the teachers still were not excessively paid, with $800 a year for a high school headmaster, $600 for a public school principal, with salaries rapidly sliding down to pittances below those ranks. There was scarcely a meeting of the joint board of trustees but a letter was read asking for an increase — sometimes "praying" for a raise. Usually the prayer went unanswered.

Upper and lower schools operated with their own sets of trustees at first. Occasionally, there were union boards of trustees, until the two boards permanently united in 1921, with the establishment of the Board of Education.

Meanwhile, the influx of families in 1871 for the railway's motive power shops made necessary the establishment of ward schools — and the arrival of yet more teachers.

By 1878, there was a brand new High School on St. Andrew Street, and, in 1879, Egerton Ryerson, now retired, made his last appearance on a public platform to officially open it. Headmaster Macgregor marched his teaching staff of three across the river to the new building on the hill and requests started coming to the board for permission to pasture cows on the old school grounds on Norman Street. The year Stratford became a city, 1885, there were 230 pupils on the roll of the newly designated Stratford Collegiate, a title it had earned by having a staff of more than four teachers, with all department heads qualified to prepare students for college.

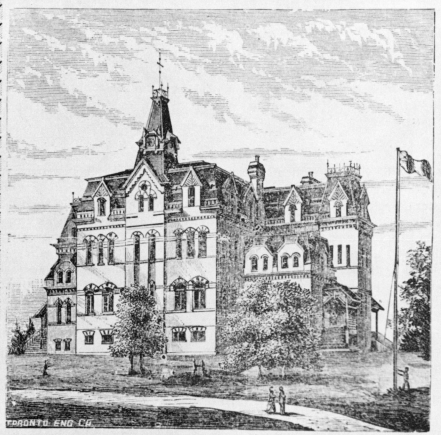

Stratford Advertiser Print

By then, the scope of its studies had tremendously increased as had its non-academic life, with military drill on the flats, a Literary Society going strong, and two large choral societies meeting after 4 p.m. twice a week. The School's Announcement for 1884 also noted the school was "One of the Dominion Metrological Stations" with instruments provided by the government and Headmaster William McBride as the observer.

With this increasingly complex collegiate system, Headmaster McBride ran afoul of one of the parents, lawyer John Idington, whose son attended the school. Idington questioned McBride's credentials and, in the following bitter exchange, accused the headmaster of "espionage, injustice, unmanliness, brutality, lying and chicanery". A judicial inquiry was held in 1886, and McBride was vindicated, while it was found that Idington, the man who would later become a Senator, had displayed "personal animus" in his attack.

By 1902, as the newspaper supplement, *Stratford Illustrated,* noted, the city had eight schools, 44 teachers and over 2,000 students. In addition to the collegiate and the separate school, there were six public schools: Avon, Falstaff, Romeo, Shakespeare, Hamlet and the original old Central Public School.

The publication commented with approval on an expansion of the school curriculum, and the imminent demise of corporal punishment as meted out by the hickory stick and the strap. "Greater stress is now laid upon the mental and moral discipline arising from the pupils' wisely directed self-activity," wrote the editor unctuously.

The *Illustrated* shed no tears either for the end of the "hardships" of pioneer schooling:

> There are no footsore and weary children now, buying knowledge with pain. Our public schools are scattered throughout the town and . . . our children coaxed onto and along the path of learning by sweet and devious ways undreamt of by the simple and direct dominie of long ago. . . .

On the Collegiate flats, the schoolmaster would put the school cadets through their drills, with as much precision as he could get. The fire bell would obligingly ring at 8:45 a.m. for the benefit of both teachers and scholars. Soon there was a need for the schooling of the teachers themselves.

The Normal School of Stratford, built in 1908, attracted students from miles around. In the prospectus, the claims were far from modest: "It would be true to say that this district, including Oxford, Perth, Huron and Bruce, has produced more scholars, professional men and teachers than any district in Canada. . . ."

And further: "Educationally, Stratford is in the forefront. It was the first place in the Province of its own initiative to establish a school of Manual Training and Domestic Science, and it was one of the pioneers in introducing the Kindergarten. These institutions could be utilized for Normal School purposes."

This they were, when the school was built! Stratford Normal School was one place where the lady teachers, along with the men, could wield hammer and saw and also coach the hockey teams. They also taught the fine arts and culture, and Mrs. Mayberry, the colorful and statuesque wife of the Collegiate's principal, was an art teacher *par excellence*. She drilled her class on basic rules, then launched them into the free form art she favored.

The educationalists were paternalistically concerned that the future young teachers should remain at home under the parental roof as long as possible, and made much of the city's rail accessibility when putting out their prospectus. Trains, they promised, arrived morning and evening, thus "making it convenient for the students in a large district to live at home, continuing their home associations and materially reducing the cost of their education."

The tidy little brochure pictured a handsome Stratford, including one view of "Ontario Street West, newly paved with asphalt block (100 feet wide)."

There were some memorable teachers in Stratford . . . Rose McQueen who taught English with love and excitement for 34 years and retired in 1946 . . . Margaret Addison, who went on to become Dean of Women at Victoria College, Toronto. In the 1920's, when the only man on the public school staff was usually the principal, Ida Easson coached hockey with outstanding results for Romeo School and May Patterson did the same at Falstaff, both of them alternately threatening and cajoling their young players, and cheering for them when they won.

At St. Joseph's separate school, where the Loretto Sisters taught the classes, two laymen took over the team coaching and the fund-raising for school teams. Soon after Immaculate Conception School opened in 1922, the pastor of the church was out coaching the boys and the "Immacs" were romping home with trophies.

There were changes: in 1905, the double seats in the collegiate giving way to single seats, to do away with copying . . . the start of the bus service for farm children coming in to the collegiate, in 1947 . . . the Normal School becoming the Stratford Teachers' College in 1953, and it in turn moving out to accommodate Conestoga College in the same foursquare brick building alongside the Festival Theatre.

School sports developed astonishingly. There were no organized leagues before 1890, and the first Athletic Association at the collegiate was formed in 1910. Its minutes soon traced some problems:

> March 20, 1912. "Motion to buy a basketball rescinded. Motion passed to buy a soccer ball, which will be suitable for both basketball and soccer."
>
> October 9, 1912. Among bills approved for payment: "Twenty cents to repair the football."
>
> April 30, 1919. "The meeting was called back five minutes after adjournment to consider buying a new football because it has just bust."

Schools increased in size and in numbers, and so did the enrolment. Northwestern Secondary School opened in 1963. The collegiate became Stratford Central Secondary School in 1962, with emphasis on courses in arts and science.

As for the young man who had gone trudging about the dusty streets of Stratford in 1882, C. A. Mayberry continued to pursue his dedicated calling, and eventually bought himself a rakish, mustard-yellow Studebaker which he drove about town with considerable flair. He also found time for whatever public affairs he deemed needed his attention. Among other things, he was on the committee that planned the opening ceremonies for the new city hall. The year 1922 found him pleading with the congregation of St. Andrew's Presbyterian Church to allow the Board of Education to continue using the Sunday School rooms to relieve over-crowding in the collegiate. The church evicted the classes all the same.

But the city named "Mayberry Place" for the schoolmaster. And the newspaper called him "the beloved citizen" when he died in the summer of 1938, when he was 82.

18

Sports-Conscious City

STRATFORD GREW UP with the tradition of home runs, the sizzle of skates on natural ice. It was known for its sports before it was famous for its Festival.

The first team sport played was probably cricket, brought out by the early settlers. Oldest Canadian sport, historically, was the Indian game, lacrosse. A game similar to soccer was played by the Chinese as early as 400 B. C., and Stratford played soccer, too.

But the sport that brought the city its widest reputation was hockey, with an impressive string of championships. Its most famous player was the man the hockey world called "the Canadian Comet", "the Hurtling Habitant", "the Mitchell Meteor" and "the Stratford Streak" — Howie Morenz.

Two Perth County communities claimed this player with the dazzling speed and style. Born in Mitchell, in 1902, he came to Stratford when he was 14, as his father moved the family to the railway town where he was to work. Howie himself became an apprentice machinist in the motive power shops.

His name became internationally known, yet once it nearly cost him a stunning series of goals.

The youngest son in a family of six children born to a clothing store clerk of German descent, the young Howie was a goalie for the hometown Mitchell Juveniles in 1915, but was soon switched to a forward to make full use of his phenomenal skating abilities.

On his arrival in Stratford, he joined the Midgets and, in a single game against Seaforth, he scored nine goals. A disgruntled Seaforth protested the game on a technicality, claiming the birth certificate produced was that of *William Francis* Morenz, not Howard. His father, however, testified that Howie's Christian name had been changed after the birth had been registered, and the Ontario Hockey Association took the elder Morenz' word for it. The protest was thrown out.

While here, he was a member of the junior OHA champions in 1921 and the intermediates in 1923; the Northern League juniors in 1918 and 1919 and the seniors in 1922. After he joined his father in the shops as an apprentice machinist, he played for the G.T.R. Apprentice Hockey League in 1922 and 1923 and, by the time he was 20, he was attracting notice from the professionals.

From then on, his star rose swiftly. In 1923, he signed a contract with the Montreal Canadiens, to the indignation of Stratford fans who resented his being lured away by commercial hockey. For the next 14 years, he remained in the NHL, 12 of those years with Montreal. The National Hockey League had been formed in 1917 and, when the Stratford Streak started, there were only four teams: the Ottawa Senators, Toronto St. Pats, Hamilton Tigers and Montreal Canadiens.

Both the Morenz stick-handling ability and the brilliant, often reckless, rushes down center ice drew fans wherever he played. The box office hummed. His annual salary went up to $7,000, tops in the league. But Howie Morenz had an obsession to win so strong it could keep him awake at night, if he felt himself responsible for a team's loss. It was a characteristic that would eventually help kill him.

In 14 NHL seasons, Morenz scored 291 goals and had 208 assists. He led the league in scoring in 1928 and 1931, and was on three Canadien Stanley Cup teams, 1924, 1930 and 1931. Three times he won the Hart Trophy, as the league's most valuable player, and in as many years was named an all-star.

The 32-year-old player was traded to the Chicago Black Hawks; he was traded again to the New York Rangers. In 1936, he returned to the Canadiens. Toward the end of January, 1937, in a game against Chicago, he was checked at full speed, slammed into the boards and broke his leg in five places.

Morenz, high strung, already worrying about the decline of his career, had earlier had a nervous breakdown. Now, in hospital for a broken leg, with time to brood and too many visitors, he died of a heart attack, on March 8, only 35 years of age.

On March 11, the body of Howie Morenz was returned to center ice at the Forum, to the spot where he had faced off so many times, while crowds of mourners filed past. Later, on Mount Royal, as the coffin was lowered, a large floral figure "7", the number he wore on his sweater, was placed upon the coffin, with the promise that that number would never again be worn by a Canadien player.

In Stratford, on March 9, prior to a scheduled junior game, a memorial service was held at the Stratford Arena. At center ice were arranged crossed hockey sticks and other paraphernalia, including sweaters in the colors of the Midgets and the Canadiens. A searchlight pierced the darkness and Walter "Butch" Kelterborn, a former Midget linemate, placed a floral wreath.

Stratford paid further tribute in 1961 when a new street, a continuation of Nile, passing in front of the arena, was named Morenz Drive. In 1975, his home town, Mitchell, dedicated a park to his memory, the Howie Morenz Memorial Gardens. He was elected posthumously to Canada's Hockey Hall of Fame. In

The "Stratford Streak",
Howie Morenz

1950, a Canadian Press poll voted him most outstanding player of the first half of the 20th century. Others in the family followed him, a son-in-law, Boom Boom Geoffrion, who also made the Hall of Fame, and a young grandson, Danny Geoffrion, coming up fast behind his immortal grandsire.

In the schools, young players dreamed of the Stanley Cup, hero-worshipped Howie Morenz, and hoped to make the junior ranks of hockey and have a chance at the big time in the professional league.

School hockey in Stratford was under way in 1898, when the Romeo "Stars" trounced the Central Public school team. After that, school hockey became the nursery for upcoming talent.

When J. H. "Mac" MacQueen arrived in 1924 as physical director of the Y.M.C.A. and, later, as director of physical education in the schools, he insisted the players help pay their own way, even if it was only five cents a game. Boys would be more interested if they had something at stake, he said.

"Mac" could gain the confidence of young people, and the Rotary club helped with funds to organize inter-school hockey, soccer, baseball and softball leagues. It also built an open air rink on the river. The Rotary-Y School Hockey League was formed, absorbing the old school league.

When, at the end of the 1926-7 season, the first annual school hockey league championship game was played at the arena, there were more than 1,000 spectators to see the "Immacs" defeat Shakespeare 4-3 in overtime. Under different names over the years, the operation has been known as the Rotary-Y School Hockey League since 1946.

By the 1975-6 season, there were 46 teams, in five divisions, with about 750 students chosen for ability, not for their home school. Sports-minded citizens, every year, continued to give freely of time and ability for coaching and managerial duties.

As for the hockey dreams of the youngsters, Rotary-Y hockey proved a stepping stone to the professional leagues for some: for Al Murray, former New York Americans; Jud and Norm McAtee, Henry Monteith, Nick Libett, Jim Uniac and Rick McCann, Detroit Red Wings; Bob Armstrong, Boston Bruins; Bob McCully, Montreal Canadiens; Phil McAtee, Springfield Indians; "Farmer" McFadden, Philadelphia, in the American Hockey League.

Rick McCann was a member of the Canadian National team at the World Hockey Championships in 1965-66, and Steve Monteith, who became a laywer in Stratford, played on the Canadian team in the 1968 Olympics Hockey series.

The minor hockey system in Stratford became outstanding, with all teams sponsored by local business firms and a regular schedule of play.

Organized hockey started in Stratford almost as soon as organized hockey in Ontario. The provincial governing body of amateur hockey, the Ontario Hockey Association, was formed on November 27, 1890; the Stratford Hockey Club on Friday, November 6, 1891.

Since then, Stratford teams have played in 26 OHA final series, winning 12: two senior, two intermediate, six junior, one junior "B" and one junior "C". In only one season, 1958-59, did the city fail to have an entry in the OHA.

Between 1917 and 1927, it had teams winning titles in the Northern Hockey League, later defunct. In the 1920's, in the C.N.R. Apprentice Hockey League, the Stratford squad skated off with four championships. Spasmodically, since 1895, there have been girls' hockey teams, and the city also collected one professional hockey league championship. Its citizens have been on the management side of the OHA.

In 1890, John A. Barron, the Lindsay lawyer, later a judge of Perth County, was chairman of the meeting in Toronto at which the OHA was formed, and became a vice president. An outstanding hockey player in his own right, Judge Barron, member of Parliament in 1889, played for the Rebels, a government house team believed to have been the first organized hockey team in the world. It was during this time that Lord Stanley, Canada's Governor General, became impressed with the game of hockey, and, when a league was formed, he donated a trophy, the famous and coveted Stanley Cup that is presented yearly to champions of the National Hockey League.

Other Stratford men had a hand in the operation of the OHA: J. A. Macfadden, vice-president 1894-95, and president for two succeeding seasons; J. S. Makins, vice-president 1905-06; Charles Farquharson, vice-president, 1910-12 and president 1913-14; William "Sky" Easson, vice-president 1919-22, and president 1924-26. Another Stratford man, F. W. Tiffin, was secretary in 1894-96, and the city's Reg Rankin coached the Olympic gold medal Canadian hockey team in 1924.

The organization meeting of the Stratford Hockey Club was held in the Albion

Hotel. Soon, two teams were entered in the OHA, the junior Midgets and the senior Indians, but, unfortunately, few records were kept. The sketchy newspaper reports had Peterborough eliminating the Midgets and Toronto-St. George the Indians in their first season.

There was no such thing as "imports" in early days. Everyone was a "homebrew" and provided his own equipment. The youngsters learned the game on open-air rinks, usually on the frozen Avon River. Sometimes young local players threw their weight around and, by 1894, a Waterloo newspaper remarked, following a Stratford victory over rival Berlin, that "rough play will, if not eliminated from hockey, eventually destroy the game entirely".

The early years of the 20th century produced some fine hockey talent. To usher in the new century, the Midgets won their first junior OHA championship in 1900, defeating Peterborough Colts. In the first game of the semi-final, Charlie Lightfoot, the only colored player in a Stratford uniform, scored the winning goal in 10 minutes overtime to give the Midgets a victory.

Stratford's greatest success in amateur hockey was the double header championship, junior and senior, won in 1907. The Midgets defeated Lindsay and the Indians won their championship over the 14th Regiment, Kingston. But there was also tragedy during that great 1907 season. In February, a train carrying Stratford team officials and supporters coming home from a Toronto game left the track at Guelph and rolled down the embankment. Former mayor John O'Donoghue and Charles R. Rankin, a team official, both were killed and about 50 other persons injured.

In 1921, the Stratford Hockey Club turned over control of that sport to the recently formed Stratford Amateur Athletic Association. After it folded in the mid-1930's, team sponsorship by industrial concerns, business firms and service clubs became important in keeping hockey alive in Stratford.

Stratford launched into professional hockey in the 1926-27 season with the Nationals, entered in the newly organized Canpro League. The team competed against Toronto, London, Kitchener, and Niagara Falls and lost to London in the finals. Next year, the league was expanded to include Detroit, Hamilton and Windsor, and Stratford took the championship by defeating Kitchener.

The Nationals withdrew from the league in 1928 when insufficient funds were available for operation. In the spring of 1929, their former manager brought the financially troubled Toronto team to Stratford to finish the season, but the public was not enthused.

Another move into professional hockey came in 1930-31, when Stratford entered a team in the Ontario Professional Hockey League with Galt, Guelph, Oshawa, Kitchener and Niagara Falls. The team made the play-offs, but, after that, professional hockey became a dead issue here.

The Northern League was organized in 1903, primarily to provide competition for hockey clubs in small centers, most of them in Perth, Huron, Grey, Middlesex and Oxford counties. Facing a player shortage during the First World War, this, in 1916, was the first organized hockey association to adopt six-man hockey, one year ahead of the OHA.

PERTH COUNTY ARCHIVES

There was a mammoth skating rink in the 19th century.

Stratford, a Western Ontario stronghold of OHA hockey, did not join the Northern Hockey League until the 1917 season. Then, meeting success in their first season by winning the junior championship and the London Free Press Trophy, the local club continued the affiliation. Repeating as junior champions in 1918 and 1919, Stratford became permanent holders of the Free Press Trophy.

In 1922, Stratford had two championship teams, the Indians winning the senior title, and the Midgets the junior crown. Three Stratford players, all juniors, Howie Morenz, Frank Carson and Borden Norfolk, played on both championship teams.

Long before the First World War, exhibition games were played between employee teams from railway centers in Ontario and Quebec. The Grand Trunk Railway Apprentice Hockey League was formed following the war, and Stratford joined the league in 1922; on this team, too, was the Stratford Streak, Howie Morenz. Stratford Apprentices won championships in 1922, 1923, 1927, 1929, 1953 and 1954, before the league disbanded.

Women invaded this primarily man's game as early as 1895, when two ladies' teams took to the ice in the old Waterloo Street rink. Victorian modesty dictated that no male be admitted to the rink and no names were even made available to hand down to posterity. However, a ladies' team flourished between 1917 and 1919, with exhibition games played with St. Marys, Clinton, Port Colborne and Welland. About 15 games were played, and the shy city lassies lost only one.

Space for sports was wherever you found it in the pioneer days — a clearing in the forest, or the ice of the Avon River.

Curling appeared in Stratford, to the amazement of some residents, on January 22, 1872, when rinks from St. Marys and Goderich Clubs played an exhibition game on the Avon River. Commenting on the event was the *Beacon:*

> The day was intensely cold and there were many frostbitten noses and ears. The uninitiated were greatly puzzled to account for so many people congregating on the river and dexterously sweeping with brooms portions of the ice which had previously been cleared of its snow, under the direction of Mr. (John) Corrie of the Queen's Arms Hotel.

However, it did not take the energetic villagers long to bring their athletics indoors. First covered rink was Ben Sleet's, a modest little structure built by the Kentucky slave close by a flax mill on the Avon River around 1864. It gave rise to the Victoria Skating Club.

For several years, beginning in 1875, various promoters leased from the government the militia drill shed, on Albert, Front and Brunswick Streets, turned it into a skating rink during the winter, and called it the Royal Rink. The property became the Optimist playground. Next, in 1886, the provincial government issued a charter to the Stratford Rink Company and Stratford had its third covered rink roughly on the site of Ben Sleet's old rink.

The large, all-frame structure, with a steeple rising over the front entrance, was designed, originally, for skating and curling, yet it later became the home of 18 championship hockey teams. Large, hinged windows ran along both sides, providing light and ventilation (and, for the youngsters, easy access without the formality of paying at the ticket office!) When snow was piled high on the Water Street side, it was simple to reach the slanted roof, open a window and climb onto one of the huge inside girders. The early caretaker could be a pretty understanding man.

A new artificial ice arena was constructed in 1924 near the river. The last hockey game was played in the old Waterloo Street rink March 13, 1924, and, eventually, the old rink was demolished. In 1942, the city took over Stratford's arena.

The Casino — the busy lady of the Avon — opened on Christmas Day 1905, intended solely as a curling rink. After 1933, it took on many other obligations — as a summer dance hall with Flanagan's orchestra engaged for the season and participants charged a nickel a dance . . . as a home for the lawn bowlers . . . for hockey . . . a skating rink . . . a roller skating arena. For years, it was one of the most popular dance halls in Western Ontario. The curlers finally moved out; the Stratford Badminton and Social Club moved in. Finally, taken over by the Stratford Shakespearean Festival Foundation, it became the Festival Exhibition Hall and, later, the Third Stage.

When the steel building was erected in 1935 at the fairgrounds, it was designed for agricultural use, but it, too, soon became multi-purpose. It served as a skating, hockey and curling rink, a rifle range, a construction company headquarters and it also housed the trade fair, sponsored by the Junior Chamber of Commerce.

The National Stadium was a project of the depression of the '30's. Plans had started with the reorganization of the Canadian National Recreation Association in 1930. Money came from the men themselves, from pay roll contributions by everybody from supervisors down to laborers in the motive power shops, in the roundhouse, stores, freight, bridge, building, and the running trades. They bought property from the city and they built their stadium, which they opened with celebrations and celebrities.

Howie Morenz was there on opening day, July 2, 1934, and received a standing ovation. Syl Apps, who later became captain of the Toronto Maple Leafs, won the pole vault after an exciting duel with Bob Stoddart, Goderich.

Long distance runner Billy Reynolds from Galt took the 12-mile road race and the Beacon Herald Trophy. In a series of brilliant performances, George Shaw, a prominent Stratford athlete, was the most consistent race winner of the day, with three firsts and two seconds. In the evening, they listened to a seven-band tattoo, watched military manoeuvres by a platoon from the Perth Regiment and topped it all off with fireworks.

A few days later, the Nationals, Stratford's Senior Inter-county League baseball team, played their first game at the new grounds, having opened the season at Dufferin Park, their home base for several years. The same day, Mr. Borthwick, the C.N.R. employee who had won the contest to name the stadium, christened it with a bottle of coca-cola.

After the final shut-down of the shops in 1964, the recreation club turned the stadium and grounds back to the city, which made the city recreation department responsible for its operation. After a lapse of 14 years, senior baseball again became the main attraction at the stadium, under a brand new flood-lighting system.

Cricket was the favorite game of early settlers in the Huron Tract, the very *British* game of cricket, developed by the villagers of Hambledon in 1760 and played on the Broadhalfpenny Downs. It was the first organized sport of the little settlement of Stratford, but no sport had to fight harder for survival.

First documented reports of cricket games go back over 120 years, to the games played between Stratford and St. Marys. They were played regularly during the early 1850's, but reporting the results was seldom considered important. One game, played August 15, 1857, and won by Stratford by 20 runs, provoked the St. Marys *Argus* into complaining that the Stratford club was made up of "crack" players from Paris, Clinton, London and Woodstock. One of the umpires for the game was Stratford landowner W. F. McCulloch.

Early teams would travel by horse and wagon, before the Grand Trunk Railway reached Stratford, and frequently the visiting players, following after-game celebrations, would head the horses for home and trust them to get there.

By 1863, cricket was well established throughout the district, with Perth Sheriff Robert Moderwell president of the Stratford club, and club membership fee set at $3.00. The game became part of the athletic program in schools, with exchange games between Stratford Grammar School and the Victoria Club of Mitchell. County cricket also was under way.

The arrival of the railway made inter-town and inter-village rivalry possible and it developed quickly among Stratford, Seaforth, Mitchell, Clinton, Listowel, Haysville and St. Marys. The Stratford railroaders formed a cricket club of their own. Western Ontario got its first taste of international cricket in 1872 with two days of matches with a touring English team.

Cricket, the "gentleman's game", did not always live up to its name, however. A "friendly" match between Stratford and St. Marys in 1875 came to an abrupt end with a fight between the rival players.

Meanwhile, by 1877, lacrosse was coming up strong, and baseball also was monopolizing the Agricultural grounds. The cricketers were having trouble, and the club was reorganized in 1894. That season was a good one with 10 games won out of 14. However, Chatham also handed Stratford its worst defeat on record, 301 to 175. The game slumped after that, until the formation of the Western Ontario Cricket League in 1907; Stratford joined in 1912. Ten years later, following an umpire's decision, it pulled out and boycotted the league's annual dinner. The club disbanded in 1957 and, after that, the game was kept alive mainly by members of the Stratford Shakespearean Festival company.

During its existence, the Stratford Cricket Club took only two championships: the South Western Ontario Cricket League titles in 1933 and 1936.

If cricket declined, however, lacrosse gained favor. Called by the Huron Indians *baggataway,* the game, far older than Confederation, was originated by the 17th century Hurons around the Georgian Bay, and described by the French Jesuit fathers in their journals. The French, who adopted it, called it *la crosse* because the head of the stick used in the game resembled a bishop's crosier or cross. It became, unofficially, Canada's national game.

Stratford's first lacrosse club on record was formed on June 4, 1869. The first game was played the following August, when Stratford defeated Mitchell three games to none. A game in those days was decided on the first goal scored. Later the same season, New Hamburg defeated Stratford three straight.

Within a few years, lacrosse was the major summer sport in town. For the first night game, torchlights were held by spectators, to illuminate the playing field at the fair grounds and, while the lighting effect was not entirely successful, the novelty of playing at night was cheered by the crowd.

Dominion Day, 1877, an exhibition match, held before 7,000 spectators, was between two Indian teams from the Six Nations and Onondaga Indian reserves, with the latter winning three straight games in less than 20 minutes playing time.

When the Western Ontario Lacrosse League was organized in 1887, the Stratford Royals joined. The 1889 final, at Seaforth, was a fight-filled affair. As the Stratford *Herald* described it: "While Stratford players were dressing, a bullet smashed a window in the dressing room. The club president was threatened with a knife, spectators threw stones, smashing windows in the special train and injuring a brakeman." One Stratford player, injured during play, had to remain in Seaforth hospital when the team went home.

COURTESY STRATFORD CENTRAL SECONDARY SCHOOL

*The Girls' Basketball Team at
Stratford Collegiate Institute, 1921, with coach Allan Neilson. It won
permanent possession of the John Whyte Trophy.*

Toward the end of the 19th century, interest in lacrosse began to lag, particularly in senior ranks. Stratford won its last lacrosse championship in 1904.

Box lacrosse was introduced, but, after indoor lacrosse folded, there was little interest until 1971, when the Stratford Minor Lacrosse Association was organized. This was a thoroughly remarkable young group.

It was started by a high school teacher and a policeman — "Ted" Blowes of Northwestern Secondary School, and Sergeant "Bud" Graper of the Stratford Force. Two former senior lacrosse players volunteered as coaches. They borrowed lacrosse sticks from Northwestern students, and begged other equipment from the minor hockey and baseball organizations.

The year after being organized, they had over 300 boys playing in novice, pee wee, bantam and midget teams, and they were already winning divisional championships. Among the championship teams that romped home were: West Central novice "B", 1972; OMLA novice "D", Hendrickson-Tandem, 1973; OMLA bantam "D", Perth Concrete, 1973; OMLA novice "C", and Hendrickson-Tandem, 1976.

Thanks to the efforts of Stratford-born Alexander T. "Dad" Turnbull, Stratford might claim some credit in British Columbia, where the New Westminster Salmon Bellies won the Dominion senior championship and the Minto cup 15 times in 20 years, between 1890 and 1910. A printer by trade, Turnbull had gone west to become warden of the provincial prison in New Westminster. While there, he first coached the Salmon Bellies in 1898, and spurred the team to the world championship in 1900.

The first Stratford Baseball Club was organized in 1867. After that, teams went under many names: Avons, Maple Leafs, Bards, Nationals and, finally, the Hillers, named for the sponsor. Most successful were the Nationals, sponsored by the Stratford Canadian National Recreation Association during the '30's and '40's, who won 10 inter-county championships and three provincial titles.

It was a gloveless game at first, and players often suffered twisted finger joints trying to catch the ball with their bare hands. With rail connections still incomplete, the games away from home took much organization. However, you could hire a bus and driver for a two days' trip to carry a baseball team to Woodstock and Ingersoll for $7 if the driver paid his own expenses and paid for his horses' feed, or $5 if the club paid all expenses. The Maple Leaf ball team, frequently making the trip in the '70's, had hard work to raise the price.

A club was formed in 1873 by employees of the Grand Trunk Railway and named the Kerfloppers. In their first game, the Kerfloppers defeated St. Marys, 42-38. By 1875, baseball had increased in popularity. Clubs were formed in surrounding communities, both urban and rural, and the young farmers of North Easthope and Shakespeare village were organizing teams and playing exhibition games.

Semi-professional baseball came to Stratford in 1896, when a local committee sponsored an entry in the Canadian League, composed of teams from London, Guelph, Hamilton, St. Thomas and Chatham. The Stratford Baseball Club was formed with over 200 stockholders, and more than $1,000 was raised by public subscription to meet costs of the new team, the Stratford Poets. The Poets, unfortunately, folded before the season's end, and interest sagged.

When the semi-professional Western Ontario Baseball League, dubbed the "Wobbly" League, was formed in 1913, Stratford entered a team, the "Classics", and won the league championship. However, the city's participation in the league ended with the outbreak of World War I.

The Inter-County Baseball Association was formed in 1919, with teams from Guelph, Galt, Kitchener and Stratford, and it had a famous player on the Guelph team: Lester B. Pearson, who later became Prime Minister of Canada. Later, other area players would win fame. One city minor league player made it to "bigtime" and another had a tryout. Right-handed pitcher Larry Landreth signed with the Montreal Expos of the National League in 1973. In 1976, Denis Flanagan, a catcher, had a tryout with the Pittsburgh Pirates. Several imports, who once wore Stratford uniforms, went to work in major leagues, playing for Rochester, Toledo, the New York Yankees, San Francisco Giants, and Los Angeles Dodgers.

At home, the list of major championships won by Stratford teams was impressive.

Minor baseball dates back to 1878, and a four-team league for 14-year old boys: Mitchell Clippers, St. Marys, Stratford Actives and Stratford Mutuals. For the junior championship of Perth County, the Mutuals defeated Mitchell in the finals.

The first school baseball league was formed in 1921, and the boys from Hamlet School became the first champions. In 1944, a city juvenile league was formed; next year, in inter-city competition, it won the Inter-County Association juvenile championship and later reached the OBA finals before bowing out to Toronto Greenwoods.

With no organized league in 1946, the game was kept alive by gallant little teams calling themselves Riversides, Cardinals and Southends. They lacked uniforms, had little playing equipment, and often had to substitute "baseballs" made of bound rags.

In 1948, the Stratford Minor Baseball Association was formed, and it, too, was a determined group when faced with financial problems. An appeal to city council brought a $250 grant, with which they bought equipment, each team being allotted two bats and two balls at the start of the season. Sugar bags were bought from local bakeries for 10 cents each, bleached and made into uniforms for the bantam league teams. All told, Mrs. Jimmy Spence made 100 of them. With stag parties and car raffles, the association, by 1954, had raised enough funds to have pee wee, bantam, midget and juvenile leagues in operation.

Next year came the first Inter-County championship, under the Association, and it got world-wide exposure. While the National Broadcasting Company was filming the Shakespearean Festival for its "Wide Wide World" series, a minor game was in progress on the flats below the theatre, and it also was "shot". The tyke division developed well, the outgrowth of a Saturday morning pee wee house league, and players began to be selected for a Stratford "all-star" team.

There were a number of provincial championships won by various teams. Particularly gratifying was the provincial title, 1975-tyke, Flexsteel over Burlington. For Flexsteel, it had been a remarkable season. Out of 52 games played, the team won 46, lost five, tied one and accumulated 682 runs.

In 1977, the Stratford pee wee team won three championships: Inter-county, Provincial and Dominion.

When soccer gained popularity in the 1890's, a picked Canadian team was sent overseas to play in Great Britain, and on it was William Buckingham of Stratford. Another Stratford player, Ernie Clark, was a member of six championship WFA teams between 1909-15. Sam Cox, a former Glasgow Ranger of the Scottish first division, held 10 "home" International cups for Scotland besides others for games against European countries.

On two occasions, games had to be called off at the collegiate flats for odd reasons: once someone cut up the goal posts for firewood, and, next, the posts were removed to the Agricultural grounds and not returned.

In Canada's Centennial Year, 1967, the Hugh Clopton High School Soccer Team of 14 and 15 year olds arrived from Stratford-upon-Avon, on invitation and at their own expense, to take part in the city's celebrations. They were billeted in city homes for five summer weeks, while they played 12 games, and won 11 of them.

Basketball once produced championship teams, but eventually became mainly the sport of the two high schools.

Stratford individuals were busy taking off flab and getting in shape in the 1880's, and cycling was the "in" thing with the community leaders.

When James Scarff, a former mayor of Woodstock, rode his homemade bicycle, or velocipede, over the dirt and slush-filled roads into Stratford in March, 1869, he opened a new chapter in the town's vehicular and athletic life.

A pioneer in cycling, he staged a demonstration in front of the town hall that amazed those who gathered to watch it, and inspired the prominent Stratford physician, Dr. W. N. Robertson, to rush out and buy one of his own to use when making his professional calls. Scarff's visit interested a local industrialist, and, shortly, an item appeared in the *Beacon:*

> Stratford, like neighboring towns and cities, will soon have a sensation of its own — a velocipede. Mr. Michael F. Goodwin of Lynne and John C. Goodwin, a mechanical genius and enterprising citizen, are busily employed in the manufacture of one of those modern aids to locomotion. The new machine is not the trumpery 'fixing' some people imagine, but a substantially constructed conveyance made of the best malleable iron. D. M. White, of the Albion Hotel, is said to have been the first owner of a Stratford-made velocipede.

Before long, John and Alex Miller, makers of buggies, wagons, carriages and farm equipment, opened a velocipede riding and instruction school. On Victoria Day, 1869, velocipede races were included in the holiday sports program, and cycling in Stratford was away to the races!

In cityhood year, Stratford's first bicycling club had 12 members, who would go wheeling off on trips to St. Marys, Tavistock, New Hamburg, and Woodstock, when the dirt roads permitted. Observed the *Beacon:* "The bicycle travels faster than a horse and costs less to feed!"

The members were nattily attired. On one occasion, wearing blue and silver uniforms, the club won first prize for "making the most handsome appearance" at a Woodstock meet.

A bicycle in that era was of the "penny-farthing" type, with a high, five to six foot front wheel and a smaller 18-inch rear. They were difficult to handle and were as tricky as skittish horses when ridden over stones on the roads.

In the early 1890's, the Stratford club was affiliated with the Century Road Club of Canada, whose rules required a member to cycle 100 miles between sunrise and sunset within 12 hours. Three city riders won their badges, Dr. Robertson, Dr. R. McFarlane and J. H. Kenner, on a course that took them to Seaforth, Bayfield, Goderich and back home. Another record-setting rider, Tom McCarthy, once won a horse, but, sensibly traded it for a pair of shoes.

Bicycle dealers, repair shops, and the Emperor Cycle Works all flourished in Stratford, and, as the citizens became healthier and healthier, they also became increasingly enthusiastic. A plan to have Perth County Council build a cinder track to the Little Lakes east of the city was turned down, although council did experiment with bicycle paths on the shoulders of some county roads.

At one time, around the turn of the century, citizens were asked to save their cinders and ashes for pickup by the energetic cyclists. The Perth Cinder Path Association was considering a number of routes, including one to Mitchell. City Council was asked to build a path from the old post office on Ontario Street to the city limits on the west because, as one banker noted, "the main roads in the city, in most seasons of the year, are in worse shape than roads in the country".

Groups took over sections between the town line and Mitchell. Farmers en route loaned their teams to help lay the cinders, ashes and gravel — the equivalent of a $3 to $5 donation to the cyclists. It was a very good try, but the ambitious Stratford-to-Mitchell bicycle path never was completed.

Stratfordites continued to enter cycling competitions. One of them, Fred

McCarthy, made it to the 1908 Olympic Games in London, England, although he failed to bring home a medal. Another, Frank "Jigger" Brown, competed with the Canadian Olympic team in Stockholm, Sweden, in 1912.

After the mid-30's, bicycling was relegated to a transportation and recreation pastime. The Stratford Cycle Club lay dormant until 1972, when two brothers, Richard and Robert Popp, from Schweinfurt, West Germany, helped revive it. Richard was a member of the West German cycling team in the 1952 Olympics, Robert a former German junior sprint champion.

There was a fish and game club in the 1880's, and the Avon Fish Protection Society kept the river stocked with pike and trout. Tennis started around 1886, with public courts set up on the collegiate flats the next year. The first recorded match in lawn bowling — for men only — was in 1891, played on greens behind the fire hall. The women, in 1920, formed a club of their own.

Cribbage, they say, was conceived in the cafeteria of the Kroehler Company plant in 1948, and eventually grew into an eight-team league, one of the largest leagues, per capita, of any city in the province.

The figure skating club originated in the 1930's. There was a hero's welcome for skater Donald McPherson in 1963 when he returned home in possession of skating's "triple crown": the Canadian men's title at Edmonton, the North American honors at Vancouver, and the world's championship at Cortina, Italy. He was the youngest citizen ever to be given the city's "golden key" and, later, he was admitted to the Canadian Amateur Hall of Fame.

The Stratford Bicycle Club, in 1886.

Softball was growing in popularity in the 1920's. The first known team was started by the 28th Battalion Machine Gun Corps back from overseas. Kroehler Manufacturing, enthusiastic from the start, sponsored both men's and women's teams, many of which took provincial honors. Company employees in their spare time built "Kroehler Field" on property leased adjacent to Queen's Park and it was the heart of softball until 1963 when the property owners took the property back for needed expansion.

A nice tribute to those who lost their lives in World War II was the Memorial Softball League formed in 1946 by the Stratford Kroehlers and teams from Dundas, Kitchener, Brantford and Woodstock as charter members.

Sportsman of the year award dinners, which became a tradition of Stratford, grew out of a 1953 gathering at the country club to honor Lorne "Chick" Appel of the *Beacon Herald* on his 25th anniversary as a sports writer. The following year, city council provided a trophy, and other trophies were put up for the top boy and girl athletes. Since 1971, these have been the Glen 'Skin' Irwin Memorial Trophy and the Optimist Trophy. In 1976, Mrs. Shirley Barth was the first woman to win the Sportsman of the Year award . . . becoming, perhaps, the city's first sports*person*.

As always, the sports-conscious city was breaking new trails.

19

Housekeeping for a City

LITTLE THAMES SOLVED its civic housekeeping with marvelous simplicity: river water to douse the accidental fires, a constable to chase a strayed cow, and a half-moon outhouse as soon as it could be built.

The town pump provided drinking water before Stratford sank its artesian wells. The garbage was tossed out the door, and every man was his own light company, with lanterns and candles.

With the complexity of cityhood, came the necessity of providing a city's services. To the pioneers' basic trio of civic needs — fire protection, law and order, and disposal of wastes — would be added many more, providing for heat and light, street maintenance, health; finally recreation requirements and parks.

The first job to tackle, in a community surrounded by an inflammable forest, was fire and the containment of it.

The first recorded fire fighting organization was formed in 1852, the members all volunteers, who brought their own buckets and ladders to the fires. Water was drawn from the nearby private wells, and a dilapidated tin trumpet, once used by Captain Laing to give orders to his men, became a prized possession of a later fire hall.

The village, in 1854, ordered a hand fire engine from Montreal, an awkward-looking affair, named the "Victoria", which had to be pulled by the volunteers. A number of reservoirs were constructed in town: one near the town pumps on Downie Street, others near the town hall, as well as at the juncture of Erie and Ontario Streets, at the corner of West Gore and Downie, and on Huron street, near St. Vincent. Meanwhile, they still used water from the river and the wells, and, if a building any distance from a water supply caught fire, a bucket brigade formed. Such operations were the forerunners of the network of water mains and fire hydrants to come with the formation of the Stratford Water Supply Company in 1883, and its successor, the Water Works Commission.

In 1856, volunteers fashioned a hook and ladder wagon to complement the fire engine. However, one thing lacking among the early volunteer companies was permanency, and sometimes the community lacked organized fire protection altogether. Finally Reeve Orr called a ratepayers' meeting and, as a result, in the fall of 1858, the Victoria Fire Company No. 1 was formed.

The officers were elected from members of the company, and each volunteer fireman was given a $3 civic grant to help buy necessary apparel.

Judging by a minute book of the company, 1858 to 1878, the captain ran a pretty tight ship, considering he was dealing with volunteers. It was obligatory to attend regular meetings, fire drills, and, of course, fires. Four misses, without a valid reason, meant dismissal. However, proof of presence at a place of worship was considered an excuse for non-attendance. Participation in parades on the Queen's Birthday, May 24, was compulsory; absentees were fined 50 cents. On occasion, members were expelled from the force for disorderly and ungentlemanly conduct. One laddie was fined 20 cents for using disrespectful language to his commanding officer; another 20 cents for smoking on duty.

For ceremonial occasions, such as out of town tournaments, the firemen of Stratford dressed to the teeth. Enginemen sported red jackets with blue facings and hosemen wore blue jackets with red facing. To distinguish them, captains carried brass trumpets; both the captains and the lieutenants wore red sashes, with the names of their respective offices printed on their caps. The hosemen got to wear blue collars if they paid for them. However, fines were imposed for wearing new hats or jackets to actual fires and, if a volunteer didn't turn in his uniform when he left the force, he was charged $8.

Fire-fighting was a dangerous trade. Chief Hugh Durkin, only 41, died in the Knox Church fire of 1913, and thought of his job to the last, as he turned to his second in command: "Take care of things for me, Lou!" Police Chief John A. McCarthy Jr. and one of his constables died in the same fire.

They did their jobs thoroughly and swiftly, sometimes while work went on around them. When fire broke out in the hospital in 1946, not a patient had to be moved and, a few feet away, three doctors continued with a major abdominal operation.

But there was fun, too. Balls, concerts and picnics came at regular intervals. Disposition of the cash donations given in return for services well rendered sometimes enlivened the meetings. Once, when a $5 donation was in dispute, one faction thought it should go into the general fund, another thought it would be nice to spend the money on ice cream as a treat after practice. The ice cream won.

After functioning nobly for seven years, the Victoria Company disbanded in 1865 "when there was no encouragement for them to continue". Company funds, amounting to $21.36, were distributed among the members, and, in the following years, other organizations looked after fire protection.

During the Fenian raids in 1866, a detachment of soldiers stationed at the town hall took over fire fighting duties. After the railway shops were built in the 1870's, employees formed their own brigade but often fought fires elsewhere in town. There was also a short-lived salvage corps formed of concerned businessmen. Carrying axes, chemicals and tarpaulins, they would cope with smoke and water damage when business places caught fire. The merchants and householders soon were phoning the fire department every time a new roof was going on, to borrow the fire tarpaulin so that they could protect their own buildings from the rain.

When the troops left, the Victoria Company was reorganized. Later, a new hook and ladder company was started to serve a growing town. However, it took years, and a bad fire in 1875, to get a steam fire engine. During the night of February 5, a police constable discovered the blaze in the Waverley block on the south side of Ontario Street. It involved 20 business places and apartments and a loss of $90,000. A ''steamer'' had to be borrowed from London. Shortly, Stratford bought one of its own from Seneca, New York, and called it the Avon. They then renamed the company ''Avon'' also.

By 1879, the firemen, sick and tired of hauling the heavy engine themselves, bought a team of horses, without telling the town fathers. When the councilors heard of it, they were outraged. The town, they said, was getting altogether too up-to-date. That team was sold, but the town later bought another, stipulating that it be used by both the fire department and the board of works. This clearly couldn't work out. Next, a $2 prize was offered to the owner of the first team to reach the fire hall when the fire bell sounded. The confusion as teamsters rushed to the hall was colossal. Ultimately, the fire department got its own horses and, while it was fully motorized by 1923, one team was kept at the hall until 1926 — just in case.

At first, the 19th century fire fighting equipment was housed in the market building, and the horses were quartered at a nearby livery stable. It was 1897 before the firemen had their fire hall on Waterloo Street. In the two-storey red brick structure, was space for the fire apparatus and four horses on the ground floor; a chief's office, various facilities, and a hayloft on the second floor. Council would not pay for a bathtub for the live-in firemen — considering it a luxury — and the firemen had to take their baths at home until a tub was installed in 1905. There was a tower on the northeast corner for drying hose and for a fire bell. When a new market building was erected behind the hall in 1912, they used part of it to house the ambulance, operated by the firemen.

There was a double fascination about that early hall that no modern one ever had: the fire bell and the horses.

For years, the bell did more than sound alarms. The city council of 1897 was asked by the school boards ''to arrange for the ringing of the fire bell at 8:45 a.m. for the benefit of teachers and scholars''. The same year, council passed a curfew law requiring children 14 and under to be off the streets by 9:00 p.m., with the fire bell sounding the warning for this too.

The curfew law puzzled some youngsters. It was customary to stage something of a ceremony at the fire hall when the curfew bell rang. The horses would come charging from their automatically-opened stall doors, trot to the front of the hall and stand under their harness, which was suspended from the ceiling. When the

*The Grand Trunk Railway's fire brigade was an
impressive outfit in the 1890's, and the city benefited
from its presence in town.*

harness was dropped and securely fastened, the drivers and other firemen took up their stations on the vehicles but didn't leave the hall. It was a good show that drew countless children as well as adults. The horses got lumps of sugar, peppermints and humbugs, handed out by the visitors. But *how* could a child be off the street at 9 p.m. and still be at the fire hall feeding the horses?

The horses were as highly trained as other members of the crew. One team, when no longer needed at the fire hall, was turned over to the city works department. Hitched to a garbage wagon, their treats and their dignity lost, the horses gave the driver and his co-workers some bad times whenever the fire bell rang, and the garbage wagon would sometimes go charging off to a fire.

The old and much beloved fire hall eventually outlived its usefulness. Stratford got a new one in 1968. Instead of the old bucket brigade, there were two pumpers, one able to pump at a rate of 850 gallons of water a minute, the other at over 1,000 gallons.

Where once the caretaker of the old town hall had received the fire calls, sounded the bell and kept up steam in the fire engine, now in the new hall alarms were battery-powered, the alarm system housed in an oak cabinet built by the city's first full-time chief, English-born Robert Myers, who had joined the force in 1873 as a volunteer. The street fire boxes eventually disappeared, and the citizens missed them for the fire bell used to spell out the numbers of the boxes when calls came in. When the service was discontinued, it cut a link with the past. The people no longer knew where the fire was. They still cared about the firemen. Sometimes, when a crew was still on standby at a smouldering building, the Salvation Army would order coffee sent over from a local restaurant.

Policing the village also was an important concern for early Stratford. In 1855, Stratford hired George Larkworthy, its first paid policeman, as it assumed the added responsibilities of its status. Previously, policing had been the responsibility of the county and, probably, the early settler, John A. McCarthy Sr., had been the first policeman to keep the peace in Little Thames, as well as throughout the townships.

To the lot of a succession of early constables fell a variety of chores, all spelled out by a zealous young council: attending police court and council meetings; seeing that the town hall caretaker tended to the fires, coal oil lamps and candles; protecting the property of the fledgling corporation from waste and destruction; rounding up stray livestock; serving as truant officer; supervising ditching, road and sidewalk construction, and acting as health and sanitary inspector. Later, he could also be liquor licence inspector.

One policeman was himself taken to court and convicted of the extortion of two dollars over a bag of apples. Local citizen J. M. Andrew bought the apples from a man named Miles, of Burford, who failed to deliver them. Mr. Andrew complained to Constable Thomas Lunn who, the next time the apple seller appeared in town, accosted him. Miles protested he couldn't deliver the apples because he couldn't find the Andrew home, but was willing to do so now. On delivery, he was told to settle with the constable, who demanded a fee of $2. Miles indignantly refused to pay. The constable threatened to impound both him and his team. Miles charged him with extortion. A jury found the constable guilty, but sentence was deferred and Lunn was allowed bail. He promptly decamped to the United States, and John A. McCarthy Sr., took his place on the one-man Stratford police force.

When the population grew to around 5,000, the strength of the police force was doubled to two men, and McCarthy became Stratford's first police chief. The man who succeeded him was William "Fixey" Wilson, a likeable Irishman, who had a large following of friends.

When, one day in 1883, "Fixey" was fired by council for allegedly withholding fees payable to the municipality, his friends, 500 strong, petitioned to have him reinstated. Council refused. The friends were indignant. They held a dinner in his honor in the Windsor Hotel and he was presented with a medal and $200 cash.

Wilson brought a $5,000 libel suit against Mayor Roberts. While the court upheld Roberts' course of action, it awarded the fired chief $1 and costs.

Meanwhile, the town, in its turn, hauled its police chief into court over the money Wilson supposedly owed Stratford. Lawyer John Idington, acting for the defence, dug out some British statutes from the reign of King George III to show that the town had no power to make the arrangements it did with "Fixey" Wilson, and that the chief constable had been entitled to keep the fees he collected in that office. The court agreed and Wilson went home free.

Parking wasn't a municipal problem when most hotels provided stabling for horses and ample yard space for the vehicles they drew. After the establishment of the Saturday open-air market on the square behind city hall, however, there came real traffic jams. An extra constable was added to the three-man force on Saturdays to cope with the situation.

With the "horseless carriage" came an increasing need for safety measures, traffic and crowd control, parking spaces and communications. It was normal for drivers to leave their rigs and hold their horses by their heads until a car passed. Considerate motorists stopped on the approach of any horse-drawn vehicle.

Short on manpower, the force in 1917 got four traffic standards, popularly known as "silent policemen", to place at busy intersections. The first overhead traffic lights came in 1941 at Ontario and Waterloo Streets.

Until 1921, the police force bicycled about its business, occasionally hiring livery rigs or taxicabs. It got its first automobile in 1921, a used McLaughlin Buick, bought for $1,500. The department experimented with different makes of cars. In 1924, a Ford in use was "too slow for the faster cars used by lawbreakers". In 1975, the department had six cruisers and a motorcycle, as well as radio equipment, walkie-talkies, and a computerized data bank to feed it instant information from anywhere in the country.

Parking meters — the "iron bandits", "little steel thieves" or "mechanical policemen" — appeared in Stratford in 1948, 300 strong, on downtown streets.

Stratford town council protested loudly to the legislature when the Ontario Municipal Act was amended in 1873, making it compulsory for municipalities to have police magistrates. Before that, court cases had been heard by the head of the municipality, in his capacity as justice of the peace, and he had received a percentage of fines for his services. He also had a number of stand-in justices, none of them anxious to lose such easy pickings. The civic protest got nowhere.

The town's first magistrate was James O'Loane, a man large in stature, bearded and bespectacled, whose appearance lent dignity to the bench. At his death, the *Beacon* praised his qualities: "He was big in his ideas, broad in his spirit and liberal in his judgments."

The police department, as it expanded, came under two jurisdictions, the municipal council and a board of police commissioners, set up in 1900 over strong objections from council. At the turn of the century, the Ontario government decreed that all cities should have a board of police commissioners, composed of the mayor, the county judge and the police magistrate. However, when the municipality had incorporated as a city in 1885, there had been a clause in the charter giving Stratford the right to organize and maintain a police force, without commissioners, until the population reached 15,000. The population in 1900 was 10,758. Council wanted to maintain its existing arrangement, but the legislature rejected council's petition, and County Judge

John A. Barron told the mayor that refusal to form a commission might be illegal. The commission was formed. Its first bylaw ran to 98 clauses, most of them to do with regulating horse-drawn traffic. And, at city hall, successive councils tried to cope with the new body.

The council of 1900 was principally concerned with control of the police spending budget. Some succeeding councils tried, without success, to have the statutes changed. The 1918 council sought power to revise commission estimates and the council of 1920 endorsed the city of Peterborough's resolution to have the commission an elective body, composed of the mayor and two other persons.

As relations became increasingly strained between the various groups concerned with police matters, the Stratford Police Association actually took Stratford City Council to court for failing to comply with the terms of the arbitration award handed down in August, 1971. By then, negotiations had broken down over a pension clause in that year's police contract.

With the organization of the Stratford Police Association in 1949, relations between the Board of Police Commissioners and the force had changed dramatically, and now the men had the right to negotiate directly with the commission through their elected representatives. *Theoretically,* the commission paid all salaries and signed the contracts with the police, but the commission was funded by the city and it was council that had to provide the money. The supplement pensions would cost the city an estimated $264,000, over 20 years.

Council was shocked. The bylaw was blocked. All sides rushed to consult their lawyers. Eventually, council had to pass the necessary bylaw, but grudgingly, very grudgingly. For a time, it had looked as if the mayor and some of the aldermen were ready to go to jail, rather than give the policemen more money.

Among its housekeeping chores, Stratford had another continuing matter: de-scenting the city.

For years, the outdoor privies, complete with Eaton's catalogues, were the most popular spots in town, and some were works of art. There was a backyard that had one covered with hops which were given to Devlin's brewery to flavor beer (a fact Devlin's never passed on to its customers). As plumbing moved indoors, half the fun went out of Hallowe'en. There were fewer outdoor toilets to tip over.

Stratford began laying sewer pipes in 1885, the year it became a city. In 1895 the ratepayers approved $30,000 for sewers. By 1898, eight miles of pipe had been laid, but, with no disposal plants, the contents all went, directly or indirectly, into the Avon River. By 1977, this would increase to approximately 76 miles of sanitary sewers.

The early council had little information to go on at the start, and didn't want the taxpayers' money to follow the sewage down the river through the system that wouldn't work. They queried cities in Canada, United States and England. When council finally turned to the Ontario Board of Health, thinking that the Province should have something to offer, it was told shortly that every municipality would have to figure out a sewage system for itself.

Meanwhile, neighboring Downie Township began complaining to the province

*Around the turn of the century, Waddell's Livery
on Albert Street provided single and double teams and hacks for
weddings, parties and funerals. The first bylaw of the new Police
Commission dealt with licencing such stables, requiring that driving
speeds be "at least six miles an hour" and that the washing of horses
and carriages be done elsewhere than on the streets of Stratford.*

over the pollution of the Avon downstream from the city. Downie said querulously it had been complaining since 1886 and how about a treatment plant? Unable to wait for civic action, a Downie farmer, W. E. Bean, instructed the surrogate court clerk to issue writs against the Corporation of the City of Stratford, the Collegiate Institute Board, E. T. Dufton, woollen mill operator, George McLagan, furniture manufacturer, and William Gordon, hotel owner, for polluting the river. On further thought, he added the names of Perth County Council, F. J. Scholz, tanner, and Alex. Smith, factory owner.

The city had no defence. The stream was polluted and the city was responsible for it.

Mr. Bean's charges against the county and school board were upheld later in court. An injunction was granted restraining the city from polluting the river, and Mr. Bean was granted nominal damages of $1 against each, with costs. The city finally got its sewage plant west of the Old Grove in full operation by June, 1900. Although upgraded from time to time, the original plant continued to fall short of requirements.

When the Ontario Water Resources Commission came into being, designed to aid municipalities in constructing or upgrading water pollution control plants, Stratford consulted with them. With government help in financing construction of a new plant, Stratford became the first municipality in the province to initiate such a program under the Commission.

The land needed for the plant was in neighboring Downie township. But, this time, Downie Council welcomed Stratford and anything that would improve the quality of the water coursing through the township. The property eventually came within the city's new limits. On March 24, 1958, the main sewage was flowing to the new plant for primary treatment; 91 days later, the complete plant was operating. It was described as the most modern and most effective type of plant in existence.

Council was, therefore, mortified when it was told by the Water Resources Commission in 1964 that the Avon River was again contaminated by sewage "above safe levels" below the plant, and had to install expensive chlorination equipment.

Although the plant was considered one of the best in North America, with the emerging water so clear one could safely drink it, there remained problems. One was the volume of storm water entering the plant during heavy rainfalls and the resultant problem of overflow. The Ministry of the Environment in 1976 imposed a limit of growth on the subdivisions; however, Stratford was still within the allowable capacity. The Commission eventually bought the Stratford plant and the city, in turn, began renting its services.

As with the sewage, the community's garbage became a continuing headache. The disposal of it was not much of a problem in the fledgling years, when the domestic animals, the cows, pigs and chickens, roamed at will through the streets and took care of most of the table leftovers. With preserving done in reuseable glass containers, tin cans and plastics were not threatening the environment.

As the population increased, however, and livestock was banned from running at large, city council became more conscious of the need for change. A bylaw was passed making it illegal ''to throw rubbish, filth, animal carcasses or refuse into the streets or Avon River''. Nothing was said about backyards, where the refuse was usually pitched out the back door to rot. Pressured by the board of health, which was strongly supported by the newspapers, council passed an ordinance in 1904 making such practice illegal.

Dumps were opened in various parts of the town, but people simply left their refuse; there were no attendants and little supervision. They were unsanitary and the health officer received numerous complaints. One enterprising citizen launched a private collection system of his own in 1911, but it proved unprofitable. Two others propositioned council to start a system under contract, but their offers were rejected. Some butchers accommodated their customers and carted the slops off to slaughter houses. Finally, the board of health started crowding council for an incinerator system and, knowing council's spending habits, proposed that it be built on the isolation hospital grounds ''so that the hospital caretaker could man it''.

It was 1914 before a 10-year, $11,500 debenture was issued for the construction of an incinerator, not on the hospital grounds but — over the objections of the board of trade and a number of businessmen in the area — on St. Patrick Street, in the heart of the city. There it would save on haulage costs.

Six horse-drawn garbage wagons were bought. The city barn on George Street, which eventually was replaced by the administration of justice building, was enlarged for the horses. A new building was erected to house the wagons and machinery. Ashes and garbage were separated, the ashes to be used as the base for city roads and to cover the refuse at the dump.

By 1950, the incinerator was nearing the point of exhaustion. It was abandoned and all refuse went to the dump. It no longer was economical to use horses, because of the long hauls.

The final dump, in the Romeo Street-Lorne Avenue area, was used simply as a dump until 1956, with the material piled sky high and smoking. Stench from the fires floated over the city until it was on the verge of being called Stratford the Stinky, and Stratford had to do something about it. A tractor finally was bought, and a landfill operation began.

By 1968, needing more space, council optioned a 15-acre tract of land in South Easthope Township, a move that brought howls of protest from the farmers of the neighborhood and from township council. Under new Ontario government legislation, the city could have gone to the Ontario Municipal Board, but the city had previously been on good terms with the township and wanted this situation to continue. Still, it was desperately in need of additional dumping space. The township, appreciating Stratford's predicament, eventually agreed to let it use land immediately east of its existing dump. The land, about 46 acres, was bought in 1969 for $55,000.

Stratford's civic responsibilities began with a bucket brigade and a lone policeman chasing a cow. The machinery of running the city became a thousand times more complex as time went on; the housekeeping services far removed from those of the nineteenth century. Street lights came on in 1864, at first coal oil, then gas; finally, electric lights lit up downtown for the first time in 1888, although there would still be lamplighters going their rounds for some time on the outskirts. At the turn of the century, Niagara power was still in the future.

The "Gas House" began operations in 1875, owned by the two-year-old Stratford Gas Company, and operated until closed down by the Public Utility Commission in 1953. Stratford had its first water commission in 1904, its first light and heat commission in 1910; from their amalgamation, in 1915, came the P.U.C. which also took over the gas works in 1928.

The Hydro Shop, which opened in the Public Utility Building in 1921, was the city's first publicly-owned retail store; by 1937, in the depth of the depression, it was doing a $40,000 business.

The first artesian well, nucleus of a group to supply all Stratford, was sunk in 1905 — thanks to an earlier, lucky discovery of the underground water supply by entrepreneurs who had been drilling for gas and oil. The Board of Park Management was set up. A Recreation Commission, essentially a modern concept, came later and, unlike most communities, Stratford kept it separate from Parks. The civic budget climbed. The first parking meters went in. Keeping the city running smoothly had become an enormous operation, headquartered at City Hall.

As for the earliest pioneer services, they became almost unrecognizeable: the fire fighters without the horses, the underground miles of sewers, disposing of wastes; the police constables using computers and data banks in the fight against crime.

*A slashing sleet storm in December, 1959, clogged Stratford roads,
forcing telephone and hydro crews to work around the clock, and
sending reporters out to scribble down details with numbed fingers. It
was not the first such storm in the snow belt.*

20

Scoops, Scribes and Scholars

ONE NOVEMBER DAY IN 1928, Police Chief Joseph Bradley called the newsroom of the *Beacon Herald* and told a young reporter it might be to his advantage to be around the Woolworth corner at Downie and Brunswick Streets, across from the Bank of Montreal, in the early evening. Plans for a bank robbery, simmering away for weeks, were about to come to a head.

The plot for the Great Bank Heist in Stratford had been dreamed up some time before, in a prison in Detroit. There, serving time and with little to occupy his facile mind, Freman J. Talbot mulled over information he had received that the Stratford bank carried over $50,000 in cash at times. He devised a scheme. When he was released, Talbot headed for the Classic City and tried to enlist a likely bank employee as accomplice. However, Walter Martus told his manager who, in turn, informed the chief of police.

With the supposedly willing employee as bait, a trap was set for Talbot, who was to be provided with a bank key and the vault's combination. November 7 was set as the date. Up cruised Talbot, with a partner at the wheel of the getaway car. Walter Martus, the bank employee, emerged on schedule to give Talbot the key to the bank and the combination to the vault.

But the whole Stratford police force was concentrated in the center core, and Chief Bradley and staff descended on the surprised Talbot and accomplice, and hustled them off. Thanks to the chief's thoughtful tip, reporter Tom Dolan was able to write a fine eyewitness account of the whole episode. Talbot was convicted and given three more years in jail for conspiracy to rob. The alert reporter, numerous scoops later, became managing editor of his paper.

The Stratford papers, often many of them publishing simultaneously, covered everything from the coming of the railways in the 1850's, to the birth of the city in 1885, from Festival opening nights to the visit of Princess Juliana and Prince Bernhard to the Netherlands troops at Juliana Barracks in World War II. In wartime, the reporters would see telegrams from the war office at the telegraph office and would have to follow them up — hoping they did not arrive at a home before the gentle ladies of the Patriotic Association had visited first and broken the bad news.

Once, King Edward VIII, when Prince of Wales, was persuaded to take a night off, accompanied by a considerate reporter in cahoots with the prince's own aide-de-camp. They all went partying to a dance hall in London, before returning to official Stratford duties of that 1919 visit.

But meat and drink to a reporter was the "scoop", the fast-breaking story of fire, murder, mayhem or theft. The driver of the local fire hose wagon would slow down if he saw a reporter legging it after him, and the newsman would climb on. Or the chief of police might take a moment to place a quick phone call. Many a reporter sat on a hot tip until the appropriate time to break the story.

The press usually got along fine with the citizens too, although a reporter had to watch his news sources. Dr. Joseph Dunsmore Monteith — Member of Parliament and one-time mayor of Stratford — was not always to be relied upon.

This worthy gentleman once told a *Herald* reporter about seeing patients with a rare new disease: lint on the lungs.

"Lint on the lungs!" exclaimed the reporter, whipping out a notebook. "How do they get that?"

"By chewing the rag," said the medico, and quietly walked away.

As early as 1879, the Belden Atlas had begun calling the Stratford press "extraordinary for a place of its size". And extraordinary it certainly was, almost from the beginning.

The first newspaper, a weekly, was published in Stratford on September 14, 1849, and the coming of the press was, perhaps, the single most important event of the settlement's first half-century. Now, there would be vastly improved communication.

News gathering had begun with gossip around the town pump, augmented from time to time by the services of a town crier. Outside events were reported by the circuit riders, or travelers bumping along on the Huron Road; the news was often stale. It was October, 1837, and months after the event, before Stratford learned of the accession of Queen Victoria to the throne. When the market building went up, a bulletin board on the wall was used for public notices and scribbled announcements of coming events; later, wooden telephone and street light poles served the same purpose. Passed from hand to hand and read avidly were the outside newspapers from Guelph or York, relaying news brought across on the ships, along with reports of the doings of the Canadian parliament.

With the first issue of the weekly *Perth County News*, started by Thomas Rowland, Stratford had the beginnings of its press five years before it was incorporated as a village.

By the time the first daily newspapers hit the streets of Stratford in 1887, *seven* weeklies had been started: the *Perth County News;* the *Examiner;* the *Beacon;* the *Herald; Der Canadische Kolonist; Der Perth Volksfreund;* and the *Stratford Times.* In 1892, there was an eighth weekly paper, the *Sun.* Not all survived, but, on occasion, there were up to five of them at a time, serving up the news, simultaneously, every week, to a population still under 9,000.

There were, besides, two quasi-news publications which appeared from time to time in the 1850's, the *Challenger,* a prohibition paper, and the *Voice of the Bondsman,* which tackled the slavery issue; both were produced periodically by the energetic schoolmaster, J. J. E. Linton.

Two others papers making short appearances in the latter part of the 19th century were the *Orange Gazette,* aimed at its special readership, and the *Advertiser,* published by Pratt and Tracy until it went out of existence in 1890. Toward the end of the century, the city's women got together and produced one issue of a Christmas magazine, *Green Holly,* which led to the establishment of the House of Refuge to shelter the old people "in the Indian summer of life".

The first newspaper, the *Perth County News,* was short lived. In 1852, came the *Examiner,* sole paper in town for two years, and the political voice of Thomas Mayne Daly, who printed it in partnership with Edwin Dent. It survived for ten years in spite of formidable opposition bent on breaking its monopoly.

Its very vocal rival was the *Beacon.* The first issue of the *"Stratford Beacon and Perth County General Intelligencer"* rolled off the press December 29, 1854, all set to tear into Daly's shortcomings at every opportunity. It was a strong beginning for a paper that would, a century and a quarter later, claim title to being the oldest continuous publication in the city.

The founder of the *Beacon* was Peter Eby, son of the Mennonite Bishop, and owner of the recently established *Berlin (Kitchener) Telegraph.* As his editor, Eby put in the industrious William Mowat who, before long, owned the paper. Scottish-born Mowat, an apprentice printer, had gained editorial experience on the staff of the Toronto *Globe,* as well as a keen interest in financial matters. Eventually, he sold out to devote more time to his other venture, a private banking business, which later went broke.

The third owner of the *Beacon* was as colorful a newspaperman as ever passed through Stratford. He was William Buckingham. This Englishman came to the publisher's chair at the *Beacon* when still only 31, and fresh from founding the first newspaper in Northwest British America, the *Nor'Wester,* at Fort Garry. His first subscriber in the Red River country had been an Indian chief with six wives; and for his first issue reams of paper had frozen fast in a solid block. Among his "stringers" (news correspondents) had been Thomas D'Arcy McGee, who would be a Father of Confederation.

Buckingham at one time also published the Norfolk *Reformer.* When he bought the *Beacon* in 1863, he was, actually, returning to the town in which he had first settled on his arrival from England. He ran the *Beacon* with efficiency and with deep concern for local issues, hammering away at such things as the need for a Stratford General Hospital (which he saw built in 1891), declaring himself for civic progress and opposed to tollgates on the Northern Gravel Road. He published for ten years, then sold the *Beacon* when he was appointed private secretary to Prime Minister Alexander Mackenzie. Later, he returned to Stratford to live, but not to publish.

About the time Buckingham bought the *Beacon,* there was a fourth entry into the Stratford media scene. The *County of Perth Electioneering Monitor* appeared June 2, 1863, and, as its name implied, it was a party organ and a Conservative mouthpiece. A family monopoly, published by Samuel Vivian and Company and employing the publisher's three nephews and a brother-in-law, it changed its name almost immediately, softening the blatant indication of purpose and becoming the *Perth Herald.*

Stratford early had its bilingual press, with two German newspapers. The first German weekly, *Der Canadische Kolonist,* a Reform paper, was founded in 1863 by Jacon Teuscher and his partner, J. H. Schmidt; it continued under the latter until 1906. The second, the Conservative *Der Perth Volksfreund,* published in Stratford only one year, 1878, then moved to Listowel. By that time, the *Kolonist,* drawing its readers not only from Stratford but also from throughout the county, had reached a circulation of 1,300. The vigorous young *Herald,* in the same era, was reaching 1,700 readers and was already snapping at the coattails of the *Beacon,* with its circulation a bit over 2,000.

The *Herald* had had a number of owners as it sought to surpass its rivals in Stratford. One of its early publishers was Henry T. Butler, the man who began the town's seventh paper, the *Stratford Times,* one fine June day in 1874.

Henry Butler was a fearless newspaper man, widely liked, but with an aptitude for news coverage and editorializing that frequently landed him in trouble — a situation that bothered him little, since it usually yielded choice news items with which to lure away readers from his entrenched rivals. Inevitably, he made enemies.

In April, 1884, his *Times* printing plant was entered by night and left a shambles. Every font of type was dumped on the floor, virtually every piece of equipment ruined. While many people disagreed with Butler politically and editorially, old antagonists rallied round him in his misfortune. On a recommendation following a public meeting, town council offered a $500 reward for information leading to the conviction of the culprits, and Butler added another $200 himself. A committee solicited subscriptions and the stricken editor soon was able to buy new stock. Two men were charged, but, when a number of important witnesses conveniently left town, they were discharged.

In the mid-1880's, the *Herald* came into the hands of its final owners, the Dingmans, who would establish virtually a newspaper dynasty in Stratford.

Absalom Dingman, head of the family, had earlier bought the weekly *Strathroy Dispatch,* and, in its offices and pressroom, the three young sons gained solid knowledge of their trade. One of them, William S., became co-publisher of the *Dispatch.* He expanded into the new-fledged city of Stratford in 1886, before long bringing in his two brothers, Charles and Lewis Hervey. It was a management of trained newspapermen, well-equipped to take on the forceful, existing press.

When the *Herald* came under the editorial control of the Dingmans, it naturally became fair game for Henry Butler, who didn't relish an aggressive rival in the Tory field, and was spoiling for a fight. He had no mean talents as a writer, and these he put to use with a vengeance.

The *Herald* and the Dingmans finally had a crawful of insult and abuse, and launched a libel suit against Butler and his *Times.* In court, one particularly vitriolic *Times* article produced as evidence accused the Dingmans of being "rank imposters, thieves, pimps and libertines", and added an implication of murder against one member of the family. It came out in court that the libellous article had been written by a disgruntled former *Herald* employee, but that didn't clear Butler, who still was held responsible for using it. The *Herald* was awarded $150 and costs, amounting, in all, to about $1,800.

Eventually, Henry Butler sold the *Times* and, two years later, it was absorbed by the *Herald.* Butler started a new weekly, the *Sun,* and published it in Stratford for only one year, 1892; then moved plant and paper north to Wiarton. Yet, when Butler returned to Stratford years later, he became friends with the Dingmans, as well as a contributor to the columns of the paper whose owners he once had reviled.

The first dailies hit Stratford's streets in 1887, neck and neck. When it leaked out that the young Dingmans were going daily, Alexander Matheson, successor to William Buckingham at the *Beacon,* rose to the challenge. He rushed out the first daily *Beacon* on March 14, leaving the discomfited *Herald* to follow, three days later.

However, the daily stint was too gruelling for the *Beacon* and, after a year or so, it became again a weekly. The *Herald* was Stratford's only daily for the next three years. Then, under William M. O'Beirne and Charles A. Abraham, the *Beacon* once again became a daily on May 1, 1891. Both daily papers continued their weekly editions for some years.

The *Beacon* scooped the *Herald* again, the evening of February 21, 1922, when a sleet storm slashed the city. Trees and hydro poles fell like matches; miles of communication lines came down as if tangled threads. With no power for days, stores soon were sold out of coal oil lamps and candles, and the newspapers were in even worse straits than the citizens.

Crippled by the break in hydro, neither daily paper could publish either Wednesday or Thursday. Then a *Beacon* employee suggested using gasoline powered motors and, with a Model T Ford engine borrowed from Fred Heimrich, the presses rolled and the paper came out on Friday. The *Herald,* meanwhile, had rushed its operations to St. Thomas. It published the next day, alibiing that its equipment was too modern to use gasoline motors.

Both major political camps and many citizens in Stratford had misgivings when it was rumored that the two Stratford dailies would merge. The *Beacon* was staunchly Liberal, the Dingmans' *Herald* entrenched Conservative. Very vocal were the Liberals, and thoroughly alarmed, convinced that it would "be impossible to get a square deal for the party from the Dingmans".

Neither party believed an independent press would work. Neither wanted to be without a political organ. When the *Beacon's* William O'Beirne died, there were unsettling rumors that the paper was for sale, but it was said openly around the office that "it would never be sold to a Dingman". And it wasn't, initially. At the time, many people thought that the man who bought it, "Billy" Taylor of the

Being a newsboy could lead to greater things.
Young Tom Dolan (2nd row, 4th from left) became a crack reporter, then the
managing editor of his paper.

Woodstock Sentinel Review, had engineered the deal for L. H. Dingman for, in two months time, on May 1, 1923, the first issue of the *Beacon-Herald* hit the street and it was under control of the Dingmans. "L. H." was at the head, and Charles Dingman was its first managing director and editor. Taylor's name remained for a time on the masthead, then disappeared.

The whole story didn't come out for 14 years until, in 1937, on the 50th anniversary of daily publication in the city, Milt Dunnell, a reporter on the paper, interviewed L. H. Dingman. Taylor had not been the "front". Simple luck had brought the Dingmans to him at the right time, while an ailing Taylor was in a Woodstock hospital. He was ready to sell. He got his purchase price back, plus a $5,000 bonus, and the Dingmans began to publish the *Beacon-Herald*. The hyphen remained until the paper was redesigned in the 1960's.

A united *Beacon* and *Herald* had the resources and ingenuity of both. When a disastrous fire made the Ontario Street building unuseable for over three weeks, the paper published as usual — missing not one single issue.

Firemen fought the blaze, while the mechanical staff moved to the plant of the Dingman-controlled *St. Thomas Times Journal,* and that paper placed its facilities at the disposal of its stricken contemporary. Reporters remained behind, setting up their typewriters in the offices of an insurance broker and a chiropractor downtown in the Metropolitan Building. The first papers were trucked over from St. Thomas, just half an hour behind schedule. The shuttle service continued for 22 days, until the big press was repaired.

There were special editions during two World Wars, one of them a special morning edition in 1914 announcing Germany had invaded Belgium; there was another on Sunday, October 5, 1930, when the British dirigible R-101 crashed in France while en route to India. It was the first Sunday edition published in Stratford, distributed free to conform with the law.

The newspapers also supplied some ingenious services over the years, among them magic lantern shows to give returns on election nights, and the Playograph baseball machine mounted in front of the newspaper office, first used in 1927 to give play-by-play accounts of the World Series games.

Stratford never again had the array of newspapers that it produced in the 19th century, although new ones did appear. The *Stratford Mirror,* a weekly news and advertising publication which began in 1923, survived for a quarter century before it submerged in a printing business, *The Mirror Press.*

A new Stratford *Times* began publishing in 1964 as a controlled circulation newspaper, but dropped news coverage ten years later and became the *Stratford Times Shopping News.* Stratford became a one-paper town with its independent daily *Beacon Herald.*

Printing shops were set up, usually, in conjunction with the newspapers, and they also made a tremendous difference to community life. The 19th century Methodists were delighted when they could have their "First Annual Report of the Trustee and Official Boards for the year ending June 30, 1881", printed locally by J. H. Schmidt's plant at the *Kolonist.* Local presses also produced the macabre, black-bordered obituary notices once put in store windows or tacked to telephone poles.

As printing methods advanced, flatbed presses at the *Beacon Herald* were replaced by a rotary press — one old press going to a Chinese daily in Toronto, another to Bogota, Colombia. The rotary gave way in 1974 to the revolutionary new high-speed printing process tied not to hot metal but to photography — direct lithography. The *Beacon Herald* was the first daily in Canada to use it, and the newspaper's own employees designed and developed a special device the process required.

Also linked to Stratford was the first book in Canada produced without type, *Renown at Stratford,* composed photographically in Toronto in 1953.

Personnel changed at Stratford's one daily. W. S. Dingman, a former mayor of Stratford and a president of Canadian Press, went to Toronto. In 1944 he was vice-chairman of the new Liquor Control Board of Ontario. In the Dingman chain of command by the late 1970's, the co-publishers were the great-grandsons of Absalom Dingman: Stanford H., editor; Charles William, general manager.

Meanwhile, the dissemination of news had a new vehicle in the 1920's — radio. Although there had been the forerunner of ship-to-shore contacts in the early 1900's, the first serious radio broadcasting for the public developed in the 1920's, and Stratford was not long getting into this new field with its own radio station. It came about largely because a ham radio operator went looking for a piece of wire in Milford Higgins' store on Ontario Street.

The Stratford radio buff, Lawrence "Laurie" East, went on to become chief engineer of Canadian Pacific Telecommunications, and, later, he returned to settle in Stratford. But, in 1922, he and the store owner, a man with an electrical technician's knowhow, were hard at work in Mr. Higgins' basement. There, they fashioned a one-tube transmitter, with a horn from an old Victor gramophone to provide amplification. Higgins was granted an amateur broadcasting licence in 1923, and a commercial licence a year later for the "Classic City Radio Station".

Listeners sat at home, head receivers glued to their ears, and sometimes they heard this marvel transmitting some extraordinary things: "This is 10AK broadcasting from the 44th floor of the Knights of Columbus Building in Stratford." (The building, owned by Kilroy Columbus Company, was a towering two stories high.)

Volunteer talent included Charlie Newell, who played piano, and Father Jordan, "the silver-throated masked tenor". Jack Parr, the "medicine man", arranged programs, solicited advertising and sold patent medicines on the side. In the 1930's, the ambitious little station was assigned call letters CJCS.

In 1936, Roy Thomson from Timmins took over the lease with an option to buy. With the Stratford station, he found he had no end of irritating problems and, when a handsome young soap salesman, desperately wanting to change jobs, approached him, he hired him on the spot for Station CJCS, as manager.

Accompanied by Thomson, Jack Kent Cooke arrived in January, cold, tired, and somewhat dizzy from Thomson's myopic driving. Thomson had not bothered to tell Cooke that the Stratford station already had a manager, proposing to let the unsuspecting Cooke establish his own position, "unofficially". This muzzly situation, and the even more curious vagueness on the part of the astute Thomson, was clarified when the incumbent manager, increasingly unhappy in this impossible bind, quit — announcing he was taking the CJCS transmitter with him.

Roy Thomson was oddly stoic. By telephone, he authorized Cooke to pay $300 for it. It was, in fact, the property of the departing manager.

Jack Kent Cooke, future millionaire, worked for $25 a week, and sometimes the checks he received were not negotiable, (not unexpectedly, since Thomson had told him, "I won't always to able to pay it.") Cooke lived at the Y.M.C.A., and worked a 20-hour day. Within six months, he had the station showing a profit, to the delight of his boss. He hired Charles Trethewey for $7.50 a week, but, at the end of the week, cut it to $5. He introduced corner broadcasting to Stratford, interviewing people passing the United Cigar Store or the Whyte Packing Company outlet.

The Thomson interests sold out within a year. The man from Timmins later became Lord Thomson of Fleet, and both he and Jack Kent Cooke went on to prosper enormously. An Alberta group bought Station CJCS from Thomson, later sold to Countryside Holdings. A new antenna went up off Number 7 Highway; the original 250 watts was increased to 500 watts for daytime use in 1959.

Predating the earliest news services by a couple of decades, were other, more casual reports. The first actual words set down about the site of a future Stratford were Mahlon Burwell's: "It rained, and continued to rain. . . ." Not much of a literary introduction!

Many early Canada Company employees, however, were articulate men: John Galt, Scottish novelist as well as the man responsible for the settlement at Little Thames; Samuel Strickland, member of the brilliantly literary family that also produced his sisters, Susanna Moodie and Catharine Parr Traill; and, most famous as an early chronicler, the Warden of the Woods, Dr. William "Tiger" Dunlop. *Statistical Sketches of Upper Canada, For the Use of Emigrants,* written by "A Backwoodsman", was first published in 1832. The pseudonym was no disguise; the style was so typically Dunlop's.

No mean writer was J. J. E. Linton, who produced, in 1843, *Life of a Backwoodsman.* This beautiful little book with its marbled-blue cover and binding, and title lettering gold on tan, contained only 31 pages, and was reportedly by "A Settler, At Stratford, Huron District, Canada West".

Among his practical suggestions, Linton interspersed some lyrically lovely bits, particularly as he documented nature:

> How quickly the lightning shivers to atoms the largest tree in the
> bush, if the fluid happens to touch it. I have seen a large maple tree,
> three feet in diameter, split and shivered by the lightning, like a
> reed. . . .

The well-bred, well-educated daughters of Judge Lizars later fell under the Dunlop spell and Kathleen and Robina continued the carefully nurtured Dunlop legend in the immensely readable, *In the Days of the Canada Company,* written in Stratford and published in Toronto in 1896. The forward was by G. M. Grant, president of Queen's University and editor of *Picturesque Canada.*

Their book was a mixture of fact, gossip, sidelights and color, with no pretense at accuracy, but it caught the spirit of the early Huron Tract as probably no other book did. A second book followed, *Humors of '37,* dealing with the Rebellion of 1837. But it was the third book, a novel, that rocked the little city of Stratford. It was titled *Committed to His Charge,* and it began:

Chapter 1

Her Reverence

☆　☆

> A crisis had arrived in the history of the Parish of Slowford-on-the-
> Sluggard. And Miss Sweeting knew it. . . .

A local clergyman was said to be the model for the fictional rector, "Reverend Thomas Huntley of All Saints", who believed himself conservative in politics "but, in Slowford, found himself progressive to the extent of Radicalism".

✳ SEVENTH LETTER

Prose for the Past

What was it like in the past?

Find out in the archives of the Public Library. In a small cellar room, there they keep the tea coloured files of the town's newspapers. A shaky fading paper rope into the darkness of the past some more than a century long. You open the door with a skeleton key—the door, has it a white china doorknob? And there in the dark little room, the summer sunlight smothered by a frayed yellow drawn down window blind—there is the past.

FROM "TWELVE LETTERS TO A
SMALL TOWN", THE 7TH LETTER.
ORIGINALLY PUBLISHED AS RYERSON
PRESS POETRY CHAPBOOK NO. 200,
IN 1962, WITH DRAWINGS BY THE
AUTHOR.

James Reaney,
poet and playwright of distinction,
professor at the University of Western
Ontario, and three times winner of the
Governor General's award, never put
aside the farm images of his childhood,
nor the sights and sounds of Stratford.
His idyllic "Twelve Letters to a Small
Town" took an affectionate look, with his
own whimsical drawings, at the Avon,
Market Square, the Stone Bridge, the
high school, even the Crimean cannon
and the archives of the public library. His
play, Colours in the Dark, *was*
performed at the Stratford Festival in
1967. He wrote the centennial play for
his old collegiate in 1979, using student
research, and a theme from the 1933
furniture strike.

E. HAMILTON

Dr. J. D. Barnett gave his entire personal library to the University of Western Ontario.

There were other facile pens in some unexpected places in early Stratford. Out on the Northern Gravel Road was William Battershall, giving the city a shooting park and writing a book *Sparks of Dynamite*. William Buckingham of the *Beacon* co-authored the biography of Hon. Alexander Mackenzie . . . Dr. William "Bicycle" Robertson published an extraordinary book on his great love, cycling.

James Trow (a penniless young emigrant to Canada in 1841, but, by 1867, the member for South Perth in the Provincial Legislature) traveled in the Northwest Territories, and became enthralled by this "great lone land". His letters were published by the government, with 35,000 copies circulated in Britain, where they were acclaimed for literary excellence as well as information.

A century later, in the 1970's, two sisters, Marg Neal and Ethel Ryan of Stratford also were piling up thousands of miles across Canada, researching a history of harness racing for the Canadian Trotting Association.

The first history of Perth County was an impressive work for its time, published by William Johnston in 1903, with no commission from anyone, no financial assistance other than $200 given him by Perth County Council to include pictures of municipal officials. He wrote and published the volume at his own expense, and the *Beacon* trusted him for the printing bill. Meanwhile, this remarkable man also cleared a bush farm and served as reeve of Blanshard Township.

The wealthy and knowledgeable people of Stratford loved books. But this did not prevent many in the city from spurning a Carnegie Library. Anything touching on culture, whether book, bandshell or festival, tended to fire up the Stratfordites anyway, and many were outraged at the idea of accepting money from a wealthy industrialist — this in spite of the fact that one of their own most respected citizens, R. Thomas Orr, had asked for Andrew Carnegie's help.

At the turn of the century, not only in Stratford but elsewhere, many deplored the lavish living of the rich in a time of low wages for workers, and the inoffensive Stratford Library Board got caught in the backlash. "Blood money!" cried many at the grant of $15,000 that built a library on St. Andrew Street in 1903 — one of the first Carnegie Libraries in Canada, and the oldest still remaining in use in the 1970's. Stratford never did put Andrew Carnegie's name over the door.

"Libraries", for Little Thames, started with informal lending rings in churches and schools. There were, in addition, excellent home libraries and, in time, a Mechanics' Institute. Started in Britain to provide classes, lectures and books as an education for working men, the Mechanics' Institutes spread to Canada well before Confederation. Although started for laborers, anyone could join; the operation was financed by members' fees which, after 1835, were augmented by government grants.

In Stratford, the Mechanics' Institute was organized in 1846 in the log school, and incorporated in 1853. It then had 90 volumes, and 28 members. For a time, it occupied a small room cut off from the end of a hall in the Central common school, and, by 1879, it had acquired 2,500 volumes and a membership of 100. There were, at the same time, other libraries and reading rooms in town, including one brought by the Grand Trunk Railway at the time of the big influx of families for the shops. Another was established by the Young Men's Liberal Club in its new white brick, two-story building on Erie Street. The G.T.R. library membership, at 10¢ a month, also included free baths for its members.

The railway also brought to Stratford John Davis Barnett, a draughtsman and engineer in charge of the construction of the G.T.R. repair shops. He assembled 42,000 books, claiming his house on Douro Street was literally propped up by them. One room alone contained a Shakespearean collection of 1,500 books which became internationally famous; barely was there room in the house even for Barnett's tiny rolltop desk that wound up, eventually, in the equally crowded Perth County Archives. In 1918, when he moved to London, his whole collection went with him and was donated to the University of Western Ontario.

Before the end of the century, with nearly 300 Mechanics' Institutes in Ontario, the legislation was passed to convert them to public libraries, and most did either incorporate or close. The Stratford Public Library, like the Institute before it, moved about considerably before there was a permanent home. It was in the market building when it burned; it had, however, more fire insurance proportionately on its books than the city had on the entire building. In 1903, the salvaged books and other volumes that had been acquired at last moved into the Carnegie building.

The library built additions as it grew. Eventually, conveniently near across the street in the basement of the Perth County Court House, there also was the Perth County Archives overflowing its modest quarters but becoming one of the best small archives in the province.

There were, besides, in Stratford, individuals who loved books and valued the past: Chief Jimmy Gillespie, who helped establish a museum at the fire hall; T. J. Dolan who, some Saturday mornings, had a house swarming with students from Guelph or London researching history in his files; R. Thomas Orr, who assembled a series of historical scrapbooks. There was the anonymous contributor to the "Do You Remember" column once published in the paper, writing poignantly of an age that would never come again:

> The summers were hotter and the winters were colder than they are now, and no gardens were quite so gay as the gardens we played in and no flowers so sweet. The cherries and strawberries had more taste in those far off days and the birds' songs were louder. We go back to the old house in which we were born and the rooms that seemed large have become closets and we wonder how we ever sat on those tiny window seats or how we thought it was a long climb up those stairs. The shrubbery that was once a forest is now only an ugly column of bushes and needs clearing out. The summer house that was our castle is but a rather damp, dark room. But every time we think of those early days we see the house and garden as we saw them long ago and it is always the beauty and sunshine that remain.

☆ ☆ ☆ ☆

On Tom Patterson Island,
a new generation discovers the joys of an ancient millpond.

EPILOGUE
Floodtides of Fortune

Today, Stratford is a city of over 27,000 people, set in a gentle, rolling land, a city basking along two shores of the Avon River and Lake Victoria.

It is a place of gracious homes, tall trees, a triangular city "square", a City Hall possibly still illegal. There are lawns of sheered green velvet, except along the river after a heavy rain, when the grass squishes under the flat, black feet of the autocratic swans. There is, always, the river.

From the beginning, and a summer day in 1827, when "Tiger" Dunlop tramped along the river bank, until now, the Avon has run like a theme through Stratford, a part of its geography, an implementer of its history, with an importance disproportionate to its size . . . this coffee-colored river lazing along through its willows.

Had it, perhaps, a hand in producing a citizenry with the ability to dream and the sure knowledge of when to act?

The river is both a physical reality — and a historic fact.

A remarkable river.

A small and special city.

As Stratford grew, the old Fair Ground was parcelled up into lots.

INVENTORY of HISTORY
The old sites . . . What is there now?

The Huron Road — roughly Highways 7 and 8 via Ontario and Huron Streets

John McDonald's survey stake for the Huron road — about 66 feet in front of Festival Square (if it still existed).

The Millpond — Lake Victoria

Canada Company mills — south of the R. Thomas Orr dam

J. C. W. Daly's home — the lawn at the County Court House

First log school — apex of the Library lawn

Shakespeare Hotel — Brown's store, 70 Ontario Street

Sharman's blacksmith shop — Huron Street, opposite St. Joseph's Church

Shakespeare Square (Post Office Square) — Memorial Park

Dufton's Woollen Mills — Shakespearean Garden

The town pump — near Memorial Park

McCulloch's "Grange" — part of it in Queen's Park

The Northern Gravel Road — Highway 19, now via Milverton

Theatre Albert — Avon Theatre

Albion Hotel — Wade's Flower shop

The "Fireproof Block" — Festival Square

Rischmiller's sawmill — City Hall

and

"Little Thames" — The Corporation of the City of Stratford

Milestones of Growth

1826   Incorporation of the Canada Company, August 19.

1827   Dr. William "Tiger" Dunlop first European at site of Stratford, Wednesday, July 11.

1828   "Tavern To Be" marked on a Canada Company map.

1832   Building of Shakespeare Hotel.
Huron Road is passable.

1834   Townsite surveyed for 35,000 people.

1835   Post Office established.

1840   First church built, for the "Auld Kirk" of St. Andrew's.

1843   A log school is built.

1845   Racial riots.
Formation of first boat club, with one boat.

1849   First weekly newspaper: *Perth County News.*
Shakespeare Hotel burns.

1850   Perth established as a provisional county Jan. 1, with Stratford as county seat. (Perth a full county, 1853.)

1854   Stratford a village, Jan. 1. (Enabling legislation: Sept. 23, 1853.)

1855   One acre acquired for a "market building" — with strings attached.

1858   First meeting in new Market Building and Town Hall, May 10.

1859   Stratford a town, Jan. 1. (Canada Statutes: July 24, 1858.)
March 31, closing of the Canada Company agency.

1862   Names of Shakespearean wards appear for first time on the assessment rolls.

1863   Frame buildings banned as fire hazards downtown, in first stab at redevelopment of the center core.

1864   Shakespeare Tercentenary Celebrations.

1867   Canadian Confederation, with great hoopla in Queen's Park.

1869   Death of J. J. E. Linton.

1870   First park, Avondale, established.

1871   Locomotive repair shops attract influx of craftsmen. (Second wave of Grand Trunk workers in 1889.)

1877   First steamboats on the river.

1883   Telephone exchange in operation.

1885   Cityhood, effective March 30, (Ontario Statutes 1885, of same date.)

1886   With arrival of George McLagan, furniture industry on its way.

1887   First electricity, July 14. First electric street lights the following year.

1897   Market Building burns.

1900   First council meeting in new City Hall, Jan. 3.

1904   Parks Board established.

1905   C.P.R. launches a losing battle for the river.

1908   Stratford is one of 12 original signees with the Hydro Electric Power Commission.

1918   The swans arrive on the river.

1933   Troops called out during strike of the furniture workers and chicken pluckers.

1953   Stratford Shakespearean Festival opens.

1956   Stratford District Labour Council chartered.

1964   City launches redevelopment in earnest, starting with City Hall.

1965   New coat of arms for the city.

1972   Parks system spans the city with purchase of last link along the Avon.

1978   ''The Fireproof Block'' becomes Festival Square.

1982   150th anniversary of the founding of the settlement.

1963
The Beacon Herald is
redesigned and gets a
cheerful new motif.

Reuben

HEADS OF STATE IN
STRATFORD, 1854-1980

In 1854, five men were elected to council, with a reeve representing the village on Perth County Council. A ward system was tried for a time, and there have been as many as 15 members on Council, besides the Mayor. Today, Stratford elects ten councilors and a mayor over the city at large, and goes to the polls in November. Two-year terms are now served, under Provincial statute.

Two mayors died in office: Andrew W. Robb in December, 1881, and E. K. Barnsdale in August, 1916. Two others resigned: Stratford's first mayor J. C. W. Daly, who quit in August, 1859, to show displeasure with a new debenture issue of $20,000, and Second Lieutenant Colonel John L. Youngs, in 1919, when he was recalled for military service overseas.

The longest consecutive occupant of the mayor's chair was C. H. Meier, with eight years. (Thomas E. Henry served as mayor for 10 years but in two terms, of seven and three years.)

Five times sons have been elected to the office previously held by their fathers: J. C. W. Daly, followed by his son, T. M. Daly; W. F. McCulloch and J. A. McCulloch; John Brown and Tom Brown; Dr. J. D. Monteith and J. Waldo Monteith; W. H. Gregory and W. P. Gregory.

The first women were elected to Council in 1959: the first woman mayor was Betty McMillan, 1975-1976.

VILLAGE OF STRATFORD
REEVES
W. F. McCulloch 1854-55
A. B. Orr 1856-58

TOWN OF STRATFORD
MAYORS
J. C. W. Daly Jan.-Aug. 1859
William Smith Aug.-Dec. 1859
W. F. McCulloch 1860-62
P. R. Jarvis 1863-67
J. A. Carral 1868
T. M. Daly 1869-70
J. A. McCulloch 1871-72
Thomas Stoney 1873-74
S. R. Hesson 1875
T. M. Daly 1876-78
Alex. Grant 1879-80
A. W. Robb 1881
David Scrimgeour 1882
William Roberts 1883
William Gordon 1884-85

CITY OF STRATFORD
MAYORS
William Gordon Apr.-Dec. 1885
C. J. Macgregor 1886-87
H. T. Butler 1888-89
John Brown 1890-91
Eli Hodgins 1892
J. C. Monteith 1893-94
William Davidson 1895-96
John O'Donoghue 1897-98
James Hodd 1899-1900
James Stamp 1901-02
William Hepburn 1903-04
W. J. Ferguson 1905-06
William Gordon 1907-08
W. S. Dingman 1909-10
John Brown 1911-12
C. N. Greenwood 1913
John Stevenson 1914
E. K. Barnsdale 1915-Aug. 1916
D. M. Ferguson Aug. -Dec. 1916
J. D. Monteith 1917-18

J. L. Youngs Jan.-July 1919
John Stevenson July-Dec. 1919
John Stevenson 1920
W. H. Gregory 1921-22
Tom Brown 1923-25
D. R. Marshall 1926-27
J. A. Andrew 1928-29
C. E. Moore 1930-31
G. I. Graff 1932-33
O. J. Kerr 1934-35
W. H. Gregory 1936
Thos. E. Henry 1937-43
J. W. Monteith 1944-45
J. M. King 1946-47

Thos. E. Henry 1948-50
A. D. Simpson 1951-52
Lawrence Feick 1953-54
W. P. Gregory 1955-56
F. W. Cox 1957-58
R. S. Mountain 1959
C. H. Meier 1960-67
John V. Killer 1968-69
James C. Neilson 1970
Donald S. Davis 1971-72
Keith A. Culliton 1973-74
Betty M. McMillan 1975-76
Keith A. Culliton 1977-78
E. S. "Ted" Blowes 1979-80

THE LIFE

OF A

BACKWOODSMAN;

OR,

Particulars

OF THE

EMIGRANT'S SITUATION

IN SETTLING ON THE

WILD LAND OF CANADA.

BY

A SETTLER,

At Stratford, Huron District, Canada West.

LONDON:

PRINTED BY MARCHANT, SINGER, AND SMITH,

INGRAM-COURT, FENCHURCH-STREET.

1843.

J. J. E. Linton's lovely little book.

BIBLIOGRAPHY

The Physiography of Southern Ontario, by L. J. Chapman and D. F. Putnam. University of Toronto Press, 1966.

Indians of Ontario, by J. L. Morris. Department of Lands and Forests, 1943.

Indians of Canada, by Diamond Jenness. National Museum of Canada, 1932.

Men and Meridians, by Don W. Thomson. Queen's Printer, Ottawa, 1966.

Surveyors' field notes and diaries of survey. Ontario Archives; and Survey Branch, Ministry of Natural Resources.

Canada Company Records. Ontario Archives.

Three Years in Canada, by John Mactaggart. London, 1829.

Illustrated Atlas of the County of Perth. H. Belden & Co., 1879.

History of Perth County 1825-1902, by William Johnston. County of Perth, (Reprint Edition) 1976.

History of Perth County to 1967, by W. Stafford Johnston and Hugh J. M. Johnston. County of Perth, 1967.

Smith's Canadian Gazetteer, by W. H. Smith. Rowsell, 1846.

Canada, Past, Present and Future (2 Vols.), by W. H. Smith. Maclear, Toronto, 1852.

In the Days of the Canada Company, by Robina and Kathleen MacFarlane Lizars. William Briggs, 1896.

Committed to His Charge, by Robina and Kathleen MacFarlane Lizars. George M. Morang, 1900.

The Canada Company, by Thelma Coleman. County of Perth and Cumming Publishers, 1979.

Picturesque Canada, Vol. II, ed. George Monro Grant. Belden, 1882.

The Settlement of Huron County, by James Scott. Ryerson, 1966.

Stratford Illustrated, (Stratford *Beacon* Supplement). 1902.

R. Thomas Orr Scrapbooks. Perth County Archives.

The Oxford Companion to Canadian History and Literature. Oxford, 1967.

Macmillan Dictionary of Canadian Biography, ed. W. Stewart Wallace. Macmillan, 1963.

Dictionary of Canadian Biography. University of Toronto Press, 1966.

The Life of a Backwoodsman, by J. J. E. Linton. London, 1843. Reprinted, 1850.

Statements of Settlers, collected by J. J. E. Linton for the Canada Company. London, c. 1842.

Twenty-Seven Years in Canada West, by Samuel Strickland. Hurtog (Reprint), 1970.

The Tiger of Canada West, by W. H. Graham. Clarke Irwin, 1962.

Statistical Sketches of Upper Canada, "by A Backwoodsman". London, 1832. (In "Tiger Dunlop's Upper Canada", McClelland and Stewart, 1967.)

Autobiography of John Galt, by John Galt. Cochrane and McCrone, 1833.

The Galts: A Canadian Odyssey (John Galt 1779-1839), by H. B. Timothy. McClelland and Stewart, 1977.

Colonel Anthony Van Egmond, by G. H. Needler. Burns and MacEachern, 1956.

When the Orange and the Green United — The Stratford Riots of 1845, by Paul E. Lewis. In Western Ontario Historical Notes, Vol. XX No. 2, 1964.

The Grand Trunk Railway of Canada, by A. W. Currie. University of Toronto Press, 1957.

On Strike: Six Key Labour Struggles in Canada, 1919-1949. ("The Stratford Strike of 1933" by Desmond Morton.) James Lewis and Samuel, 1974.

Imprint of a Nation, by Eric Haworth. Baxter Publishing, 1969.

Roy Thomson of Fleet Street, by Russell Braddon. Collins, 1965.

Edison, by Matthew Josephson. McGraw Hill, 1959.

This One Thing, (A Tribute to Henry Burton Sharman). Student Christian Movement of Canada, 1959.

Public and Private Persons, by Peter Oliver. Clarke Irwin, 1956.

Stratford Around and About, by Ellen Stafford. Fanfare Books, 1972.

Twelve Letters to a Small Town, by James Reaney. Ryerson, 1962.

Stratford Central Secondary School 1853-1968 — A History, by the students. 1968.

Stratford Visitors' Survey. Ontario Department of Tourism and Information, 1967.

Stratford (Jackdaw No. 33), by James R. Aikens. Clarke Irwin, 1972.

Renown at Stratford, by Robertson Davies, Tyrone Guthrie and Grant Macdonald. Clarke Irwin, 1953.

Twice Have the Trumpets Sounded, by Robertson Davies, Tyrone Guthrie and Grant Macdonald. Clarke Irwin, 1954.

Thrice the Brinded Cat Hath Mew'd, by Robertson Davies, Tyrone Guthrie, Tanya Moiseiwitsch, and Boyd Neel. Clarke Irwin, 1955.

A Life in the Theatre, by Tyrone Guthrie. McGraw Hill, 1959.

The H. A. Showalter papers. Public Archives of Canada.

The Stratford Story, by Leonard Marquis and Margaret Rowe. Shakespearean Festival of Canada Foundation, 1955.

To Stratford With Love, by Nicholas Monsarrat. McClelland and Stewart, 1963.

The Stratford Scene, 1958-1968, ed. Peter Raby. Clarke Irwin, 1968.

Stratford Under Cover, by G. L. Shaw. N.C. Press, 1977.

INDEX

Trow, James, 78, 145, 185, 187, 291

Unions *see* Labor relations
United States *vii*, 7, 27, 32, 72, 90, 155, 164, 185, 228, 230, 246
Upper Thames Conservation Authority 140

Van Egmond, Anthony 7, 9, 13, 14-15, 16, 26, 28, 30
Van Egmond, Augustus 9
Van Egmond, Constant 23
Vivian, J. P. 46
Vivian's Brewery 86
Volunteers 212, 269, 270, 288

Warden of the Forests *see* Dunlop, Dr. William "Tiger"
Wards 49, 298
Wars: Boer 116, 117, 172; Crimean 72, 133; War of 1812-14 7, 147; World War I 156*ff.*, 159, 173; World War II 32, 140, 149, 171-75, 268, 281-82, 287
Water rights 34, 127, 138 *see also* "Land under water"

Waterworks 99, 169, 269
Waterloo County 14, 32, 69, 105, 122
Waterloo Street and bridge 79, 119, 124, 126-27, 134, 137, 141, 146, 147, 228, 274
Way, William 28
Wellington Street 85, 105, 111, 113, 166, 190, 219, 220
Wheat 4, 72-73, 86, 92-93
Whisky 23, 59, 67, 83
Whyte Packing Company 168, 169, 288
Wildlife *see* Flora and fauna
Wilmot Township 8, 27, 28, 33
Wilson, William "Fixey" 188, 273-74
Wolf, Morris Lee 107
Wolseley, Col. Garnet 110
Women's Institutes 157
Wooden Indian 68-69, 79
Woods, Judge J. P. 121, 122, 129, 243
Woods, Peter 68
Worsley, George 28

Yemens, Dr. J. G. 72
York 3, 21, 32, 224, 282

Zorra Road 33, 36